LES JACKSON

A Life Well Red

A memoir edged in black – a true tale of family, friends and football, of joy and tragedy

First edition

ISBN: 979-8-70-602396-6

This book was professionally typeset on Reedsy.
Find out more at reedsy.com

For Peanut and Lentil and all the legumes and pulses to follow.

And to the memory of your Uncle Tom.
He would love you as surely as you would him.

Life is just a minute

Only sixty seconds in it.

Forced upon you – can't refuse it.

Didn't seek it – didn't choose it.

But it's up to you to use it.

You must suffer if you lose it.

Give an account if you abuse it.

Just a tiny, little minute.

But eternity is in it!

Dr Benjamin Elijah May

Contents

Acknowledgement

My thanks to San, Dan and Liv for their love and encouragement and for providing the inspiration to write about our family. And to our Congleton Clan - you know who you are - who have inspired us for the last 30 years.

Thanks also to Marlene and Mary for their proof-reading and support.

Thanks to Rosie for her feedback and more than encouraging review, and to her agent Helen for taking the time to read my manuscript and her subsequent advice.

Thanks to my dad, Les, for being a red. I'm sorry I never thanked you when you were here dad.

And thanks to Liverpool FC for the last 50 years and more. The pleasure has all been mine.

Introduction

The dear and sadly departed Kev Rowland, an inspirational work colleague who quickly became a friend, once posed a simple question.

"How do you define yourself?"

And I simply couldn't answer it.

It eventually occurred to me that any definition could surely only be provided by the questioner himself. Kev might have thought of me as a friend and colleague, others as a husband, father, employee and myriad other things depending on our relationship.

That said...

I am a football fan. I love football. A Liverpool supporter first, last and foremost, who started going to matches at Anfield in 1968 and have held a season ticket since 1987. In my lifetime Liverpool have won 39 of their 44 major trophies to date. Indeed, I've been lucky enough to be in attendance when we clinched 17 of them.

If time spent worrying about, talking about, laughing and crying and arguing with, and generally focussing your time, effort and money on is a fair indicator, the only thing more central to my life than Liverpool Football Club is my family. My wife also loves Liverpool, especially when sat beside me at Anfield in the Sir Kenny Dalglish Stand. In fact, when I first met her as a new work colleague over 40 years ago, she was already a season ticket holder. Some things are meant to be.

And so, our kids had little choice than to love football, and Liverpool too.

Since attending my first match at Anfield in 1968, when my dad dropped me outside the boys' pen on his way to the Kop and we overcame a half-time deficit to beat Leicester City, to the end of the 2019-20 season when we finally clinched our 19th league title despite the best efforts of covid-19, both family and football club have brought me untold joy. And unspeakable tragedy.

This is my story.

1

FROM WORKHOUSE TO SILKHOUSE

I n the spring of 2020, before the restrictive effects of the coronavirus pandemic inspired health crisis fully kicked in, my octogenarian mum still managed to do a lot of her shopping in 'the Asda' Superstore on Smithdown Road in Liverpool.

It's a huge store with two floors of aisles, shelves and cabinets offering inhabitants of this bustling and densely populated area a few miles south of the city centre - many of them students from around the globe attending one or other of the three popular Liverpool universities - everything from their weekly food and personal hygiene essentials to clothing items for adults and children alike, home furnishings, electronic goods and a lot more besides. On a recent visit I even noted fireworks for sale.

You can also grab a bite to eat at the on-site café, get your eyesight checked and your new glasses from the latest, forever changing, styles available at the on-site opticians, have your prescription filled at the on-site pharmacy and top up your fuel tank at the on-site petrol station. It's a one size fits all amenity for modern living and convenience. It's also where my mum presented me to the world some time during Sunday 24 August 1958.

Then of course, it was the site of Sefton General Hospital, originally one of the numerous workhouses opened in Liverpool following the introduction of the 1834 Poor Law Amendment Act, and I say 'some time' because my mum, Jean, couldn't remember the exact time (or even which side of midday it was), and my dad, another Les, was working away at the time – roofing I believe - so neither could he be more precise.

Of only slightly less interest to my dad, and I say this not in accusation but in understanding, would have been the opening of the new football season the day before. Liverpool had dropped a point in a 3-3 draw at home to Grimsby Town in the old 2nd Division, with goals from Jimmy Melia and a brace, including a penalty, from Mr Liverpool himself Billy Liddell, my dad's favourite player.

Those lost points would contribute to another disappointing campaign, with Liverpool finishing just outside the promotion places yet again. Following relegation from the top flight in 1953-54 and an initial feet finding season where we ended up in 11th place, we went on to finish frustratingly just outside the promotion places in consecutive seasons with 3rd, 3rd, 4th, 4th, 3rd and 3rd again placings, before finally topping the table to gain promotion in 1961-62 under the inspirational leadership of Bill Shankly (who as it happens was managing Huddersfield Town to a similarly disappointing 1-1 draw at home to Derby County on the day before I first made an appearance).

During my schooldays a Chinese classmate once told me, perhaps mischievously, that in his culture they celebrated birthdays on the anniversary of conception. However, as I'm neither Chinese – despite a seemingly racist school mate once asking me if my dad was a 'nip' or a 'chink' (because the size and shape of my young eyes apparently suggested that possibility) - and nor had my mum and dad yet taken their wedding vows in November 1957, I'll stick with the conventional birth date.

Actually, my parents were married in December 1957 and I was born six weeks premature (you do the maths), weighing in at a respectable 5lb 2oz under the circumstances. For those of you at the back scoffing at this 'convenient' explanation of the timing of my entry into this world, I'll have you know that all my siblings – sister Stephanie and brothers Alan and John – were also born approximately six weeks prematurely, and were 'blue' babies to boot, enough of a trend to suggest my 'premature ejection' was indeed par for the course within the family.

That my sister and brothers were 'blue' at birth is not to suggest, however, that they were born pre-disposed to be Evertonians (or 'black sheep' as such errant family members might more kindly be known), but rather that they were born with a slight bluish tinge to their skin, apparently caused by a lack of oxygen in the blood. This potentially fatal condition was caused by the incompatibility of my mum and dad's blood, my mum being rhesus negative and my dad rhesus positive.

All three (though not me) required lifesaving blood transfusions immediately after being born. Fortunately, they all survived and, as an added bonus, also escaped that fate worse than death which might have been their lot had they indeed turned out to be of the blue persuasion on Merseyside. Brothers Alan and John, like me, were keen reds. Sister Steph hates football with a passion (perhaps she's a closet blue after all!).

As you might imagine, I remember little of substance of my early years, although I do vaguely recall being lauded for managing to meander – without falling - from the chair I had used to pull myself up from the floor, to the sofa which was a few baby steps away. These may or may not have been my first steps but the fact that I recall the event, no matter how ethereally, is perhaps early evidence of the indelible mark positive feedback and encouragement can leave on a child.

Looking back, I find it difficult to shake the feeling that my early childhood was less than completely happy. Not that I was mistreated or unloved by my parents – I know that not to be the case, just the opposite in fact – nor that I had an unhappy childhood. Just that, on a continuum between extremely happy and extremely sad, where 'content' might be the mid-point, I was probably slightly on the wrong side of 'content'. Only slightly mind! Whether this had anything to do with my being the eldest of four siblings born in the space of 5 years between August 1958 and October 1963 is impossible to say, although it is easy to imagine I may have had my nose put out of joint by the arrival in quick succession of my sister and brothers.

Stephanie did tell me that she thought I was always the blue-eyed boy, so I guess I can't have had too much to complain about, though I do have to say that I never felt particularly comfortable as the eldest in the pack. Still don't in fact. And while I have enjoyed my siblings' company more as we have moved through adulthood, I wonder if it is instructive that we have seldom visited each other's homes, always meeting up at my parents' house, usually unarranged. Even family events like weddings, christenings and celebratory meals out have rarely, if ever, resulted in the evening being rounded off with a drink or two at one or other of our homes (though that may be as much to do with the physical distances between us).

I grew up feeling closer to my brothers than my sister – though I think my brothers were closest to each other - and closer to my dad than my mum. I loved both my parents of course, but I also really *liked* my dad, the softly spoken gentleman that he was. He was as big a red as they come, his main claim to infamy being an away fan at St. Andrews in 1954 to witness our heaviest ever loss, beaten 9-1 by Birmingham City in a second division contest. Over 50 years later I felt I achieved an element of retribution on his behalf when I was at the same ground when we hammered them 7-0 in the cup. They say opposites attract – hello mother – which is just as well, or I wouldn't be here to tell this tale.

I vaguely remember my 5th birthday party (at least I think it was my 5th – we didn't have parties where friends and relatives were invited for run-of-the-mill birthdays, and 5 was the first big one we would have celebrated in that way). Jimmy Hanlon, slightly younger than me and I think it's fair to say more a neighbour than a friend, rose from the table (without asking – what was the world coming to?) and made to leave the room. On being asked why, he retorted he was "going home for a pee" (believe me, knowing Jimmy, it could have been a lot worse even at that age).

Strange how the memory works isn't it? Someone gave me a plastic golf set for my birthday and that's all I remember – the golf set and Jimmy Hanlon wanting to go home for a pee! It must have been because we had an outside toilet, and it was a good four- or five-yard walk to the bottom of the back yard to find it!

It may have been because the toilet was so far away (he says sarcastically), but the three lads often used the grid halfway down the yard (only a couple of yards to walk) when not needing to 'perform in the sitting down position' – as Sid, my gentlemanly BB captain once referred to 'it'. Well, one day I came across my mum's plastic icing set which, from memory, consisted of a plastic syringe like contraption and a number of different nozzles each of which offered the potential for any resultant icing to be produced in a slightly different shape to the others. Much to my later embarrassment – I'm cringing thinking about it even now, over 50 years on - I thought it would be a good idea to see if these nozzles would have the same effect on my wee. Little boys will be little boys after all. So, I took the icing set with me to the grid and proceeded to try each of the nozzles as I 'performed in the standing up position'.

I can state quite categorically, and needlessly I'm sure, that the nozzles had no effect other than to spray this particular body waste everywhere except down the grid. The other lasting memory of the experiment was my mum banging furiously on the kitchen window when she'd realised what I was doing – that is, that I was using the icing set (the fact I was also using the grid was nothing new).

As on many other occasions, mum threatened me with all sorts of retribution, the main one being that she would tell my dad as soon as he came home from work ("wait till your father gets home!"). Whether she did or not I don't know, but I certainly don't recall any further ramifications from the incident. Similarly, I don't recall mum ever using the icing set again either.

It was around this time that I must have started school, though thoughts of my first day at Brae Street Infants – a less than 5-minute walk away – invoke few notable memories, good, bad or indifferent. The one particular standout memory I have of Brae Street is my mum and dad forgetting I had to be there one day. I don't think it was my first day, though it wouldn't necessarily surprise me. I recall coming downstairs into the parlour where they were sitting at the table chatting over a pot of tea one morning, the ubiquitous Woodbine between mum's fingers, streaming smoke. Apparently, I was awake and out of bed earlier than usual.

"What are you doing up so early?" she asked.

"I'm going to school" was my somewhat surprised response, though it appeared to be more of a surprise to her.

"Oh, bloody hell I'd forgotten about that" she exclaimed, jumping out of her seat and rushing round to do the myriad of things that now needed doing in preparation for my day.

And that's it. I don't recall anything else about that day, my first day or any other day in particular – maybe not surprising as I'd only just turned five when I started. To be honest I don't recall much about any of the two full years I spent at Brae Street Infants before moving on to Clint Road Count Primary School. Well, apart from Mrs Owen and the wonderfully named Miss Tickle, my two favourite teachers there, though I can't remember why specifically. And I remember that school dinners were usually pretty awful, being brought in pre-cooked from I know not where. I seem to remember the sprouts were always pretty unappealing, though that clearly didn't have a lasting effect on me as they're one of my favourite veggies now, especially at Christmas.

And then obviously there's Linda Moorcroft, my first girlfriend (I think it was Linda. It was the elder of Linda and Brenda anyway, so let's settle on Linda for now). The sisters lived a few streets away in Fell Street and I know one of them was my girlfriend because she announced it at the same time as she invited herself home with me one day after school. I made her walk down the opposite side of the street until I reached our front door, at which point I allowed her to cross the street and join me. I remember her planting a smacker on me before she went home, and I'd never felt so terrified. I wonder what happened to her.

Well actually, I know she also joined the same junior school as me, the aforementioned Clint Road which was maybe twice as far away from our house, possibly a bit more, than Brae Street, but with the additional hazard of having to cross two busy thoroughfares in Holt Road and Edge Lane to reach it. To my delight, although catering for both boys and girls on the same site, the different sexes were kept completely separate to the extent that we might have been in separate establishments. Separate playgrounds, separate buildings, separate classes and separate teachers were the order of the day, and I couldn't have been more pleased. Physically I was a late developer and always a bit shy and introverted, and not having to deal with, or even be near the opposite sex at this stage of my life suited me down to the ground. In fact, that state of affairs really wouldn't change until I started work in 1976, some eleven years later.

If my first two school years were not the happiest of my school days, the next four at Clint Road were very much the opposite.

It was here that I blossomed academically, particularly under the tutelage of my all-time favourite teacher Mr (David) Matson. He was my third-year class teacher, and following a couple of fair to middling performances in years one and two where I continued to find my educational feet, Mr Matson seemed to take a shine to me and my school performance consequently rocketed to put me at the top of the year rankings (there were two classes of pupils per school year).

He also introduced me to the game of Chess, at which I represented both the school and, later on, the Boys Brigade. My Chess arch-nemesis was John Manning – commonly known as 'Mandy' by his mates - who beat me in the tournament final during our final year in Junior school, and regularly in tournament finals at the BB. Nevertheless, it was a game I thoroughly enjoyed playing in my younger years although never a serious competitor to football (watching or playing).

It would be remiss of me not to mention another chess player from my junior school days at this stage. Michael Bouey was also an excellent young player and the third and final member of the Clint Road County Primary School Chess Team, and we had a fair amount of success playing against other schools in the area. Chatsworth Street, from the other side of Wavertree Road, were our closest rivals in that respect, their star player a chap called John Carney I recall, and it was always a feather in our cap coming away from those matches with a win under our belts.

In later years me and 'Mandy' formed two thirds of the BB chess team which, with Paul Walsh – or Wolla - as our third team member, reached the quarter finals of the Boys Brigade National Chess Tournament. Along the way we'd beaten teams from Liverpool and Dublin (that I can remember) but lost to a team from Stoke-on-Trent and consequently missed out on a trip to London for the later rounds, an exciting prospect in those days. This defeat was particularly tough on Mandy as he won all three of his games, with me and Paul both losing all three of ours.

In my defence, I had been stricken with a bug in the days leading up to the game in Stoke and, much to my embarrassment, even threw up during lunch at the home of the Captain of the Stoke company we were due to play. I soldiered on but my mind was never fully on the games. Paul was doing us a favour by even playing and, if blame were to be apportioned, none could be laid at his door. I felt like I'd let the team down.

* * *

Apart from a short spell in Crosswood Crescent in Huyton, where the family moved temporarily while our home was being renovated, I spent all my life as a single man and boy – up to the age of 23 – in our terraced house in Wedgewood Street, Liverpool 7, number 16 to be precise. Wedgewood Street wasn't very long, running as it did (and still does) between Holt Road and Quorn Street. Our house was in the middle of the 'T' junction opposite the end of Adderley Street which ran parallel to Holt Road and Quorn Street, and joined Wedgewood Street to Edge Lane, the main thoroughfare which now links the M62 to the city centre. At the top of Wedgewood Street, on Quorn Street, was the entrance to Brae Street Girls School and St Cyprian's Church Hall.

As kids, Quorn Street seemed to go on forever, as it linked Edge Lane with Kensington, metamorphosing into Gilead Street along the way. The Kensington area of Liverpool has been portrayed as one of the most deprived areas in the country, featuring in one of the first showings of 'The Secret Millionaire' TV programme. However, I can't say it registered as such to us. True, we never had a bathroom or inside toilet (until the aforementioned renovation was completed in 1981), but that was par for the area. Our Edge Hill constituency at the time had the highest percentage of housing without indoor bathroom facilities in the country. And all four of us kids qualified for free school meals at one time or any§other. I read recently of someone who similarly qualified for them professing they'd rather not eat than suffer the stigma, but that was never the case for me. We didn't even think about it (at least I didn't), it's just the way things were. In fact, for a long time we never even had a timepiece.

I remember the days when, as we were all getting ready for school or work, I would step out of our front door and walk the ten yards or so to the other side of our cobbled street, from where I could see the clock on the Littlewoods building, just off Edge Lane, in the distance. Back in the house I'd update the family with the time, and wonder why my parents hadn't called me Tim (one for the oldies!). Looking back, we were also probably a bit overcrowded. Our terraced home consisted of three rooms downstairs and three rooms upstairs, and for much of my early childhood provided shelter for four adults and four children (and Champ the dog).

Downstairs, we had the parlour at the front of the house with its big bay window looking out onto Wedgewood Street itself, the kitchen and the 'back' kitchen. The back kitchen was where all the cooking and washing took place (personal ablutions as well as clothing and dishes), while the kitchen was where we used to eat and live from day to day, with the parlour potentially reserved for special occasions. However, with my beloved Nanny Jackson (Edie) and Auntie Nellie – my dad's mum and her sister - living with us during my early years, they resided and slept in the kitchen and nominally the rest of us lived in the parlour, although certainly us kids spent as much time with Edie and Nellie as anywhere else – they did spoil us rotten after all.

Upstairs was possibly even more crowded, as for a long time only two of the three bedrooms were habitable. The small back bedroom - which overlooked our back yard and the back yards of our adjoining neighbours, as well as those of the terraced houses in Brae Street which backed onto ours, and the 'entry' that ran in between - had a serious damp problem which made it unsuitable for occupation. Try as they might, my mum and dad could not get the landlord to make the necessary repairs, and it was only after they eventually bought the house and obtained a grant to modernise it, that the necessary renovations were made.

This meant that my mum and dad had one of the bedrooms – the slightly larger back bedroom - and us four kids shared the front bedroom which was the biggest of the three. (The kitchen served not only as a living area for Nanny Jackson and Auntie Nellie, but also as their bedroom at the end of the day). When we were very small, mum and dad had the largest bedroom at the front of the house but as we grew older (and bigger) they moved into the smaller bedroom and us kids replaced them in the larger one.

Bath time for the pre-pubescent kids was Sunday night in a big tin bath in front of a roaring coal, and later luxurious gas, fire. For a long time, we did not have instant hot water, so my dad used to heat the four largest pans full of water on the gas stove before carrying them through to fill up the tin bath in front of the fire in the kitchen. On reflection, the potential for serious injury (or worse) through scalding must have been huge, but we all survived bath times unscathed (and un-scalded). Health & Safety would have something to say nowadays I'm sure. Our weekly bath was always timed so that we were freshly scrubbed and clad in our pyjamas just in time to watch the weekend's second episode of Batman and Robin, which went out early on the Sunday evening. Then it was off to bed ready for school the next day.

As we grew older, and were naturally more demanding of our privacy, we started to follow our parent's example of using public facilities for our personal bathing. The public wash house was at the top of Gilead Street, very close to the Kensington thoroughfare, and for a few pence you had a full-size bath to yourself with an endless supply of hot water readily available on tap. Although obviously well used, each bath was properly cleaned (by someone employed for that purpose, not just the previous occupant) before being handed over to the next bather in line.

As you can imagine, we spent a lot of our spare time outside of the house and, as far as the lads (and one notable girl – take a bow Franny Hanlon – Jimmy's sister) in the neighbourhood were concerned that meant playing football pretty incessantly. Which brings me to Wimpole Street.

Wimpole Street, which was effectively a cul-de-sac off Quorn Street, ran parallel with Edge Lane and linked Quorn Street with the 'bowlie' – a crown green bowling club which had three immaculate bowling greens. The 'bowlie' had an entrance at the top of Wimpole Street and another on the path that led through Kensington Park, joining Jubilee Drive and Brae Street. Although we occasionally managed the odd game of footy on one or other of the greens (shocking I know), it could be quite a stressful pastime, what with the constant lookout for the green keeper and potential assault from opposing 'gangs' from the other side of Jubilee Drive, or even Anglezark Close which was situated towards the top end of Gilead Street and had a fearsome reputation.

So, much of our time, certainly pre-senior school, was spent playing footy in Wimpole Street. We played there a lot because, on one corner at the bottom of the street was the huge side wall of an end terrace house in Quorn Street and on the other side of the street was the similarly huge side wall of St Cyprian's church hall. (St Cyp's – the church itself – was, and still is, about two minutes' walk away on the corner of Durning Road and Edge Lane, though its facade now provides the exterior shell for student accommodation rather than the promise of spiritual nourishment for the soul).

The set up in Wimpole Street was further enhanced by the contrived appearance of a couple of goalframes on either side of the road, one painted on the side of the end-terrace and the one opposite made by a couple of drainpipes 9 or 10 feet apart connected by a line of chalk about 6 or 7 feet off the ground. Ideal for kids not yet out of junior school, and playing the likes of 'attack and defence', 'three and in' (where the idea was for the first outfield player to score three goals to swap places with the goalkeeper before the whole process started again) and '60 seconds' (where the goalie counted up to 60 and the outfield players were allowed to score only with an increasing number of headers. Starting with one, each time the requisite number of goals were scored the goalie would start the count to 60 again and the number of goals to be scored in the ensuing 60 seconds increased by one from the previous target. Where the keeper was particularly adept – or more likely the ability of the outfield players not up to the mark! – a variation of the game allowed goals to be scored 'on the volley' – the ball not allowed to touch the floor after being played by the last man before being struck by the would-be goal scorer).

These games necessitated the participation of at least 3 players – the goalkeeper and at least two outfield players who invariably shared the burden of 'assisting' or 'scoring' the requisite number of goals in '60 seconds' - who were split equally – by numbers if possible, or by ability if the number of outfield players was odd – to play in either 'attack or defence'; or to play individually against each other in a mad free for all when playing 'three and in'.

We spent many a happy hour in Wimpole Street honing our footy skills as kids, and on many occasions were joined by one or more of the adult neighbours for a kick-about. On one memorable occasion we even had a professional footballer join us. Stephen Wills was in the same year as me at school – we went to Brae Street infant's school and Clint Road junior school together - and was one of our footy playing group. 'Willsy' had a number of brothers and an older sister, Pamela, who dated Terry Darracott for a while. Terry hadn't quite made the first team at Everton at this stage, but we all knew who he was (probably because the Willsies – all keen reds by the way – never stopped going on about him).

Anyway, the Wills family lived in Quorn Street, just a couple of doors away from Wimpole Street, and one day Terry, who evidently was visiting Pam at the time, came out for a kickaround with the lads. He had his best gear on ready to go out, so didn't stay long, but showed enough prowess with a football at his feet to suggest Everton was the ideal club for him.

Many years later, after Terry had retired from playing with Everton and I had progressed to the grandiose heights of playing in the I Zingari League for Collegiate Old Boys, I played in a pre-season friendly match against a local Sunday League team, called Lister if I remember correctly. Terry was at centre half for Lister, sweeping up behind the rest of the back four and attempting to play in a sophisticated manner he'd never quite managed to achieve as a dour, somewhat limited, left back with Everton (no offence Terry). He never quite managed to achieve it in the game against us either. Sadly, it gives me a great deal of pleasure to report that we beat Lister 5-1 in that game, and that Terry had a nightmare while I, playing for one of the first (and one of the few) times in a similar position to Terry, pretty much excelled (though I say so myself) for Collegiate OB.

And yes, for the avoidance of doubt, any comparisons I may have just made between my ability with a ball at my feet and that of an actual professional footballer are for hyperbolic reasons only and stated with tongue firmly in cheek. Mostly.

On the rare occasions when nobody else was available to play, I would take a tennis ball and play right outside our house. Immediately opposite, on the other side of the street, was the massive side wall of one of the end terraced houses in Adderley Street. As luck would have it, there was also a streetlight – in my very early years one of the original gaslights, eventually replaced by a more modern electric one – and a manhole cover immediately outside our front door, about five or six yards apart. In my football obsessed imagination then, the area outside my home became a ready-made penalty area, the extent of it delimited by the end terrace opposite, the Adderley Street T junction a few yards to the right, and the busy thoroughfare of Holt Road about 50 yards to the left at the bottom of our street.

Okay, the dimensions (and the symmetry) may have left a little to be desired, but it meant that, between Wedgewood Street and Wimpole Street, with or without available teammates or opposition, I always had somewhere immediately and handily accessible which afforded me endless opportunities to participate in some of the greatest feats ever performed on a football pitch (or street). Liverpool, with me as top scorer of course, never lost a match in these single player games, and I also used the wall opposite to hone my heading skills and perfect my ability to make one-twos or, as it is otherwise aptly known, the wall pass.

Thinking about it, these one-man games outside the house were not without incident. I remember a chap – an acquaintance of my dad's, let's call him Doug – who would always walk up Wedgewood Street to his home in Quorn Street after work. During the summer months especially, this would sometimes coincide with my playing football in the street. On one such occasion, so confident was I in my ability with the tennis ball by this stage, and so caught up in the drama of the closing stages of the latest Cup Final I was destined to win, I decided to ignore the fact that Doug was making fairly speedy progress up the street towards my penalty area, and carried on regardless (normally I would have taken a breather and waited for him to pass).

Having just scored the equalising goal with a couple of minutes remaining (a right foot scorcher from just inside the box which went in off the inside of the lamp post), I was so eager to press on for the inevitable winner that I picked the ball out of the net (or front 'area' as the small space around our bay window was more traditionally known), and immediately turned and threw the ball at the opposite wall, planning to take the rebound on my chest before turning and volleying into the opposite corner – a bit like Fernando Torres would do against Blackburn at Anfield some forty odd years later, the best of his first fifty goals for us, according to the striker himself.

Unfortunately, the ball never reached the opposite wall. 'Doug' had unwittingly made a last ditch 'headed' clearance, sending the final into extra-time and possibly an unwanted replay. Amazingly though, Doug failed to appreciate the significance of his intervention. Not for him the warm satisfaction of denying the opposition a last-minute goal scoring opportunity, not even an ounce of sympathy at the crushing of a young boy's dreams of almost (well, in my imagination, literally) single handedly winning the FA Cup for his beloved Liverpool.

Oh no, having been taken unawares when this young hoodlum had, without warning, smashed a tennis ball into the side of his face from a distance of no more than five yards, Doug's immediate reaction was to want to knock seven shades out of me. Thankfully, probably because he couldn't catch me, he satisfied himself with nicking my tennis ball and promising that my dad would be receiving chapter and verse about this 'incident' at the earliest opportunity.

Extra time and a replay would have to wait.

* * *

Hubert Octavius Spink was born in Dulwich, London on 20 January 1878, the eighth in a line of ten offspring born to Joseph Simeon Spink and his wife Lucy Dorothea (nee Critchett). After leaving Dulwich College, he followed in his father's footsteps to work in the City, but soon left his position at Lloyds Bank to join Durham University at the start of a journey to fulfil his religious vocation.

Having taken orders in 1904, he started his first curacy at St. Philip's, Litherland, in North Liverpool and from 1905 to 1909 was the curate at St. Cyprian's Church in Edge Hill, also in Liverpool. He subsequently moved to Hong Kong to be incumbent to St. Andrew's, Kowloon before returning to Liverpool three years later to be vicar of St. Clements in Toxteth. The St. Clement's congregation at the time was quite unique in that it was largely made up of young men who immediately joined up in the various Liverpool and Lancashire battalions at the outset of the Great War.

Finding it impossible to sign up as a fighting man himself – specifically forbidden to do so by his bishop – he eventually went to France as a Chaplain in January 1916, where he was attached to the 5th Battalion South Lancashire Regiment. In July of that year, he took part in the first battle of the Somme and on 9 August, at Delville Wood, he was killed by a shell while tending to the wounded and burying the dead. He had been slightly wounded three times during the previous 48 hours but refused to remain at the rear despite orders to do so, as he believed he could still be of use to his own men. Throughout his division – the 55th – he was loved and respected by officers and men alike.

It probably won't surprise you to learn that I gleaned the information for the brief pen picture painted above from the internet. You won't find anything on the internet, or at least I couldn't, about his founding of the 43rd Liverpool company of the Boys Brigade, nor about the Captain of the company during the time I was a member (and had been for over half my life at the time I left), Sidney James Rannard. Which is unsurprising but nevertheless a great shame in my humble opinion.

It was during his time at St Cyprian's in Edge Hill when the Reverend Spink laid the foundations of what, unbeknown to him, would have a significant impact on the lives of many impressionable young men, including mine, in the years to come. For it was as curate at St Cyp's that he founded the 43rd in 1906.

One day, when I was eight, I'd just finished playing footy with my mates in Wimpole Street and was on my way home, when I heard the faint sounds of what seemed like playful activity coming from the church hall, which appeared to be locked. I peered through the keyhole on the huge entrance door to no avail and was then startled to hear a soft Irish burr behind me.

Startled because, up until that point, I don't think I'd heard anything other than a scouse accent on the streets of our neighbourhood.

"Can I help you, young man?" caused me to turn from the keyhole, at which point I was further startled by the fact that the owner of the voice was wearing a dog collar.

"I was just looking to see if there was anybody in there. Thought I'd heard someone playing" I nervously replied.

"And do you like to play?" the Reverend Richardson, for it was he, went on, which was a bloody stupid question I thought as I was standing there with a ball under my arm.

"Yeah" I said, a bit more confidently now, and continued "what are they playing?"

"Oh, they play lots of different games in the Boys Brigade" he replied, "but you have to be a member".

"Can anyone be a member?" I asked and he replied with another question of his own:

"How old are you?"

"Eight and a half" I responded hopefully, resulting in, much to my delight:

"Just the right age then, you'd better come in".

Such was my introduction to the BB and a better decision in my young life I'd have been hard pushed to make.

I joined what was actually still known as 'The Life Boys' at the time, in 1966 shortly before it was rebadged as the 'Junior Section' of the Boys Brigade (back in 1926 it had been known as 'The Boy Reserves'). Although Mr Rannard was captain of the 43rd company as a whole, he was most heavily involved with the more senior boys in the Company Section – those aged eleven and above who were already in secondary education – and my first recollection of him, though I must have met him before, was a visit he paid to our home in Wedgewood Street one early Sunday evening in 1969.

1 June to be precise, and the reason I know that is because I recall England, reigning football world champions at the time, were playing in Mexico, in a televised game which ended 0-0, when he visited, and a quick internet search confirmed the date. Live televised football outside of FA Cup Finals,

and indeed any football on a Sunday, were very rare occurrences back then and I remember my dad not exactly being thrilled at the interruption to his viewing.

Mr Rannard had come to ask my parent's permission for me to attend the forthcoming BB summer camp, which would be right at the start of the school holidays in July, for ten days starting from the Saturday after school broke up for the summer. Money was tight, and the cost of £6 – unbelievable value even in those long-ago days, given that it covered return transportation, lodging (in classrooms at a school in Portishead near Bristol which had been procured for the duration), and all meals – was still prohibitive for the family coffers to spare, despite the potential attraction of having one less child to entertain for a reasonable chunk of the summer break.

Mr Rannard remained adamant however, and agreed to cover half the cost himself, such was his belief in the importance of summer camp, and his devotion to the BB, the 43rd in particular, and the boys in his charge. He'd been a member himself all his life, starting as a young boy and progressing through the ranks as an NCO, then a Commissioned Officer before becoming Captain in the early to mid-1960's when his predecessor, Mr Potter who he revered, had finally retired. It was the first holiday I'd ever had, and I absolutely loved every minute of it.

Except for the bit where all the gifts I'd bought for the family where stolen from the staff room, where they had been stored for 'safe keeping'. Not removed you understand, but another lad had marked them all with his initials (DK) and then proclaimed that it was merely a coincidence that he had bought all the same gifts as me. No-one believed him – he was a known miscreant - but we couldn't prove otherwise, and it took some of the shine off the last couple of days at camp.

It never dampened my enthusiasm for summer camp though. I can still remember them all now, over 40 years after I attended my last one. Portishead in 1969 was followed by Cheltenham in 1971, Nailsea 1972, Keswick 1973, Cheltenham (again) 1974, Barrow-in-Furness 1975 and my final camp at Sandhead, near Stranraer, right on the nose of Scotland, in August 1976. (I never made it to Prestwick in Scotland in 1970 as my parents forbade it, having already agreed for me to go on my first foreign holiday – my first time on a plane – which would be a school skiing trip to Finkenberg in Austria during the Christmas holidays later that year. Their not unreasonable argument was that I'd been to summer camp in 1969 and had the skiing trip to look forward to, as well as our first family holiday, to Butlins in Pwllheli, in the summer of 1970. My holiday drought was in danger of becoming a glut).

Sandhead was my only tented summer camp, though we also had shorter Easter camps which were all under canvas. Summer camps had always, in my experience, provided us with lodgings in a school or college in the locality (Portishead, Cheltenham, Nailsea, Barrow) or in log cabins on the banks of Derwentwater when we went to Keswick. Thankfully, as I'm sure older readers may remember, 1976 delivered a glorious summer, one of the driest, sunniest and warmest in the 20th century (though that also meant a severe drought) and I returned home as brown as a berry, ready to start my very first job, courtesy of the government sponsored Job Creation Programme, in Liverpool Social Services Department.

Throughout these years, and for a number of years after my membership of the BB lapsed, Mr Rannard was the ever-present Captain. I cannot readily recall a single company event which he did not attend. In fact, not just attend, he would also be heavily involved in organising and running most of them, albeit with assistance from a number of similarly dedicated stalwart officers, and undoubtedly making significant contributions towards their cost. Summer or winter season, whether it be gym night or swimming; snooker, table tennis, or tuck shop at '21' or cricket at Gleneagles; football on a Saturday or bible class / church service on a Sunday, Mr Rannard was there. As dependable as night following day. He stocked the tuck shop, refereed our football matches, umpired our games of cricket, prayed with us on a Sunday as well as for us every other day of the week I'm sure. He cajoled us when we needed it and was unceasingly supportive.

I had as much reason as anyone, and possibly more than most, to be thankful for his patronage. As well as subsidising attendance at my first summer camp, he also bought me a pair of football boots I desperately needed (Gola mouldies, I loved them), arranged an interview for me with a friend

18

in Liverpool at an accounting firm in Rumford Place when I was looking for my first job (after which I was rejected because they were 'trying to move away from the provincial accent' – he was not happy), as well as many more contributions to my well-being that I took for granted and the particulars of which I have long since forgotten.

His support and guidance throughout my adolescent years undoubtedly helped to keep me on the straight and narrow when there were plenty of opportunities to stray and plenty of examples of my contemporaries who were not as fortunate. I, and undoubtedly many others, owe him a lot.

Be in no doubt that he genuinely loved all the boys in his charge. I don't believe you can provide the public service he did, for as long as he did, without sincerely believing in what you do and caring for those you do it for. Reverend Spink would surely have approved, for Mr Rannard was certainly cast in his mould.

For as long as I knew him, he lived alone in Westway, off Thingwall Road, in what is now the 'Wavertree Garden Suburb' Conservation Area in Liverpool. He died in the mid 1980's when I was in my mid-20's, he in his late 60's. His was a great loss, for he was a great man. He had never married, though I always considered him married to the 43rd, who were blessed indeed to be led by Sidney James Rannard.

I salute you, my Captain.

* * *

From when I was eight years old until after I turned eighteen, the 'BB' catered for pretty much all the needs outside those provided by the home environment (and even some of those) that most young lads – or certainly this one at least – growing up in inner city Liverpool might otherwise have struggled to have met.

The 'Junior Section' of the BB catered for boys aged from about 8 to 11, after which they progressed into the Company Section. Although there was plenty to keep you occupied as a member of the Junior Section, progression to the Company Section once you'd turned 11 years old opened up access to a full programme of events. During the autumn, winter and spring months – let's call this period the 'season' – these events consisted of gym night on a Monday, '21' on Tuesday, Thursday and Saturday evenings, and organised 11-a-side football on Saturday afternoon's against other Liverpool 'BB' companies.

As the 'BB' was also a Christian organisation, Sunday mornings meant bible-class and the occasional church service, which although technically a compulsory condition of membership, were generally not as well attended as some of the other 'offerings' of the company, though I have to say I always made sure I attended them (occasionally with a little help from my dad who was determined that I didn't pick and choose what I attended, but instead met my 'responsibilities' as a member. Perhaps needless to say, my dad had been a member of the 43rd when he was a lad).

'21' actually refers to a building in Deane Road, Liverpool 7 – number 21 would you believe? – which had facilities for playing snooker, table tennis and various other indoor games as well as a subsidised tuck shop. Gym sessions on a Monday evening were provided courtesy of the local Edge Hill Secondary Modern which allowed us to use the school gymnasium, and were run by Walter Pleasance, one of the company's longest standing officers.

I recall Mr Pleasance as the gentlest, most softly spoken gentleman who, as well as running the gym sessions which included all manner of games, exercises and exercise equipment, and always finished with a couple of hard-fought 5-a-side games, also attended the annual 'BB' summer camp, wherever in the country it was being held, and for the full ten days never ventured out of the kitchen, such was his dedication to ensuring that all camp attendees, staff and boys alike, were kept well fed and watered. His devotion to the cause was typical of all the officers I had the good fortune to encounter during my ten years in the 'BB'.

Friday evenings during the season were dedicated to 'Inspection and Drill' night and involved staff and boys in full uniform – including pill-box hats (which were soon replaced by the 'thunderbird' variety) when I first joined, pressed trousers with jacket and tie and polished shoes (that was the aspiration anyway). The boys' turnout was inspected – hence the name – for cleanliness and smartness, following which a number of marching drills were practiced in readiness for those few special occasions during the year when we would march from the church hall in Quorn Street to St Cyprians Church, situated on the nearby corner of Edge Lane and Durning Road. On these occasions we would be led by the 'BB' band - made up primarily of marching drummers, trumpeters and a solo bass drummer - who also practiced their instrument playing at the end of some (not all) of the Friday evening sessions.

Saturday afternoons were the highlight of my week though. Between the ages of 11 and 17, most Saturday afternoons would involve an 11-a-side game against another Liverpool company. These were normally high scoring affairs, and it isn't difficult to understand why. Competitions were divided between two age groups – Intermediates aged 11 to 15 and Seniors aged 16 to 17 – and the difference in physicality between an underdeveloped 11-year-old and an early maturing 15-year-old would be huge.

With certainly the younger age group being made up of a wide spread of ages and the varying abilities and physical attributes that entailed, double figure victories or defeats were not uncommon. So much so in fact that particular details of the many high scoring games are difficult to recall. Indeed, the one game that I do remember with any clarity is a cup match played at 'Greenhill' playing fields in Allerton against the '20th' company (I think, if not it was the '32nd'). The game resulted in a 2-1 defeat, a particularly low scoring affair in my experience of these matches (I recall a single 1-0 win a couple of years later which was the only lower scoring game I was involved in with the 43rd), and which had gone into extra time after yours truly floated an equaliser into the top left corner from the edge of the box.

There must have been a dozen or more pitches regularly used at Greenhill on a Saturday afternoon and I'd love to be able to tell you that the ball nestling in the back of the net was a sight to behold, given the relative paucity of the goals scored that day, and the fact that it was such a late, important goal in the cup. We didn't play with nets then though, the existence of an actual goal frame (rather than more portable poles, with no crossbar) still being relatively novel. The sight of one of the goalkeepers from the pitch immediately behind ours hurriedly collecting our ball and returning it to us, while their ball was in the opposing penalty area, would have to do.

As a particularly late developer, those very early years – whether on the winning or losing side – were far from enjoyable, particularly in the winter months when I would spend most of my time out of the way standing on the wing. I hesitate to suggest I was 'playing' on the wing, as my involvement in many of these games was little more than cursory and many were the times I struggled to fasten my shirt buttons after changing out of my football kit, so numb with cold were my hands.

Nevertheless, I was happy to be involved in the camaraderie these games engendered with my mates and as I grew older and started to bloom, from a technical football ability perspective first and then physically, my influence in, and enjoyment of, these games similarly blossomed. By the age of 17 my physique and ability had developed enough to be chosen to represent the Liverpool Battalion of the Boys Brigade in games against other representative sides from London, Bradford, Oldham and Dublin.

I still didn't look my age, but I was quick, could head and pass the ball, and loved a tackle, especially the sliding variety. The fact that I was representing my city, my Liverpool indeed, albeit with only a subset of its inhabitants available for selection (that is, the 'BB' members across the city which, to be fair, was a pretty significant number in those days) was a huge thrill and is something of which I remain proud to this day. Indeed, over 40 years on I still have the representative blazer badge all squad members were required to wear when 'on duty' before and after the games.

If there was no game to play on a Saturday afternoon, there was a fifty-fifty chance that Liverpool would be playing at Anfield, and on those occasions I headed that way. I recall on occasion a decent sized group of us would end up in the Anfield Road end before graduating to The Kop. At different times this group would have included some or all of the likes of Derek Slater (my best mate at the time), his brothers Keith and Brian, John Manning, Paul Walsh, Stephen West, Dougie Drinan, Barry Griffiths and either or both of the Kenwright brothers (Henry and David), but more often than not I remember going mainly with Derek (Sledge), and sometimes John (Mandy), and I certainly wasn't averse to going on my own.

I know for many football fans these days, certainly Liverpool fans who are well travelled and I would imagine for plenty of others too, the whole 'going the match' experience is enhanced by travelling and socialising with mates and like-minded supporters before and after games, with endless pre- and post-match discussion adding to the occasion, as well as the actual fare served up on the pitch. Not for me. An ideal world would see me teleported into my seat five minutes before kick-off and back home five minutes after the match has ended. In these podcasting days, pretty much all my other match related needs can be satisfied with judicious listening to The Anfield Wrap.

When the lighter nights and longer days of the approaching summer months heralded the end of the BB 'season', as they did the football season, the sheer volume of BB activities reduced only slightly. Swimming at Lodge Lane baths in Toxteth replaced gym night on a Monday, and cricket at the playing field at the top of Gleneagles Road near Bowring Park replaced '21' on Tuesday and Thursday evenings (it's called the 'King George V Playing Field' these days, and may have been even then, but we always called it 'Gleneagles'). Although regular Friday and Saturday activities took a break, Sunday Bible Class remained a staple, and of course BB Summer Camp had to be prepared for and attended. There was still plenty to keep us all occupied.

* * *

I was exactly 9 and a half years old, not that the half year held any significance and I certainly wasn't aware of it at the time, when I made what was actually my *second* pilgrimage to the shrine which is Anfield.

I'd already visited a virtually deserted Anfield when my dad took me to see the reserves lose 1-0 to a Manchester United reserves team playing incongruously (to me) in all blue. Only the main stand and the paddock were open for the reserve matches and, although we started off in the stand (where we could sit), at half time I noticed someone being allowed to move through the 'eye of the needle' (a gate within a larger gate) which separated the area below the main stand from the area behind the paddock (where refreshments and the like could be purchased).

So fascinated was I by this 'spectacle' (what an innocent life I must have been leading) that I persuaded my dad to try and get us through this gate. He asked the gatekeeper (okay, a steward) to let us through and so I watched the second half standing in the Paddock in the freezing cold. And that's about all I remember of the evening, except that I'd missed a session at the BB that night and felt a bit guilty about it. Still, it was my first trip to Anfield and one of the few times that I actually stood with my dad at the match. He was a confirmed Kopite, having himself started in the boys' pen when it was situated at the side of the pitch on the Kemlyn Road side of the ground, and, for my first few games, he would walk me to the boy's pen, giving me enough money to get a match programme and pay for my bus fare home. This enabled me to get home under my own steam while he went for his post-match pint.

I don't remember the date this game was played, but it was on a Monday night – BB night at the time – and I must have been at least eight but certainly no older than just turned nine, because the first time I visited Anfield for a first team game is indelibly printed on my brain. Saturday, 24 February 1968 was the glorious date when my dad first dropped me off at the entrance to the boys' pen. The time would have been about 2 pm I suppose, giving my dad enough time to nip to the pub for a couple of pints before kick-off. I remember the long (to a skinny nine-year-old) walk up the wide, deep concrete steps at the side of the pen, before turning the corner at the top of the steps and espying that wonderful green carpet laid out before me, seemingly miles away.

In truth, the boys' pen was a great spec to watch the game from given its location in the top left-hand corner of the Kop (or the top right-hand corner when viewed from the pitch). And if the game was occasionally less than riveting, you could always amuse yourself watching some of the lads bunking into the Kop by climbing out of the pen up onto the girders which stretched the length and depth of the huge old standing terrace. Looking back, these were really death-defying escapades as a plummet from the girders to the terracing would undoubtedly have left you with more than a severe headache. But I don't ever remember an incident which resulted in serious injury in the three or four years I followed the reds from the pen. Plenty of incidents of intimidation and petty larceny mind you, but no serious accidents.

My first game didn't start so well. Roger Hunt, who was my first Liverpool hero, was missing through injury and we were playing our bogey side of the time – Leicester City who, if I remember correctly, included a very young Peter Shilton in goal. Despite playing well, we were a goal down at half time, so had it all to do in the second half. Would my 'debut' turn into a nightmare? Was I a Jonah? I should have known better, had more faith.

We blitzed them in the second half and won comfortably with goals from Ian Callaghan ('Cally'), Geoff Strong and Tony Hateley (I must confess, though I still remember the score, I had to look up the names of the goal scorers in my trusty copy of Brian Pead's 'Liverpool A Complete Record 1892 – 1986', an invaluable source of information – though surpassed now by the marvellous LfcHistory.net website - on Liverpool FC's playing history from its birth at Anfield following Everton FC's acrimonious split with the then landlord, John Houlding, up to the end of the season when Liverpool achieved the coveted League Championship and FA Cup double, by pipping Everton to both honours. What a glorious final illustration of our usurping of their long-gone position as the leading football lights on Merseyside).

Actually, the incident I remember most from the game came in the second half when we had already turned the game around and were leading. Ron Yeats conceded a free kick on the edge of the penalty area by deliberately reaching high above his head, both feet off the ground, to handle the ball, and Tommy Smith gave him a right bollocking for it. Made an impression on me anyway – can't remember the goals at all!

* * *

So, my Anfield career was off to a flier. That season we finished third in the league behind the two Manchester clubs, City winning it for the last time before a 44-year drought which ended in spectacular fashion after being bought by an Arabian Sheikh. A season later, a very creditable performance for an ageing team saw us finish as runners up to Leeds United, but the warning signs were there.

Unfortunately, the warning signs weren't heeded, and it took a shock defeat in the quarterfinal of the FA Cup at second division Watford the following season to herald the changes in personnel that were clearly required. Ray Clemence replaced the 'Flying Pig' Tommy Lawrence in goal, Larry Lloyd took over at centre-half from the colossus Ron Yeats and slowly a younger, more vibrant team began to take shape. The following season Liverpool reached the Cup Final only to fall short as Arsenal completed the double, and the season after that only a hotly disputed offside decision at Highbury ruled out a late John Toshack winner and stopped Liverpool winning the league.

With Derby County sitting at the top of the table, and a point clear of Leeds United having completed their fixtures for the season, Liverpool took to the field against Arsenal at the same time as Leeds, who'd defeated the Gunners in the Cup Final just two days earlier, were setting up at Molyneux against Wolves. Leeds, with a better goal average than Derby, needed just a point to add the league crown to their cup win and complete the double. Liverpool needed Wolves to win that game and a victory themselves to emerge as Champions. Wolves, somewhat surprisingly, did the honours while at Highbury referee Roger Kirkpatrick's decision two minutes from the end to disallow John Toshack's goal for offside - the linesman never raised his flag – ultimately denied us that reward, and the Derby squad, enjoying an end of season break in Majorca, celebrated on the beach.

Unbelievable as it is to think now, but the first me and my dad heard of any of this was at the end of the 9 o'clock news on the BBC. No live TV coverage then. The fact that both Leeds and Arsenal were expected to play season defining matches scarcely 48 hours after the cup final barely entered the public consciousness. My dad stormed out for a pint. If you can call tight-lipped silence storming. But if you knew him, you knew. It was one of many traits I admired about my dad, that ability to keep his emotions under control at times of stress or strain. And though I like to think I inherited a lot of his traits, unfortunately that isn't one of them.

(His dry and mischievous wit on the other hand? By way of example, I grew up believing he'd had a lucky escape when, in the performance of his national service duties in Egypt, he'd been nicked by an 'arab bullet' which had left a scar on his neck that was plain to see. It was my mum who'd told me this and warned against raising the subject with my dad, such was the clandestine nature of what had happened. Anyway, one day in a rare moment of insight, I plucked up the courage and asked:

"Is that really where you got hit by a bullet in the army, Dad?"

"Who told you that?" he answered with his own question.

I glanced nervously at mum, herself wide-eyed at my apparent faux pas.

Sensing the game was up, my dad burst out laughing and replied to the effect that "you shouldn't believe everything your mum says son, she'll believe anything".

My mum, on the other hand, was mortified. They'd probably been married ten years or more at the time, and she'd met, married and had four children with him, all the while under the impression he'd been involved in some secret post-war gun battle, narrowly escaping with his life, before they'd even met. Turned out the 'wound' was from an old shaving injury or something equally mundane. Yeah, I like to think I inherited some of that!)

So, we were trophyless again. But this team was just getting started. The first game of the following season saw Manchester City visit Anfield. I was in the Anfield Road end with a mate watching a relatively comfortable 2-0 win, memorable for the sendings off (no red cards, their introduction was still two years away) of our Larry Lloyd and City's Wyn Davies, one half of the Davies twins, Southampton's Ron being the other. It was memorable because sendings off were virtually unheard of back in those days, and even bookings weren't much more common. So, two sendings off in a single game on the opening day of the season was particularly newsworthy, and indeed did make the national news bulletins.

During the first half of the season, Liverpool and Arsenal battled for league supremacy, and when the North Londoners won at Anfield in early February to go top of the table, this 14-year-old boy's dreams looked close to being crushed. We hadn't won the league since before I'd started going and last season's last gasp disappointment had only whetted my appetite for this. Thankfully, my fears proved to be unfounded.

Five years to the day since I'd attended that first game against Leicester at Anfield, Ipswich Town were the visitors and probably deserved something from the game. But they didn't get it, and Liverpool's 2-1 win put them back at the top. The following week I watched from the Gwladys Street as two Emlyn Hughes goals saw Everton beaten 2-0 at Goodison and steam rising from the sea of celebrating Liverpool fans in the Park End (some nine and a half years later I was in the Gwladys Street again, this time as Ian Rush scored four and Mark Lawrenson the other as we handed out a 5-0 hammering to the home team. With another two goals disallowed and the woodwork struck three times, Everton could count themselves fortunate it was only five).

At the end of March, I watched from the Anfield Road End as Tottenham's Pat Jennings saved penalties from both Tommy Smith and Kevin Keegan, the great Irish keeper eventually beaten only by a mis-hit Keegan shot which looped over his diving form to give us a point on Grand National day, the game having kicked off in the morning to avoid a clash with the world-famous steeple chase. Only a point, but a welcome one. We were in the end game now.

Ten days later, we played Tottenham at Anfield again, this time in the first leg of the UEFA Cup semi-final, when Alec Lindsay's left-footed strike gave us a slender advantage to take to White Hart Lane. Eleven days after that, during which time we recorded two more narrow league victories, we entered an intense eight-day period which would settle the league one way or another and determine our progress in the UEFA Cup.

Easter Weekend in those days always meant Easter camp with the BB for me, a much smaller camp than the main summer one. This year we'd set up camp at Capel Curig in Snowdonia and, on the Easter Saturday about a dozen of us, all teenagers and almost all reds, were traipsing around nearby Betws-y-Coed when we came across a football pitch in the centre of town, complete with goals and corner flags in place, and two teams preparing for kick-off. One of the teams was from Trawsfynydd and the other, I assume, was from Betws-y-Coed itself.

I am unequivocal about the team from Trawsfynydd because, like Liverpool, they played in all red and so we asked their goalkeeper where they were from.

They became our team for the day and, coincidentally, their opponent's shirts were adorned with black and white stripes. And I say coincidentally because Liverpool's first game in this eight-day period was also about to kick-off, at St James Park against Newcastle, probably the most famous English club to don the magpie colours (though followers of Notts County, the oldest professional football club in the world having been founded in 1862, a fact which inspired Italian giants Juventus to adopt the colours for their own kit in 1903, may disagree).

It was a cold miserable day in this particular corner of the Caernarfonshire countryside, and we kept ourselves warm by basically singing and clapping non-stop, in favour of the away team of course, throughout the game. At the end of it, the 'team from Trawsfynydd' had triumphed by six goals to two and their goalie, behind whom we'd expended most of our energy, came over to thank us, saying they'd never had support like it. It had been a good day.

Until we found out Liverpool had lost at Newcastle. A blow – especially having taken the lead - but the league was still in our own hands.

Two days later (yes, just two days!) on the Easter Monday, old foes and bitter rivals Leeds United were in town. Unfortunately I wasn't, and listened to the second half of the game on the radio in a minibus on the way home from North Wales. Not only would a Leeds win give Arsenal the upper hand with just one league game remaining, but it would also put Leeds, who had a couple of games in hand, within striking distance themselves. Goals from Keegan and Cormack, who also assisted each other, put Leeds out of contention and one of our hands on the Championship trophy, with just one game left to play, and that at home. The reaction in the minibus would have been rivalled only by the reaction on the Kop when each of the goals went in.

Two days later (yes, just another two days!) Liverpool were in North London for the second leg of the UEFA Cup semi-final against Spurs. Steve Heighway equalised in what was eventually a 2-1 loss, but the away goal was enough to see the reds through to the final and deny Spurs the opportunity of winning the trophy for the second year in succession, having triumphed over Wolves in the two-legged final the year before.

Just three days after that I was again in the Anfield Road End as Champions-elect Liverpool needed just a point against Leicester City who, to be fair, were still a bit of a bogey team. In the first weeks of the season they'd come from two goals down to beat us 3-2 at Filbert Street with a Keith Weller hat-trick, so we couldn't take anything for granted. Indeed, Leicester's Mike Stringfellow (if I remember correctly) did have a goal disallowed in the second half which may have denied us the point on another occasion.

But with a superior goal average to second placed Arsenal (the use of goal difference to differentiate between teams with matching points totals was still three years away – and we had a better goal difference too for good measure), it wouldn't have mattered anyway, especially with Arsenal also dropping points in their remaining games. It finished 0-0. Champions again, but for the first time in seven years, the first time this decade, and the first time in my relatively short match going experience. My 14-year-old spirit soared. I was walking on air.

We completed a double with the UEFA Cup joining the League Champi-onship in the trophy cabinet following two exceptional games of football over the next month. I was in the Anfield Road End again, on consecutive nights, for the first leg of the final against West Germany's Borussia Monchenglad-bach. A filthy night on Merseyside as the first game kicked off only got worse as the rain continued to batter down, with the referee's decision to abandon it during the first half due to a water-logged pitch, the only logical conclusion to the evening.

The weather having abated, for the princely sum of ten pence I was back in the same spot the following evening for the rearranged game. Shankly changed the team slightly, bringing in our six-foot plus striker John Toshack in place of the diminutive Brian Hall, having detected a German defensive weakness in the air the previous night. It worked a treat, our opponents unable to deal with Toshack's aerial prowess or the annoying presence of his effervescent side-kick Kevin Keegan. Two first-half goals from Keegan (who also missed a penalty), assisted by Toshack, set us up nicely and another giant, centre-half Larry Lloyd, rounded the evening off perfectly by making it 3-0 with a free header from a corner in the second half. Ray Clemence's save from a Jupp Heynckes penalty a few minutes later was merely the icing on the cake. Or so we thought.

In the second leg two weeks later, Heynckes did his utmost to make amends for that penalty miss with two goals before half-time. With Liverpool on the ropes, Keegan's penalty miss from the first leg was starting to look like it may prove more significant than it had seemed at the time, Clemence's penalty save at least ensuring that our opponents didn't have the away goal which would have given them the edge.

But Monchengladbach, having put so much effort into the first half to get back into the tie, visibly tired in the second. Gradually, Liverpool took back control and ultimately saw the game out more comfortably than looked possible at the break. It was our first European trophy, and the first time an English club had triumphed in Europe in the same season they finished as English champions. Shankly's pride at our first European success was obvious. We weren't going away. Sadly though, Bill was.

* * *

But at least we were to get another season and another trophy with the great man.

For a short while, it looked like it might be another double but Leeds, who'd started the season with a record run of 29 games unbeaten before giving up a two-goal lead at Stoke in an eventual 3-2 loss, recovered from a spring wobble, and became Champions when Arsenal extinguished the dying embers of Liverpool's faltering challenge at Anfield. Ironically, it was Ray Kennedy's final goal and appearance for Arsenal which did the damage in front of the Kop. The following season he'd be lining up for Liverpool.

I'd watched the game from the Kop that night, and can still remember the sense of utter bemusement I felt when we failed to recover from going a goal behind. After the double success of the previous season, we'd reached the Cup final this time around, and although it had become highly unlikely we would win the league even before the Arsenal defeat, the mathematical removal of the possibility was a bitter pill to swallow.

Certainly, Leeds becoming champions after a mid-week evening game at

Anfield was nothing new. Five years earlier I'd watched from the boys' pen as Leeds claimed a 0-0 draw which clinched the title at Liverpool's expense, and earned them a standing ovation from the Kop. This time round, it was Arsenal doing the honours on Leeds behalf. I consoled myself with thoughts of my pending trip to Wembley for the FA Cup Final against Newcastle.

It would be the first of many visits to the appointed home of English football, a dream at last come true, but I have to report my sister Stephanie had already beaten me to it. A school visit to watch an international schoolgirls hockey match had been the occasion, maybe a year earlier, and I'd been green with envy. Not anymore.

In those days, non-season ticket holders at Anfield were given a voucher on the way into the ground for one of the preceding league games, after which the club would announce a single digit which, if your voucher serial number ended with it, entitled you to a ticket for the final. If I remember correctly, this year the magic number had been 4, and I didn't have it. However, my dad's mate Frankie Wheeler did. A seasoned traveller with the reds, he unbelievably kindly let me have it.

I travelled to the game with Dougie Drinan, a friend of mine, and an older friend of his family who was planning to drive down with his own mate. For some reason, which I still can't fathom other than this was clearly a special occasion, I wore a suit and tie to the game. Made to measure from Peter Pell on London Road, the suit was a stylish aubergine three piece, with turnups on the trousers, complete with lilac shirt and matching tie. And me not yet 16. I dread to think what my denim clad fellow teenagers surrounding me on the Wembley terraces must have thought. Or my travelling companions for that matter. Not that sartorial elegance, or lack thereof, was high on our conversational to do list, which was basically football, football and more football.

We parked close to Stanmore tube station where a Geordie with a very happy disposition, clearly alcohol enhanced, pleasantly informed us that we were wasting our time turning up, such was his team's obvious superiority. I shared his happiness, if not his opinion, with my first footsteps inside Wembley now just a few minutes away. I have to say, the rest of the day went swimmingly. For me if not for our friendly Geordie.

A goalless first half belied Liverpool's growing dominance, and when left back Alec Lindsay's stunning left foot drive from an acute angle was ruled out for a marginal offside call, fleeting thoughts that this may not be our day did briefly surface. But a superb volley from a more central position a few minutes later by Kevin Keegan set the ball rolling and signalled the beginning of the end for Newcastle.

Rather than trigger a response from our opponents, the goal seemed to urge Liverpool onto even greater heights and long before Steve Heighway had slotted a headed flick-on from Toshack past Toon keeper Iam McFaul, the outcome was no longer in doubt. The party on the terraces had been in full swing for a good ten minutes when Keegan added the third and final goal a couple of minutes from the end, tapping in from a few yards after a series of passes switched play from wing to wing more than once. A glorious end to a glorious performance on a glorious afternoon. And we even arrived back in Liverpool in time to catch the end of the highlights on Match of the Day. I was already looking forward to the following season.

Barely two months later I was in Southport for 'Orange Lodge Day' (as we called it). On 12 July each year, the Liverpool Lodges of the Orange Order emptied from the city to the coastal resort on the Irish Sea about an hour's train journey north of Liverpool, for a day of celebration. I am not a member and, born to a non-practicing catholic mother and protestant father, have little inclination towards either denomination, though if pressed would declare myself 'Church of England', a legacy of my BB days.

But I'd enjoyed these days out in Southport as an onlooker in the past and, having recently completed my 'O' levels, my schooldays were over at least until September. So, I'd arrived fairly early to spend a few hours savouring the ambience of the occasion before I needed to catch a train to get me back in time for my paper round. After all, the Liverpool Echo wasn't going to deliver itself around the Holt Road, Edge Lane, Wavertree Road area of Liverpool 7.

On the way to Southport station, I noticed a guy standing on a chair outside a newsagents, attempting to put a poster in a newspaper billboard frame (for want of a better description). He was having some difficulty maintaining his balance and I assumed he'd probably had a bit too much to drink, as many in the town centre had on this annual day of merriment. That assumption quickly became fact in my panic-stricken mind when it registered what was written on the poster. Just two words: 'SHANKLY RETIRES'. What explanation could there be other than a deranged and jealous Evertonian attempting to wind up his red supporting mates?

Having dismissed the terrifying possibility with my unerring logic, I was curiously unable to put it out of my mind on the journey home, and found myself anticipating my paper round – and the opportunity to see the Echo for myself – rather more than I usually would. In fact, anticipation was turning to dread the closer to home I got.

And with good reason as it turned out. 'SOCCER BOMBSHELL – SHANKLY RETIRES' screamed the headline on that sunny summer evening. It must have mocked me more than 50 times as I posted each copy of the Echo through the letter boxes of its many customers, most of whom would be affected in one way or another, red or blue.

Many, like me and Dougie, who also had a paper round with the same shop and was there waiting for me when I arrived, would be devastated by the news. Some may have thought "Thank Christ for that", like the Evertonian responding to Tony Wilson on Granada TV's news magazine programme Granada Reports.

A few may even have agreed with the Liverpool fan on the same programme who declared "If he has (retired), Liverpool's had it", though that turned out to be somewhat premature as Liverpool went on to enjoy the most prolific two decades in their history. (In that time, eight league titles became eighteen, two FA Cup wins became five, a single European success became six, four of those in the continent's premier competition. The league cup even made Anfield its home four years on the spin, having never graced us with its presence before. And though the best part of another three decades has passed since that period of hegemony, and the trophy haulage rate has diminished somewhat, another league title, two FA Cup wins, four league cup wins and three European successes, not to mention the FIFA Club World Cup, have been added to the list of honours at Anfield. Not quite 'had it' it seems).

Whatever your football allegiances were in 1974 though, Bill Shankly's rapport with and respect for the club's supporters was an accepted, dare I say envied, phenomenon of the English football landscape. It was impossible not to empathise with his admission that deciding to resign was "possibly like going to the electric chair".

* * *

Shanks had been my hero for as long as I could remember, certainly spanning my school years at Clint Road juniors and secondary education at Collegiate Grammar School in Shaw Street. (Fun fact: Charles Dickens was once a guest lecturer at the Collegiate - though many generations before my attendance I hasten to add!).

A plethora of other luminaries connected with the school over the years included the former Everton captain Brian Labone, he of the "one Evertonian is worth ten Liverpudlians" quote, a logic which probably goes a long way to explaining some of the paltry attendances they've pulled in over the years. Holly Johnson, of 'Frankie Goes to Hollywood' fame's time there overlapped mine, younger than me but in the same form as my brother Alan for a couple of years. And many years before, one of our finest comedy actors, Leonard Rossiter – 'Rising Damp', 'The Fall and Rise of Reginald Perrin' etc – also attended and, like me, played for Collegiate Old Boys first eleven when his schooldays were over.

This statistic may have changed since I stopped playing for the Old Boys 40 years ago, but I believe he played in the only team (certainly the first) to win the quadruple of I Zingari League, I Zingari Challenge Cup, Liverpool Amateur Cup and Lancashire Amateur Cup in the same season. He was obviously a talented sportsman, being a highly ranked squash amateur at national level before he died and also excelling at cricket and tennis. In another equally tenuous personal link, he was brought up around the corner from my mum in Cretan Road, Wavertree. So, clear family connections there then.

The Collegiate provided a much different experience for me than junior school had. For a start, I was no longer the star pupil, the learning experience not quite as straightforward. The school building itself was very imposing, a grade II listed building with a pink Woolton sandstone facade, designed in Tudor Gothic style by Harvey Lonsdale Elmes, the same architect responsible for Liverpool's St. Georges Hall.

Compared to my junior school experience, I initially found the number of pupils quite intimidating, probably three to four times as many, with five streamed forms for each school year, the 'A' stream containing students judged to be furthest forward in their educational development, and the 'E' stream those who had furthest to catch up.

I started in the 'B' stream, form '1B', so not just no longer a star pupil, but not even in the top form, a blow to my confidence which was perhaps reflected in my performance during the first term where I finished 21st out of 30 students. I evidently regained ground in the remaining couple of terms, enough that by the end of the school year my 'promotion' to the 'A' stream was justified, and I started the next school year in the 'A' stream, form '2A'. And that's where I remained throughout my remaining years at the school, leaving, perhaps prematurely, with five 'O' levels in 1974 just before my 16th birthday.

I say prematurely because I had every intention of returning to the sixth form after I'd finished my 'O' level exams, but a visit to the Careers Office during the summer holidays, which included some form of aptitude or psychometric test, persuaded me to opt for a place at Millbank College of Commerce to study for a diploma in Business Studies instead. Not that I regretted that decision either, as I added to my 'O' level count with good pass marks in Law, Accounts and British Constitution – subjects I'd never have the opportunity to study at school – and also scraped a pass in Economics and 'A' level Law.

College also provided a more adult learning environment than my school days, where students were treated as grown-ups and there was more onus to be self-motivated, though I suspect the sixth form environment at school may well have provided the same.

Curiously, throughout my time in secondary education I never really got involved with the school football teams, except for one occasion when

Collegiate were desperately short of players and I answered an emergency call to help plug the gaps, scoring in a 7-0 rout of a Liverpool Institute High School team, who evidently were even more desperate for player numbers as they turned out without a full team, hence the one-sided score line. It's not as if I tried and failed to be selected for the school team, more that I played regularly on a Saturday afternoon for the BB, which was where my loyalties lay in that regard. I did play chess for the school team, and represented the school at cross-country during the winter and athletics in the summer, and football was my only activity during school breaks in the morning and at lunchtime. I just never really considered turning out for the football team.

A constant throughout of course, was my pre-occupation with Liverpool FC. I've already mentioned the successes we enjoyed during my time at Collegiate. My two years at college saw us draw a blank in the first, finishing runners-up to Derby County in the league and relinquishing our hold on the FA Cup to a late Mick Mills goal at Ipswich in the 4th round.

That's a long way to go to get kicked in the teeth late on, and I felt the pain all the way home on the seemingly never ending 'special' train journey. (We returned that favour four years later when Ipswich were FA Cup holders themselves, Dalglish scoring the only goal of the game at Portman Road to knock them out.

I travelled to that one on a supporter's coach in such a poor state of repair that it struggled to get up Brownlow Hill in Liverpool city centre a few minutes after setting off, eventually deposited us at the ground after breaking down on route and after Dalglish had already scored, and back in Liverpool city centre in the early hours of the following morning. But only after I'd been attacked by rival fans outside the ground – a consequence of our late arrival and ending up in the wrong end – and an encounter with members of the local constabulary after a handful of my fellow passengers thought it a good idea to help themselves to various unpaid for items from a petrol station we stopped at on our way home.

The cheeky buggers – passengers not police - even suggested a whip round to recompense the garage owner. I wasn't the only one of my fellow innocents to disabuse them of that idea).

Our European adventure in the Cup Winners Cup initially promised something more as it started with the club's record victory, 11-0 at Anfield against
Norwegian amateurs Stromsgodset, nine of the ten outfield players scoring,
with Brian Hall the only one to miss out. Despite the lowly nature of the
opposition, it was an entertaining watch from the Kop, but ultimately a futile
exercise as we exited in the next round, losing on away goals to Ferencvaros
of Hungary.

The final game of the season, at home to QPR, found most supporters in
celebratory mood during a 3-1 win with "Europe Europe Here We Come"
rolling down from the stands as we finished runners-up to Derby County,
themselves Champions for the second time in four seasons.

Sadly, a tiny minority of 'fans', I guess no more than a couple of dozen or so
standing immediately in front of me on the Kop, thought it was an appropriate
time to start a "Paisley Out" chant. Predictably, they were immediately left
in no doubt what the rest of us thought of that sentiment and it was never
heard again. And just as well, or we may not have had the eight seasons which
followed! (For the avoidance of doubt, it's *never* appropriate for the Anfield
crowd to call for the manager's head - unless the manager's name is Roy
Hodgson!).

Cutting to the chase, in Paisley's second season we won the double of
League title and UEFA Cup for the second time in four seasons, and three
personal experiences from that season spring to mind, only one of which
involves my attendance at a league game, and none involve the UEFA Cup –
though I did attend the home legs against Dynamo Dresden, Barcelona in the
semi-final and Bruges in the final.

In the fourth round of the FA Cup, we were drawn to play Derby County
at their 'Baseball Ground' home. I travelled to the game with a couple of
college friends – Chris Evans and Robert Potter – and Gerry, a mate of Bob's
– in Chris's mini. It was a bit of a squeeze, but we weren't breaking any laws
with just the four of us in the car, and we set off from Liverpool early in the
morning, in plenty of time for the 3pm kick-off, travelling cross-country
to pick up the A6 which would take us in to Derby. The home team were the
reigning champions and near the peak of their powers, and though the game

wasn't ticketed, a full house was certain. So basically, it was get there early to guarantee entry. Hence the early start.

A cold, crisp start to the late January Saturday morning on Merseyside translated into snow on the ground and freezing conditions as we approached the Peak District, and with them a creeping sense of foreboding. Which crystallised when the sub-frame on the mini 'went' as we approached Bakewell in Derbyshire. I don't really know what that actually means, other than that we were unable to progress much further in the car and had to leave it at a local garage for attention, while we decided what to do next. Which didn't turn out to be much of a decision as we were all pretty much skint. We'd have to give the match a miss and concentrate on getting back to Liverpool.

The Peak District is a beautiful part of the world, and especially scenic when decorated in snow. Not ideal for road travel though, even at the best of times. Our trek home saw us take a long, lumbering bus ride from Bakewell to Buxton, a rattling train journey onto Manchester Piccadilly station and then a coach from Manchester to Liverpool's Pier Head, at which point we all split up to catch our respective local buses home. At least we managed to get back in a reasonably timely manner, which had been by no means certain when we'd abandoned the car.

Adding insult to injury, as I entered the living room my dad, listening to the match on the radio, looked up with a mixture of surprise and disgust on his face. Surprise to see me, disgust that Roger Davies scored the only goal of the game for Derby as I closed the door behind me. You couldn't make it up.

Mum rounded things off nicely when, noting our increasingly dark humour as the game progressed to its dismal conclusion, blithely espoused the view that it was 'only a game' and that we 'shouldn't take it so seriously'. She was right of course. And very wrong.

Easter brought with it the climax to the season, both Liverpool's and the BB's. Glenmalure Park, often simply known as Milltown, was the home of Irish club Shamrock Rovers in 1976, situated in Milltown on the south side of Dublin. It was also where the representative team for the Liverpool Battalion of the Boys Brigade were due to play against our Dublin counterparts on the Easter Saturday.

As a member of the Liverpool squad (I've always wanted to say that!), I travelled on the overnight ferry from Liverpool to Dublin on Maundy Thursday with my teammates, giving us a day to recuperate from the crossing before the game the following day. As I recall that day of recuperation was sorely needed, as most of us found it impossible to get any meaningful sleep on the boat.

It was an enjoyable trip. I was selected in my usual left back position and the momentum of the game swung between the two teams, Liverpool taking a 2-0 half-time lead, then falling behind 3-2 before equalising with a few minutes remaining. Honours even and an exciting final game for me, as my age – I'd be eighteen in the summer – would rule me out of any future appearances.

We caught the ferry home that same night and, to my delight, Match of the Day was shown in one of the lounges, with the headline game being Liverpool against Stoke City. It was more nerve wracking than it should have been because for some reason I didn't know the score despite the game finishing hours earlier, but it turned out to be a cracking match, Liverpool triumphing 5-3 to take over at the top of the league with just two games to play. Two days later on Easter Monday we won 3-0 against Manchester City at Maine Road, leaving us a point clear of second placed QPR, both teams having a single game left. Next up, Wolves away.

It's unthinkable these days, but QPR played – and won – their final league game a week and a half before Liverpool's final game at Molyneux, so were top by a point and watching from their collective armchairs as our game kicked off, with a few hundred of their fans adding their support for the home team from inside the ground, having travelled up for the game from the capital.

Again, I travelled to the match with my mate Dougie (and seemingly half of the city), this time on the 'special' from Lime Street. Again, a full house was guaranteed but the match wasn't ticketed, so we were there hours before kick-off queuing to get in, and only just making it minutes before the turnstiles were closed – it was like a home game for us with so many reds in the ground. Again, match-going supporters treated abysmally. 'Twas ever thus.

For added spice, Wolves own perilous league position provided another dimension to the occasion. They needed to win and hope that Birmingham City were beaten at Sheffield Utd on the same night, results which would see Birmingham take Wolves place as one of the relegated sides. Liverpool needed a win or a low scoring draw (any draw other than 0-0, 1-1 or 2-2 would see QPR take the league on goal average).

And for a while, it looked like everything was falling into place for Wolves and QPR. Steve Kindon scored a fine goal inside the first 15 minutes to give Wolves the lead, and Sheffield United took the lead against Birmingham. At Molyneux Liverpool dominated, but half-time came and went with the score unchanged. The second half was even more one-sided than the first had been, but we entered the last quarter of an hour still needing a goal. Then, like Merseytravel buses, three arrived at once.

Kevin Keegan equalised courtesy of a flick-on by John Toshack and the Liverpool end erupted, fans behind the Wolves goal spilling onto the pitch in glorious rapture. That would have been enough in itself, but with five minutes to go, Toshack himself took a pass from Ray Kennedy to score our second and a few minutes later Keegan put Kennedy in for the third. Final score 3-1 and champions for a record ninth time.

If it was any consolation to Wolves (I'm sure it wasn't), Birmingham had also rallied against Sheffield United to earn a draw, so their loss hadn't cost them. They were down anyway. A couple of weeks later Liverpool clinched the UEFA Cup, a 1-1 draw in the second leg of the final in Bruges enough for an aggregate victory, after coming from two goals behind in the first leg at Anfield a week before the Wolves game, to take a 3-2 lead to Belgium. What a fantastic season. How could we follow that?

Well, with eleven more trophies, including four more doubles, before Bob decided to call it a day, as it happens!

* * *

In the summer following that memorable Molyneux evening I joined the world of work, which would see me fill a couple of roles with little opportunity to advance, before accepting a more promising offer to join an insurance brokers in Silkhouse Court in Liverpool city centre. Nothing too taxing, a reasonably gentle introduction to an activity that would sustain me, and later my family, over the next 44 years. Financially at least.

I also responded to a notice in the Liverpool Echo inviting former pupils at the Collegiate to join up with the Old Boys football club, which ran six teams. The first eleven in the I Zingari League, the seconds in the I Zingari Combination, and the remaining four teams in various divisions of the Old Boys League.

I'd played for the BB since I was 11 years old and always assumed that I'd simply stop playing organised football regularly once I'd reached their 18-years-old age limit. However, playing for the representative Liverpool BB side had whetted my appetite for more senior, organised football, and when I saw the notice in the local paper I didn't think twice about turning up for training, as instructed.

I made my debut as left back for the thirds in the first division of the Old Boy's league, a 3-1 victory on a filthy day somewhere in South Liverpool, the torrential rain and sodden pitch unable to dampen my enthusiasm for the task in hand. I did love a slide-tackle! Glowing references from the third's Captain Dave 'Dicko' Dickenson at the weekly selection meetings meant that I quickly moved up to the seconds, and before the end of the season, despite flitting between the seconds and thirds for the majority of the it, I'd broken into the first team.

Which may sound a bit of a grandiose way of putting it, but to my 18 year old self at the time it did feel like an achievement, sharing the stage with a mixture of experienced old heads, some of whom had been playing at this level for almost as long as I'd been on the planet and were well acquainted with the dark arts of amateur football (stand up Dave 'Waz' Walkden); enthusiastic cloggers who were more than happy to try and physically intimidate a raw and still not fully developed newbie to the scene (mentioning no names here); and one or two genuine superstars who simply stood out at this level (take a bow Paul Bennett).

I even ran the gauntlet of psychological abuse from the touchline at times, opposition entourages (yes, there were a few!) keen to test the mettle of the skinny young kid at the back. I wallowed in "Get at the left-back, he's only about 12!", and similar comments shouted from opposing managers on more than one occasion, revelling in the moments they eventually substituted their 'marked out of the game' right winger (me and right wingers have never got on!)

I loved every minute.

We weren't particularly successful, in fact we became a bit of a yo-yo team when I played, too good to stay down in the second division, not quite good enough to stay up in the first. But without fail I looked forward to playing every Saturday, followed by a few drinks afterwards, usually within the environs of West Derby village, just down the road from our home pitches at Holly Lodge, behind the Jolly Miller pub on Queens Drive. Although the Jolly Miller car park was our regular pre-game meeting point for away fixtures, it was never an after-match destination, our usual haunts being the Halton Castle, until the whole club was banned for the undisclosed misdemeanours of a few, and then the Hare and Hounds.

It was at the bar in the Hare and Hounds one after-match Saturday when I said a passing hello to Johnny Miller, one of my first eleven teammates, who was having a drink with another guy I hadn't seen before. He in turn was accompanied by his dog sitting quietly at his feet (which I also hadn't seen before), and said hello before complimenting me on my performance a week earlier, playing on what is now 'The Bill Shankly Playing Fields' on Eaton Road.

A few minutes later Johnny, who had been on Liverpool's books as a kid, came over to where I was enjoying my first post-match pint.

"You know who that was, don't you?" Johnny asked.

"No idea, never seen him before" I replied, "or his dog".

"Liverpool scout mate. Said you had a cracking game last week".

Which was true, I had played particularly well though I say so myself. And though it never led to anything more, along with being selected for the I Zingari League representative squad and receiving a glowing write-up in the now defunct 'Liverpool Weekly News' around the same time, it invokes a feeling of pride I never experienced at the time, along with no doubt exaggerated thoughts of scorned opportunities. It seems the older I get, the better I used to be!

My time with the Old Boys was all too short, coming to an end when a career move took me briefly to the States after a few years, but I did manage to fit a couple of Easter excursions to 'the island' in when I was playing. Every Easter the club organised a trip to the Isle of Man, travelling on the Thursday ferry to Douglas, staying at The Princes Hotel on the sea-front there, and catching the return ferry home on Easter Monday, with the odd football match played against a variety of local sides and a lot of drink taken in between times! The ferries, and indeed the island itself, were always rammed with visiting sports teams from the mainland with football, rugby and hockey all well represented.

There is a tradition, or at least we had one, of avoiding bad luck by always saying hello to the fairies as we passed the fairy bridge on the way to Castletown for our annual fixture. Everyone on the coach would greet the fairies as we passed. Except once as I recall. One of our group, Johnny Hawkins if I'm not mistaken (though I may be), decided that this year he wouldn't play ball. In fact, he went a step further by mocking the fairies as the bridge receded through the rear window of the coach.

Arriving at our destination, the coach parked up, Johnny got off and, with no-one within yards of him, promptly fell over and landed face first on the concrete floor, breaking his jaw. Now, I'm not suggesting the affronted fairies had anything to do with the mishap. But I'm certainly not ruling it out either! Suffice to say, on our way back to Douglas after the match the fairies were roundly greeted by everyone on board (though Johnny *was* still at the hospital, and wouldn't be 'playing ball' for a long time!).

The Old Boys' relative lack of success during my time with them was in stark contrast to that enjoyed by the city's, indeed the country's, premier club. The domestic and European double referenced earlier was emulated a year later, although this time Liverpool's first success in Europe's premier competition, confirmed with a 3-1 victory over Borussia Monchengladbach in the final of the European Cup – replaced the UEFA Cup in the trophy cabinet, the League Championship trophy staying exactly where it already was, thank you very much.

A year later FC Bruges were beaten, a lot more comprehensively than the 1-0 score line suggested, as the European cup was retained at Wembley (the first time by an English club and emulated only by Nottingham Forest since, in the following two seasons), and for two consecutive years after that the League Championship returned to Anfield, having taken a sabbatical at Forest for a year following the 1977-78 season.

The European Cup and League Cup double achieved in 1980-81 was accompanied by a disappointing final league position of fifth, an uncharacteristically low finish which Mr Paisley clearly took personally, as he rounded off his time as manager with the League Title and League Cup double in each of the following two seasons. Shanks would always be my hero, but Bob's record was beyond reproach, almost faultless in nine years, the only omission being success in the FA Cup.

Playing legend Kenny Dalglish would eventually remedy that by winning the League and FA Cup double in his first season as player manager a few years later, but not before Bob's successor, Joe Fagan, had guided his charges to the treble of League, League Cup and European Cup in the first of his two seasons, though his second season would end trophyless despite finishing as runners-up in the league and reaching the European Cup final. And sadly remembered primarily for culminating at the Heysel stadium and the tragedy which unfolded there.

2

THE LEAVING OF LIVERPOOL

One day in the winter–cum–spring of 1976, I attended an interview in pursuit of a place at Liverpool Polytechnic to study Law. I was in the second and final year of study for an Ordinary National Diploma in Business Studies at Millbank College of Commerce in West Derby, during which I'd particularly enjoyed the 'General Principles of English Law' element of the course. With an 'O' level in the subject after the first year, and an 'A' level exam to come, I figured that along with the diploma I'd have a good basis for taking my interest further.

The interview went reasonably well, and towards the end the interviewer asked me where else I was looking at to further my education. To which I didn't really have an answer other than that I probably wouldn't be looking beyond the Liverpool city limits. And in answer to his querying my response, I truthfully replied that I'd never even considered moving away, why would I, my family and friends were here. And more to the point, so was my football club.

Six years later I was on my way with a new wife to a new job and new life in New York, and have never actually lived in Liverpool as a responsible adult other than with mine or, for a few months after we married, my wife's parents.

I occasionally wonder how my life may have turned out if I'd actually gone on to study Law at the Poly. But though I scraped a pass in the Law 'A' level, I found studying for it a lot less enjoyable than for the 'O' level a year earlier. I also failed to get my diploma. My course marks were generally fine, most of them at distinction level, but failing the mandatory Economics module, albeit narrowly, scuppered any immediate prospects of, not to say appetite for, staying in education and so I took advantage of the government's Job Creation Programme – a forerunner to the Youth Training Scheme (YTS) – and started, with five other school leavers, at the Social Services department in Liverpool's Hatton Garden, where we were tasked with transferring details of the city's register of disabled citizens from Kalamazoo sheets onto index cards. All done by hand, there were no computers, digital data, or data protection issues to be considered back then.

It was tedious stuff, but the novelty of working and getting a weekly wage, no matter how meagre, and the making of new friends – one of whom would be best man at my wedding – was enough to hold my interest for six months or so. I moved on from there to another pretty much dead-end but enjoyable job where I lasted a few months longer, before I decided it was time to move on again. This time to Alexander Howden Insurance Brokers in Liverpool City Centre. It was a decision which had enormous ramifications for the rest of both my personal life and my career.

On my first day, I met my wife Sandra. It would be a little over two years before we started dating and maybe another 18 months after that until our nuptials, but we did hit it off immediately despite my new boss Alan Mason, jokingly I'm sure, warning San before I'd even started the job, to "leave the new boy alone". Though I wasn't aware of it at the time, the first step towards the most important, and best, decision I'd ever make had been taken.

From a career perspective? Well, I'd never thought too much about even having a 'career', and to be honest, now that I've retired from the workplace, I'd say that always remained the case. Of course, I'd always had it in mind that I'd need to make enough money to support a family and live a reasonably comfortable life and that I'd probably need a decent job to provide that. But the thought of identifying a career path and progressing along it step by step had never appealed to me, and never did. Which is perhaps where my failure to progress further with my Law studies was rooted - the 'Law' being heavy career material - and where the diploma course I'd studied paid unexpected dividends in spite of my inability to pass it.

One of the course subjects I'd taken was 'Computer Studies' and I achieved a reasonable pass mark in the final exam, which came as a bit of surprise, both to me and the tutor if I'm being honest. I didn't particularly enjoy the subject and it certainly didn't whet my appetite for using what I'd learned in the future. It did however give me something to talk about when Howden's decided to implement a new computer system. When I'd started the job, we had a couple of NCR accounting machines which the operators would use to enter information via a keyboard – no screens – onto cassette tapes. On a regular basis, and with a big push at the end of each month, the information on these tapes was used to update our ledgers – one for each of our clients (the customers we sold insurance to) and one for each of the actual insurance companies (whose insurance we sold, and from which we received commission).

Having been in and out of the office on numerous occasions as a consultant for our IT capability supplier NCR, Dave Berry had just started a new contract with Howden's, brought in to oversee the implementation of the replacement system. We'd already met a few times during the Sales phase for the new system, when NCR had been on their charm offensive to clinch the deal. Not that I'd had any involvement in that other than being taken out for lunch on a couple of occasions with the rest of the team – no more than half a dozen or so – who worked with the current system.

"What language does the new system use Dave?" I enquired, hoping I sounded like I knew what I was talking about, which was pushing it a bit to say the least.

"COBOL" he replied. Dave was a man of few words.

"Oh, I used that at college".

This was actually true. I had written some syntactically error free code, which didn't do anything useful, in fact anything at all, but followed the correct syntax rules which meant that no errors were reported when the source code I'd written was compiled – converted – from English-like statements, which could be understood at the most basic level by any English-speaking person, to machine code which would be used to instruct the computer what to do. My code didn't instruct it to do anything.

"Really?".

Dave could not have laced his response with any more disbelief.

"Yeah. I did Computer Studies as part of the course".

"That's interesting" Dave replied.

And that was the end of a conversation which left me in absolutely no doubt that Dave hadn't found it 'interesting' at all. So, no-one was more surprised than me when, a few weeks later, I was offered an aptitude test to determine my suitability for a trainee computer programmer role, which I found straightforward enough, and soon after that I was enrolled on a course to find out about the operating system for our new minicomputer. My new 'career' was up and running.

What really excited me with this latest development though was that the one-week course was going to be held at NCR's London Offices in Balcombe Street. First, I'd hardly ever visited the capital before (one FA Cup final notwithstanding). Second, and most importantly, the first day of the course would be the Monday after Liverpool, as League Champions, were due to play Arsenal as FA Cup holders, in the new season's Charity Shield curtain raiser. Although my boss Alan was a blue, he wasn't of the bitter variety, and he added his own weight to my request to spend the weekend before the course in London, which thankfully the powers that be agreed to.

Liverpool comfortably won the game 3-1 with a couple of long-range efforts from McDermott and another goal from Dalglish, who put the Arsenal keeper Pat Jennings on his backside before planting his shot in the opposite corner, Alan Sunderland scoring a late consolation for the gooners. It was a supremely dominant performance from the reds which foretold another successful season at the end of which we were duly crowned league champions again. It was also the only game in seven encounters with Arsenal in that 1979-80 season where we'd come out on top. They managed to dash our hopes of the double later in the season after four attempts in the semi-final of the cup, while both league games ended in draws.

Back in the office after my course, I settled into my new role somewhat slowly. Christmas came and went, as did a memorable New Year's Eve party at San's house. Memorable for the others present that is, less so for me. It must have been a good one, her dad's home-made punch certainly was. Early in the new year I completed another course in Balcombe Street – this time a two-week introduction to the latest version of COBOL, the computer programming language I'd shortly be expected to start writing code with – and was immediately tasked with using it. Which was when I realised most of what I'd supposedly 'learned' on the course had gone in one ear and right out the other. In the meantime, the company had taken on another experienced programmer, and her obvious knowledge and expertise only served to throw my lack of both into sharp relief.

I've come to realise over the years that I can be too unforgiving of myself when faced with a task which I've never attempted before and for which I don't currently have the know-how to resolve, for some reason believing that if I'm expected to complete it, I must surely have the inherent knowledge and ability to be able to do so. It means that on occasion I have become quite stressed, especially in a work situation where I'm actually being paid to achieve something, regardless of the fact that an objective observer might be more than happy with my progress. And a result of that has sometimes been a spiralling lack of confidence which further inhibits performance, to the extent that it seems almost impossible to make any progress at all.

Of course, as my experience and self-awareness has increased over time, I have been better able to control and rationalise similarly stressful situations. Which is all well and good now that I've retired from the daily need to make a living, but back in my new role at the end of the 1970s it was almost enough to stop my fledgling career in IT before it even got off the ground.

As well as Bev, the new programmer, a couple of more senior consultants, Roger and Neville, were also taken on temporarily, with Roger given line management responsibility for me. Shortly after, he took me to one side and asked if I'd liked to return to my previous role as an accounts clerk, as I didn't appear to be enjoying my new role, that it wasn't for everyone, and that there was no shame in 'giving it a go' but realising it wasn't what you wanted to do. I was in an enviable situation he said, whereby I could simply pick up my old job where I'd left off. Looking back, it was a real 'sliding doors' moment.

I was tempted to accept the offer, to cut my losses and run, if you like. And who knows what the ramifications of that decision, for better or worse, might have been? But I knew IT, as an industry, was as future proofed as any at the time. If I could just settle into it, I probably wouldn't have to worry about gainful employment for a while, and the financial rewards where not to be sneezed at either, certainly above average.

As much as anything, I didn't want to be perceived – by myself as much as anyone else - as failing, as giving up this chance of being able to pursue a more rewarding, at least financially, occupation. 'Working in Computers' also carried a certain cachet at the time which would certainly have appealed to my developing sense of self-esteem. I still had no career path in mind, but it was clear to me that working in IT would potentially give me a lot more options in the future than simply knuckling down in an accounts department. So, I politely declined Roger's offer and resolved to at least prove my mettle as a computer programmer. Which I did, to the extent that a year later I was in a position to accept a job offer from a software house in New York.

San and I were already engaged at the time I received the offer, and we married a good six months before my new job eventually started, such was the length of time it took for our visas to be granted.

In the space of a few days just before we left for the States, Liverpool won twice in Manchester to hammer home their rediscovered title credentials after an inconsistent start to the 1981-82 season had seen them sitting in 12th place, nine points off the leaders Swansea after a 3-1 defeat at home to Manchester City on Boxing Day.

A 1-0 mid-week victory at Old Trafford, where Craig Johnstone scored the only goal after Frank Stapleton had missed an early penalty for the home team, was celebrated appropriately in "The Scotch Piper Inn" – the 'oldest pub in historic Lancashire' (and possibly the smallest!) – where me and San were having a farewell drink of sorts with San's brother and sister-in-law, Tom and Carol. A few days later, City paid a heavy price for having had the temerity to win at Anfield, on the receiving end of a 5-0 home drubbing.

Having arrived in New York mid-April 1982, we were back home less than six months later, a combination of my father-in-law's ill health, and a recession inspired dearth of clients for my new employer contributing to our decision to cut short our stay in the States. But we'd cut the apron strings to our motherland and, though we would always hold it dear, and look forward to visiting as often as we would any familial gathering, we also acknowledged that the world was a big place and we'd be better served not limiting our immediate horizons to a very small corner of it, no matter how warm and welcoming.

While in New York, we were kept up to date with 'soccer' news by the regular arrival of the 'Pink', or the 'Football Echo' as it was otherwise known, a weekly football only version of the 'Liverpool Echo' which came out immediately after each Saturday's fixtures had been completed. Without fail, my dad sent it out to us after he'd finished with it.

This was more important than it may sound. Although technically the internet was 'started' in 1969, we were still a decade and more away from it being available for anything like public use, and common use of mobile phones by the masses was similarly some time away. Other than small print in the results section of the New York Times on Sunday, we had nothing else to go on.

Through the NYT we got to know of Liverpool's comeback from an early two goal deficit at Spurs to grab a draw, and of Liverpool's comeback at Anfield against the same team for a 3-1 victory which clinched the league title. This completed a noteworthy treble of sorts against the men from White Hart Lane, Liverpool having also come from behind to win 3-1 at Wembley in March and take home the League Cup for the third consecutive season.

After a couple of unemployed months following our return home, which we were grateful to be able to spend living with San's parents, we were off on our travels again. Not so far this time, but still a big step for us. That there London town beckoned, another software house for me, another accounts department in another insurance brokers for San. Six months or so living in a rented flat in Palmers Green, with a reasonably short commute into the City, were followed by the best part of four years living in our own first home near the Essex coast, with an expensively monster commute thrown in for good measure.

We still managed to get home to Liverpool a few times each year – Easter, Christmas and summer holidays at least – and always managed to take in a few games at Anfield. A combination of being in New York when the season started and a temporary lack of finances after we'd returned meant that the first game I managed to attend in the 1982-83 season was actually at Goodison Park, the 5-0 derby rout of Everton. It was a good omen for the rest of the season.

Just over a month later, my last game at Anfield before I started work in London was against a Watford side managed by Graham Taylor and graced by future red John Barnes, both of whom were helpless to prevent us running out comfortable 3-1 winners, a sublime turn and pass from Dalglish to set up Ian Rush for the first goal a particular highlight for me. A good, if unspectacular win, and not particularly noteworthy except for the fact that captain Phil Thompson, a Liverpool legend by this time, was injured and had to be replaced. Although he returned briefly later in the campaign, it was the beginning of the end of his Liverpool playing career, which wouldn't make it into the following season.

Two weeks later I was back in Liverpool for the Christmas break and still in the queue for the Kop on Boxing Day when Liverpool scored three of their five goals that day against Manchester City. Final score 5-2. Technically 2-2 after I eventually managed to get in!

During the next four and a bit years, our football club was as successful as at any time in its history. Success followed success, home and abroad, and we were destined to watch it primarily from a distance. Living, working, and more significantly, playing local amateur football where I did, meant that my path regularly crossed those of supporters of other clubs, especially the senior London clubs like Arsenal, Spurs, Chelsea, West Ham. Even Queens Park Rangers figured.

The day after Spurs won at Anfield for the first time since 1912 springs to mind, as their supporters in our Sunday League team queued up to gloat. One win in 73 years didn't seem much to celebrate to be honest, but even then, there was a potential silver lining of sorts with Spurs being the closest challengers to our bitter local rivals Everton for the league. Of course, they still bottled it, Everton winning it comfortably with Liverpool eventually finishing as runners up.

The following season, QPR knocked Liverpool out in a two-legged league cup semi-final, both their goals at Anfield in the second leg 2-2 draw scored by Liverpool players, before Oxford United, with future reds John Aldridge and Ray Houghton in their line-up, wiped the floor with them, 3-0 in the final. Sadly, I was delighted at this vicarious revenge.

By then, Liverpool had already recovered from the setback to reach the FA Cup final, and a couple of weeks later we won at Chelsea to clinch the league, player manager Dalglish predictably the hero with the only goal. I celebrated the win by screaming my head off as I ran around a car park in Maldon after the final whistle had blown. No rival fans queuing up for my attention the day after that one.

A week later the coveted double was in the bag following a 3-1 victory over Everton to win the FA Cup at Wembley. Having managed to get to White Hart Lane for the semi-final victory over Southampton, I'd watched the final in our living room. Dave 'Sandy' Howard, a mechanic by trade, manager of our Sunday League team by unpaid vocation, and a West Ham fan, came round to service my car in the morning and stayed for the match, enjoying my antics after each Liverpool goal.

Which is more than can be said for our six-month-old son Tom. Propped up in one corner of the sofa, dressed in a home-made red and white outfit including woolly hat, he clearly didn't share my sense of euphoria when Ian Rush equalised Gary Lineker's opening goal, dissolving into startled tears at his father's unseemly and hitherto unattested behaviour. So guilty did I feel that, when Craig Johnstone scored our second a few minutes later, I simply jumped up and ran out of the house before letting any sound escape from my lips. When Rushie scored our third, his second, with just a few minutes to go, putting the result beyond doubt, all was relatively calm. Job done, pressure off, no way back for Everton now. It was joyous!

One more adverse result stands out for me before we left our Essex home for the last time. Less than three weeks before the move, we were again in the

League Cup final, this time against regular foes Arsenal. When Rush scored the first goal of the game halfway through the first half, a customary victory seemed likely. Liverpool had never lost a game in which Rush had scored, a fact even alluded to by Everton's Gary Lineker after our Cup final victory the previous season (I'm sure the Evertonian's were delighted with that observation!). But two goals from Charlie Nicholas put paid to that statistic and won the final for the gunners. A week later, Rush scored the first goal at Norwich in a game we again lost 2-1. That spell had been well and truly broken.

A personal 1-0 cup final defeat as my Quay Sports FC of Maldon lost, undeservedly in my opinion, to local rivals Purleigh Queens, followed a week later, and with that final disappointment behind us we were off back up North.

3

FAMILY MAN, LUCKY GUY

Where to start? How do you begin to find the words which adequately describe your thoughts, feelings, emotions about those without whom your life has little meaning beyond the shallow confines of material achievement and maybe the vicarious pleasure, or otherwise, of following your favourite sports team, for example? Both may be undeniably all consuming at times, but eventually pale into unfulfilling insignificance. For me anyway.

Well, let's start at the beginning.

I took my first step on the road to my own family – that is the immediate family I have been privileged to bring up with my wife (as opposed to my parents' family which I share with my siblings, if I can put it like that) – on Monday 12 December 1977. Somewhere between 8.30 and 9.00 am on the day I walked into the accounts department of Alexander Howden Insurance Brokers' Liverpool office, on the 6th floor of Silkhouse Court in Tithebarn Street, to be even more precise. An office which seemed to me - a shy, fresh-faced, 19-year-old introvert of a lad who barely looked as if I'd entered my teens when in fact I would shortly be leaving them behind - to be over-stocked with oestrogen.

These were long before the hipster years of facial hair, no matter how sparse and ragged, being a popular male accoutrement, yet I hadn't shaved for my first day on the new job. There was no need. Regular daily shaving was still half a lifetime away at that stage (I didn't shave on my wedding day nearly four years later either) and, having been in all-male education establishments throughout junior and senior school since I was seven, and a member of the obviously all male Boys Brigade until I was eighteen, I was painfully uncomfortable in the presence of any group of females which didn't include my mum, sister or other family member.

In echoes of my first day at college three years earlier – for a male dominated business studies course at a primarily female dominated secretarial college, where at least 95% of students at first day registration appeared to be young women – my first inclination was to flee. At college I'd temporarily escaped towards the welcoming sight of double doors at the end of a long corridor, adjacent to the assembly hall where registrations were taking place, only to find that the doors led solely to the enclosed college gym and were locked anyway. I eventually registered 30 minutes late after waiting for my heart rate to return to normal and the hall to start emptying.

On my first day at Howden's, the thought of running down six flights of stairs to make my escape did fleetingly cross my mind, but by then I was made of sterner stuff, if only slightly. This was my third job, and the previous two – at Liverpool Social Services Department and in the Transport department of Graham Gratrix, a builders merchants situated on Great Howard Street – plus the best part of 18 months and a couple of girlfriends since leaving college, had improved my appreciation (or should that be tolerance?) of the fairer sex, at least enough to enable me to push through the gathering panic and make it, under the guidance of Alan Mason, my new boss, to my new desk which at least was at the end of a row. I wasn't *completely* surrounded.

Sitting opposite was Ruth Oldfield, soon to become Ruth Cowell by marrying Paul, coincidentally a former junior school classmate of mine; next to her was Carol Brizzel, and immediately to my right Jean (Ogden, if I remember correctly, which I may not) who would go on to marry her soldier sweetheart and become a Lunt. Glancing over my right shoulder allowed me to observe Denise Blundell who, perhaps not unreasonably, fancied herself as the glamour puss of the office and next to her was San, who I immediately took to. Friendly, easy to talk to, certainly not playing second fiddle to anyone in the glamour stakes herself and a Liverpool season ticket holder to boot. Be still my beating heart!

San was born, less than two weeks after I made my own first appearance a few miles further south, at the family home in Dumbarton Street, just off County Road in Walton, within an overhit Jordan Pickford clearance of Goodison Park, and was actually christened in St Luke's, the church located between the Gwladys Street End and Goodison Road stands. Thankfully her family's allegiance to the reds was stronger than the gravitational pull of our near neighbours – laudable given the respective statuses of the two clubs at the time she was born in 1958 – or our relationship may never have got off the ground.

I had a steady girlfriend at the time, in a relationship which was very serious for a while, until it wasn't, and it was time for me to move on. From then on San was the one for me, a subsequent girlfriend notwithstanding (sorry Janet, my heart was never in it), though she rejected my nervous advances more than once before agreeing to go on a date. But long before that first date we had become close friends, spending pretty much all our lunchtimes together – often with Pam Hughes, another work colleague and friend – and frequently socialising outside work, especially when celebrating birthdays, weddings and the like of other work colleagues. So much so in fact, that it is difficult to pinpoint what our first date actually was. It certainly wasn't before we'd spent a week together, along with my best mate Phil New – who would agree to be my best man – at the home of San's Auntie Lisle, who lived with her son Michael just outside Antwerp in Belgium.

San had mentioned her Auntie Lisle, a Germany lady who had married San's late Uncle Stan, during a conversation in the office, revealing that Lisle always looked forward to receiving visitors from the family in England. After a chat on a night out with Phil the following weekend, I cheekily suggested to San that perhaps her aunt would be prepared to put me and Phil up for a week. A couple of days later we'd settled on the dates and San had decided to come with us, having already cleared it with her auntie.

We subsequently travelled overland via the midnight mail train from Liverpool to London, coach to Dover, hovercraft across the Channel, then another coach to Antwerp where we enjoyed a great week with Lisle and young Michael, the perfect hosts, at their lovely home on the outskirts. A visit to Brussels enabled us take in the Manneken Pis – the famous 'Peeing Boy' water fountain statue (not an icing kit in sight!) - and the Atomium, a landmark silver structure built to resemble a giant atom for the 1958 Brussels World Fair.

It was much more of a landmark than the football ground we espied from a window within one of the 'electrons' in the 'atom', which I remarked must be a local neglected amateur ground as it was clearly in such a poor state of repair. It actually transpired to be the Heysel Stadium which would sadly become a well-known landmark for all the wrong reasons five years later when it hosted the European Cup Final between Liverpool and Juventus, and 39 people, mainly Italian, would be killed when a crumbling wall collapsed following clashes between rival fans.

Hindsight is apparently a wonderful thing, but it surely didn't require much foresight to determine that stadium wasn't a suitable venue for any high-profile fixture. Following the disaster, it was deemed to be in such poor condition that it was completely demolished and rebuilt, and is now known as the King Baudouin Stadium, though it will always carry the stigma of being 'Heysel'.

But that was all in the future, and travelling home after a wonderful trip – only my second one abroad - I reflected on the week's highlights and realised, though there were many, that the main and most exciting one was the growing closeness I shared with San. Things were starting to look up.

Not long after we arrived home San and Pam – I don't know who had the original idea - suggested a night out in Liverpool with Pam's fiancé Tony making up a foursome, and we enjoyed a few drinks while 'clubbing' it in Wood Street. That must have gone well enough as not long after San invited me for tea and a stay over at her home in Maghull where she lived with her mum and dad.

I'd already met her parents a few times – celebrating her twenty first birthday, both at home on the actual day and then the following weekend for the big birthday bash at the Bradford Hotel in town, and when invited for a New Year's Eve celebration where I did myself no favours by drinking far too much of her dad's home-made punch. It was equally delicious and potent, and I suffered the consequences the following day, having apparently already introduced myself to a few neighbours by running drunkenly round the streets just after midnight, knocking on doors and wishing anyone who wasn't too wary to answer a Happy New Year. I'd also met San's mum about a year earlier at the Emlyn Hughes testimonial match which we attended together, so it wasn't a massive deal meeting her parents again.

It was a good weekend. Liverpool beat Spurs at White Hart Lane in the sixth round of the cup courtesy of the only goal of the game by Terry McDermott, a volleyed screamer into the far corner of the net from the edge of the penalty area, the match fortunately being featured on 'Match of the Day'. After dinner (beef risotto if I remember correctly) prepared by San, the four of us popped into the local 'Coach and Horses' pub for a few drinks to round the day off, and I left for home later the following day happy in the knowledge that me and San were slowly starting to become a couple.

Following the victory over Spurs, Liverpool were drawn against Arsenal in the semi-final, the game to be played at Hillsborough in Sheffield. As a season ticket holder San was entitled to a ticket for the game and was happy to let me have it, as well as the ticket for the subsequent first replay at Villa Park following a tedious 0-0 draw, both of which I attended with George Brash, another friend and work colleague. However, when the replay ended in another draw – this time one goal apiece in a much more entertaining game, with David Fairclough's opener for the reds being cancelled out pretty quickly by the gunners' Alan Sunderland – San decided she was up for attending the second replay, again to be played at Villa Park. Obviously, George was quickly ditched in San's favour (sorry mate) and we travelled to the game on a coach full of expectant reds fans, though we split up on arrival as our tickets were for opposite ends of the ground.

Our hopes were dampened pretty much as soon as the game kicked off, with Arsenal taking the lead, again through Sunderland, within the first fifteen seconds. Liverpool retaliated feverishly, and it made for a compelling spectacle with Dalglish scoring a much-celebrated equaliser deep into injury time after the 90 minutes were up. Although no-one else troubled the scoreboard during extra time Liverpool had remained dominant, with Pat Jennings excelling in goal for Arsenal, and we travelled home in high spirits and looking forward to the third replay, this time to be played at Highfield Road in Coventry.

Less than a month after the first game at Hillsborough, and for the fifth time during that period (the same teams had drawn a league game at Anfield just after the first replay), the two great rivals faced up for what turned out to be the final time in their quest to reach the FA Cup Final, where the winners would face second division West Ham who had accounted for Everton in the other semi-final, needing only the one replay to dispatch their Merseyside opponents. An uninspired performance from Liverpool, in the face of a gritty one by Arsenal, led to an all London final (when all the talk after the draw had been made was of a potential first all-Merseyside final), with Brian Talbot capitalising on a rare Ray Kennedy error to head the winner from the resulting cross.

San and I had again travelled by supporter's coach for the game and the trip back was a sombre one – we weren't used to losing big games. But we had a league game against Aston Villa to look forward to at Anfield less than 48 hours later, where a victory would clinch yet another league title. And best of all, me and San we're definitely 'going out' now, as the hugging and kissing, dare I even say canoodling, on the walk home from the coach demonstrated.

* * *

As spring turned into summer, so our relationship blossomed further. I had lived all my nearly twenty-two years on the planet to this point in Wedgewood Street with my parents and siblings (and for a while my nan and great aunt).

The small terraced house was rented, and we could never persuade the landlord to provide a bathroom. Eventually, my mum and dad were offered the chance to buy the house from the landlord, an offer they jumped at, encouraged no doubt by the asking price of a mere £1400. They subsequently obtained a grant to add an extension which would house a new bathroom, including inside loo. Luxury to us. However, that entailed us moving out to temporary accommodation a good few miles away in Huyton while work on the extension was carried out. San's parents kindly offered to let me stay at the family home – separate room to San of course – and I eagerly accepted.

Now we were living together – in a manner of speaking – working together, obviously socialising together, and pretty much spending all our waking hours together. And we were enjoying that and becoming even closer. Our friendship had proved to be a solid basis to become more intimate and serious and eventually asking San to marry me became simply the most natural thing to do. Thankfully she said 'yes' and having asked her dad Tom for her hand in marriage – he happily rubber-stamped his consent – we were officially engaged on Valentine's Day in 1981 when San's parents held an engagement party for us at their house.

They'd invited my parents to meet them for the first time at their home just three weeks earlier, on the Saturday evening after Everton had come out 2-1 winners against the reds in an FA Cup tie at Goodison Park. On the day of our engagement, we drew 2-2 at Anfield with Birmingham City, despite taking an early two goal lead. At least the results were trending in the right direction, so the omens were good!

Joking aside, 1980-81 was shaping up to be an unusually poor league season for Liverpool and we would end up in fifth place, the first time in nine years we'd finish lower than second. It would be another eleven years before we finished lower than second again. The ignominy of this lowly league placing was soothed somewhat though, when we won the league cup for the first time in our history – and the first of four consecutive triumphs in that competition – and the European Cup for the third time. More than reasonable compensation I thought!

Not long after we were engaged, I accepted the offer of a job in New York. My new employers would cover my travel expenses, and those of my wife if married, but not those of my fiancée, and our wedding plans rapidly changed accordingly, from a fairly nebulous 'in a year or two' to 'as soon as possible this summer please'. Eventually we settled on a midweek date, it being almost impossible to book a weekend date at such short notice. So, Wednesday 2

September 1981 it was. And anyway, Prince Charles and Lady Di were married on a Wednesday in the same year. If it was good enough for them...

It feels almost heretical to admit in these somewhat hedonistic days of hen and stag party extravaganzas, bridal showers and the like, but neither of us even considered having a pre-wedding celebration. I guess money was tight, not that we were contributing much to the wedding ourselves, thanks primarily to San's parents Tom and Gladys, but moreover it just wasn't *that* big of a thing, in our circles at least.

The night before the wedding we were both in the Anfield Road end as Liverpool gained their first point of the season with a 1-1 home draw against Middlesbrough who'd led at half time. This followed a single goal defeat in the season opener against Wolves at Molyneux the previous weekend, an inauspicious start to a campaign which would end with us as Champions (once again) and League Cup Winners (once again).

San's cousin Richard, who lived in the Midlands and is a baggies fan, with Liverpool a close second in his affections, had arrived in advance of the wedding and attended the game with us. We also bumped into Arthur Good, another of San's cousins and a dyed-in-the-wool red, in the ground. He quipped that I was the first man to have 37000 at my stag do. Which turned out to be an exaggeration anyway, as the evening's attendance was a good five thousand below that. After the game, San caught the bus back to Maghull with Richard, and I departed for the family home which was back in Wedgewood Street now that the building work had been completed. My best man, Phil, joined me there and we went to The Grove, one of our many local pubs, for a couple of pints. And that was my stag.

Again, it feels strange to acknowledge now, but me and Phil actually spent my last night as a single man by sharing the double bed in my mum and dad's bedroom. Phil was staying the night in preparation for the big day tomorrow and it was the best we could do. I mean, no-one questioned Morecambe & Wise when they regularly did likewise (another one for the oldies), so no problem right? To this day, I've no idea where my mum and dad slept. In the morning I was off into Town to get my hair cut – just a trim – and then one of the wedding cars arrived to take me and Phil to the church, with my extended family and a few friends following behind us on a charabanc.

On a gloriously warm and sunny day, we'd arranged for the wedding ceremony at St. Andrew's church in Maghull to 'kick-off' at 3pm, giving us enough time for the service, the signing of the register and enough photos to shake a stick at, before heading for the Bradford Hotel, the same venue which had hosted San's 21st party a couple of years earlier, for the wedding breakfast and evening reception. As Wagner's Bridal Chorus erupted from the church organ, me and Phil, along with the rest of the congregation, jumped to our feet in eager anticipation of the bridal party's arrival. On time, naturally.

Shimmering down the aisle on her dad's arm with Carol, her sister-in-law and maid-of-honour bringing up the rear, San was radiant. In all white (obviously) save for a splash of blue flowers on her matching white pumps, no heels to avoid walking taller than the groom, visage coquettishly concealed beneath her bridal veil, a delicate crown of silken petals and a bouquet of salmon pink roses completing the ensemble. Beneath the veil, all evidence of a particularly nasty stye which San had suffered in the lead up to the wedding (which I am assured had absolutely nothing to do with any stressful thoughts of a lifetime ahead with yours truly), had gone. She looked simply stunning. I was breathless.

San and her dad had been delivered to the church in the bridal car, a gorgeous cream-coloured vintage Rolls Royce complete with Spirit of Ecstasy on the bonnet, and convertible to boot. After the ceremony and the photographs, the weather continued to bestow its blessings on us, and we set off for the wedding breakfast venue, a good 30-minute drive away, with the top down. What a thrill. I've never enjoyed being the centre of attention, and clearly San was most deserving of that scrutiny, but the journey was great fun and we arrived for our first public appearance as a married couple at the Bradford, on the corner of Tithebarn Street and Pall Mall in Liverpool city centre, slightly windblown and very excited.

The office where we both worked was no more than 200 yards away, and a small group of co-workers had turned out to welcome us, snapping their own mementos of the occasion, with some of them then rushing off to change and return for the evening reception. Sadly, we couldn't invite everyone from the office, much as we'd have liked to.

Getting on for 50 guests sat down for the four-course wedding breakfast which I can still remember; it was of its time and superb. Spring Vegetable Soup, Prawn Cocktail, Sirloin Steak and accompaniments, and Black Forest Gateaux – none of that nouvelle cuisine nonsense. My dad, admittedly a soup enthusiast, enjoyed it so much he even asked one of the waitresses for the soup recipe.

I am ashamed to say that I was woefully ill-prepared for the groom's speech, an unforgiveable state of affairs especially given my known discomfort at speaking in public, but I did at least manage to utter a few words of thanks to various members of the wedding party, as tradition dictated. The father of the bride speech on the other hand consisted of a raised glass and "You'll get no speech from me. Here's to the bride and groom!".

Tom was a lovely gentleman, and even more terrified of speaking in public than I was. Looking back, it was the speech of the day.

Fortunately, my best man Phil – who at the church had been mistaken for the groom by the photographer as, in his opinion I looked too young to be getting married (he was probably right!) – loved to chat and loved an audience and turned out to be a natural entertainer. As a Legal Executive he was more than comfortable standing up in court and arguing a case, so a few dozen wedding guests held no terrors for him, and despite having nothing formally prepared he quickly struck up a rapport with the 'gallery', concluding the nuptial banquet with his effortless wit and charm.

After a short break, guests started to arrive for the evening reception, most of whom had actually been invited. A few of my dad's work mates made up the bulk of those who hadn't been, but they spent most of the evening in the bar upstairs celebrating with my mum and dad away from the disco and dance floor, and I was delighted to welcome them over a couple of pints.

The evening buffet seemed to go down very well, with the spareribs and chips in particular the subjects of a number of compliments, and there was hardly a morsel left at the end of the evening (I think that was a good thing). The dance floor was busy for most of the evening, so the disco appeared to get the thumbs up too, though not quite top marks as the resident DJ called time 15 minutes earlier than planned when Frankie Wheeler, a lifelong family friend and one of my dad's best mates, got rather too enthusiastic in his dance interpretation of Shakin' Stevens 'Green Door', and sent the record deck flying. Game over.

It had been a long and tiring day and we retired to our room actually ready for a good night's sleep, which we had to delay due to the fact that some kind souls (alternative interpretation: pains in the arse) had followed the long-standing wedding night tradition of making an 'apple pie' bed for the happy couple. For the only time since either of us had risen from our beds for the last time as single people, the 'happy couple' were less than completely so. But it was a minor blemish on what had been a great day.

The following day we were off on honeymoon. Not for us the sun-kissed beaches of the Mediterranean (or even further afield as is the current vogue). Instead, we spent a couple of nights in a B&B – The Cottage - in York, the highlight possibly being the meal we enjoyed at the Bonding Warehouse on the banks of the river Ouse. Nowadays it's an apartment block, but back then it was an old warehouse which had been converted into an impressive steak restaurant. San ordered sirloin which arrived just before mine, and I eyed the look and size of it enviously until my porterhouse arrived moments later. If San's was big, mine was enormous. Size isn't everything though, and the first mouthful confirmed the serendipity of my choice. Nearly 40 years on I'm drooling just remembering it.

The weather continued to be kind to us, and it was a pleasant enough couple of days ambling around the centre, where we took in York Minster and The Shambles, while we also enjoyed a couple of walks along the riverbank. It was a short stay though, and we were on the train back to Liverpool's Lime Street station late on the Saturday morning, arriving back in Maghull as Liverpool completed a 2-0 win over Arsenal at Anfield. Results continued to trend in the right direction, always a good sign.

To be fair, though the honeymoon was short, we had already enjoyed a fortnight in Cala Millor in Majorca at the beginning of July, our first holiday together. We had booked the holiday before we became engaged, and long before I'd been offered the job in New York, and we decided it made little

66

sense to lose money by cancelling it, only to book another holiday for a couple of months later. We still didn't have a departure date for the States as our visas were being organised by my employers-to-be, something over which we had no control, and we reasoned it made sense to have our holiday as planned, giving us the flexibility to up sticks as swiftly as necessary after the wedding. So, we had a week off around the time of the wedding and were back in the office on the following Monday as Mr & Mrs Jackson.

As it transpired, we needn't have worried about the timing. It was April the following year before our visas were ready and San's brother Tom dropped us off at Manchester airport to catch an internal flight to London, switching to a Pan Am jumbo at Heathrow, on route to JFK.

* * *

Our first year of marriage was eventful enough, both personally and on the football front. Before we'd been married a full month, Bill Shankly, my hero and to all intents and purposes the man on whose values the foundations of the modern Liverpool FC were built, died of a heart attack, a massive shock to Liverpool fans the world over.

Just before our first Christmas together as a married couple Liverpool played in their first World Club Championship final, a consequence of having defeated Real Madrid to land our third European Cup in May. It was the early hours of the morning in Liverpool when the game against Flamengo, the South American Champions from Brazil, kicked off in Tokyo. I had planned to listen to the game on Radio City – no live TV for this fixture then – but only woke up just before half time and went straight back to sleep on discovering we were trailing 3-0. No more goals were scored by either side and it would be 37 years before Liverpool finally became World Club Champions by turning the tables on Flamengo, this time in Doha, Qatar in 2019.

Before our first anniversary had arrived, we'd left our jobs, travelled to America, moved into an apartment in Manhattan, and returned home due to San's father's ill health. But not before I'd called the New York Times Sports Desk from a Manhattan payphone to enquire as to the result of

Liverpool's final home game of the season against Spurs. A win, and the League Championship would be ours for the 13th time. In response I was told, in no uncertain terms, to buy the paper the following day and look for the result myself!

Our, or perhaps more accurately San's, return home just a few months after departing for a hitherto indeterminate length of time, appeared to have a wonderful, almost miraculous, effect on her dad. She decided to stay at home when I returned to New York after a couple of weeks, and Tom's cancer soon went into remission, giving him and us another six precious years before he eventually succumbed to its ultimate dreadful consequence.

I'd worked for a software house in New York and I have to say I found them to be a bit 'cowboyish'. They made their money as a supplier of software development staff to clients of various industries and in 1982 the software industry in the States was in, or only slowly coming out of, a deep recession. When I arrived, along with a number of other ex-pats, we were immediately tasked with coding and testing computer programmes in a training environment which were then disingenuously – as far as I'm concerned - added to our CVs as if they'd been developed commercially for other US clients.

From when I arrived in April until I returned home with San in July, actual work for which my employer could charge me out was non-existent, which meant a lot of time spent in the office basically twiddling my thumbs. At the same time, San's visa never allowed her to work which meant that, while I was in the office, she got to know Macy's, Bloomingdales and a plethora of other Manhattan department stores previously known to us only through the medium of celluloid, very well.

Though exciting and novel at first, the sense of wonder we had started our American adventure with quickly dissipated, enjoyment faded, the experience somewhat chastening. As we moved from the fresh and temperate spring into the notoriously hot and humid New York summer months, the lack of air-conditioning in our studio apartment (it had been stolen by previous occupants apparently) began to, perhaps disproportionately, have a further increasingly negative impact on our appreciation of the great metropolis, and our shopping trips, albeit primarily to browse, increased in volume simply because the department stores were all air-conditioned.

I had paid for our 'emergency' flights home on hearing of Tom's health problems using an American Express Charge card, the balance of which needed to be cleared at the end of each month. With the trials and tribulations of our first three months in New York obviously fresh in our minds when we returned home, the decision for San to stay with her mum and dad rather than return to the States with me was made easier by the simultaneous decision that I would only return long enough to enable me to pay off the card debt.

On my return to the office, I managed to negotiate a salary advance which allowed me to clear the card balance on time and repay my employer over a six-week period (we were paid fortnightly. Otherwise known as 'very weakly'). Consequently, San and I were still the best part of three and a half thousand miles apart when our first anniversary dawned, a month away from being reunited.

In the end it was only six weeks apart, but it felt like a lifetime. I finished repaying my salary advance and caught a flight from JFK to Heathrow the following day, all preparations for my departure having been planned since the day I arrived back. I'd moved from the company apartment for couples in Manhattan to share an apartment with other ex-pat work colleagues in Queens and, on our anniversary, simultaneously celebrated and drowned my sorrows with a pitcher of Michelob at McNicholls, the neighbourhood Irish bar which had been adopted as the ex-pats local. There was little melancholy on my part as I said goodbye to my fellow work colleagues at the beginning of October, anticipation of my reunion with San casting all other considerations to the wind.

The company tried to make a big deal about me leaving without having stayed the requisite amount of time to avoid the contractual need to reimburse their expenses for relocating us, but they knew I had no funds, and I was costing them more by staying on, as the market still hadn't picked up sufficiently to get many staff out of the door and fee earning.

Once home, a letter arrived demanding a couple of thousand dollars from me, a letter returned thanking them for their kind thoughts and offering to pay them back a few dollars a month once I had found employment in the UK, and a further letter received insisting that they didn't want to appear vindictive in the present economic climate, and we could discuss repayment again when my financial situation improved. That was the best part of 40 years ago and the last I heard from them.

The day I arrived back in the UK, Liverpool suffered their first defeat of the season, 1-0 at Ipswich, and my superstitious self did briefly wonder if I'd come back a Jonah. I needn't have worried. The football season proceeded in customary fashion. Liverpool won the League Cup for the third season in a row, defeating an admittedly injury weakened Manchester United in the final, and a second successive League Title (we'd win both trophies again the following season, and add our fourth European Cup for good measure).

Our team this season, Bob Paisley's final one as manager, was one of the great unheralded ones in my opinion. Liverpool finished 11 points clear of second placed Watford, despite only taking two of the final 21 points available. A more focussed run-in may well have seen us win the league by 30 points but, having long since turned the title race into a procession (16 points clear with seven games to play, and with a game in hand) the team appeared to simply lose interest.

The economic outlook continued to be pretty grim, and I signed on the dole for a couple of months, applying for and failing to get a number of roles in Liverpool before eventually landing a position with a software house in London. CAP – originally an acronym for 'Computer Analysts and Programmers', but now just a name I was informed – took me on as a developer in their High Holborn London office in early December 1982, starting the week after I passed my driving test at the second time of asking (having initially failed the test a few days before we left for New York).

It was a great relief to be earning again, and Christmas immediately became something to look forward to, rather than something to get through. I had two working weeks to navigate before the Christmas break, during which time I travelled home at the weekend, having spent the intervening evenings in the spare room of a flat in Palmers Green which was rented by a work colleague planning to move into a new place in the new year. This worked very well for us, as it meant I could then take over the lease of the rented flat and San could join me there.

San immediately found herself a position at another insurance brokers, Gibbs Hartley Cooper, and settled in very quickly, her office based in the City a few minutes' walk from both Moorgate and Liverpool Street stations. So, for the next six months San and I had the relatively easy commute from Bowes Park station in north London into Moorgate and Kings Cross respectively.

It was a good walk for me, getting on for 30 minutes and a large part of it through a fairly seedy area. During the rush hours at either end of the day, with office workers aplenty traipsing through the streets on their way to work or back to the station, the more salacious elements of the neighbourhood remained largely out of sight. At least to my delicate eyes. Consequently, it was quite a shock to the system when, arriving on a later mid-morning train one day – I can't remember why I was running late – and following my usual walking route, a young lady, antipodean if my analysis of her dulcet tones was anything to go by, suddenly materialised seemingly out of thin air, and asked me if I was "..on business John?".

My first thought was a case of mistaken identity. There's definitely a strong family resemblance between me and my brother John, and in my innocence, I almost pointed out her error. But it dawned on me as I opened my mouth to speak that that was *my* mistake and her 'business' was very much not mine. My face must have been a picture as it glowed bright red – I can still feel the heat - and I managed to impart, somewhat timidly, "no thanks, I'm on my way to work".

How humdrum she must have thought.

We only spent six months or so in the North London flat, though I can assure you that had nothing to do with my chance encounter with the 'doxy from down under' in the back streets of Kings Cross. We wanted to buy our own place and, as soon as I picked up my first car in the April, we drove out to a new Wimpey housing estate under construction just outside Maldon in Essex. It took us ages to get there – I was still a novice driver and found the London traffic, even on the outskirts, quite stressful – but we were immediately attracted to the quaintness of the little town centre as we passed through it on the main drag from Chelmsford towards the site at Heybridge, no more than a couple of miles further on.

We have discovered over the years that the bigger a decision there is to be made, the quicker we tend to make it. So, it was no surprise when, less than a couple of hours later, we were on our way back to north London having paid our deposit on an end-terrace two up two down plot due to be completed in the July. Not for us any consideration of the cost, both in time and money, of the potential daily commute to and from our office jobs in London. Both of which turned out to be quite hefty by the way.

On reflection, we could probably have bought a flat near to where we were currently renting for a similar, perhaps even lower, price, and without the monster commute. It would have meant we'd have been able to see more of London too – though to be fair we didn't spend a lot of time doing the tourist thing during the six months we actually lived there – and probably made more of a killing when the time was right to sell up and move on.

But we were enchanted by the semi-rural location, its proximity to Heybridge Basin with its sea lock connecting the Chelmer & Blackwater Navigation canal to the muddy River Blackwater estuary (which featured in an episode of Lovejoy once, much to our delight) and the prospect of being well away from the capital when we weren't actually working. And the deposit was only £50 so, nothing ventured nothing gained eh?

We loved it there. Even the address was made for us and we ended up spending nearly four happy years in *Redshank* Drive on 'The Saltings' estate.

Recollections? Well, there are a few. We moved in with virtually nothing to our name in the way of furniture or appliances. San's brother Tom and his wife Carol hired a van and brought our bed and a few other bits and pieces from San's parents' house in Maghull, and during the first week the major kitchen appliances we'd ordered– cooker, fridge, washing machine – arrived. The house was fitted with new carpets, curtains and kitchen units as part of the purchase deal, but we missed out on the improved deal which included kitchen appliances, by a couple of weeks.

Christmas was approaching before we replaced the small portable black & white television, which belonged to San's mum and dad, and the tea chest it perched on in the corner of the room, with something a bit more modern and attractive, and indeed watchable. Similarly, it was a while before a new dining table and chairs arrived to replace the garden chairs and ironing board we'd been using at meal times, with the arrival of a double sofa bed eventually relegating the garden chairs back to service outdoors.

I joined a neighbourhood football club, Quay Sports FC – the name a remnant of a by then defunct Sports shop in the town centre - in the local Maldon & District Sunday League. Team Manager Dave 'Sandy' Howard named me Player of the Year in my first season and my teammates twice voted me their Player's Player of the Year, though my old boss from Liverpool, Alan Mason, jokingly (I think!) downplayed the awards on the basis I was playing with and against a 'bunch of southern softies'.

'Purleigh Queens', Quay Sports rivals from just down the road and against whom we had a number of bruising battles during my time there – including a cup final in which they narrowly triumphed by a single goal in what was my final game before returning 'up north' - would dispute that character assassination I'm sure, regardless of any personal attributes which might uncharitably be assumed from their chosen appellation, a clever play on the more well-known 'Pearly Kings and Queens' though it may have been.

(I say 'uncharitably' without wishing to cause offence. An informal use of 'queen' is described in the Oxford dictionary as "a gay man, especially one regarded as ostentatiously effeminate", and while such attributes are as valid and endearing as any, I'd suggest they're not top of the list of qualities you'd expect to find in many, if any, football teams at any level of competition. And who knows, maybe that's football's loss).

* * *

On the way to Colchester zoo one weekend, a relatively short trip along the road which linked Maldon with Colchester, and accompanied by San with her mum and dad in the back of our old Austin Allegro, I suffered my first road accident just outside Tiptree, a place famous for its conserves and jams produced by the Wilkin and Son family-run business since late in the 19th

73

century. In our house it's now also notorious for the stubble burning which takes place in the late summer and was the direct cause of the accident.

A sudden change in wind direction caused the dense smoke to smother the road in front of us and, as I slowed down, the driver of the car in front, which had completely disappeared from view, slammed on the brakes. Within seconds of entering the blanket of smoke I'd careered into the back of the now visible again car-in-front, amidst a cacophony of breaking glass and grinding metal. It was a frightening experience, disoriented as we were through the lack of visibility, and unsure of what else might come at us through the smoke from either direction.

Thankfully, only San's dad suffered a relatively minor injury – cuts and bruises to his shins – and though shaken none of us needed any medical attention. The trip to the zoo was off though, and we arrived home courtesy of the pickup truck which also dropped the car off at a nearby garage. It was more than a month later when the insurance company officially wrote the car off and provided the funds to buy a replacement. In the meantime, the convoluted nature of our daily commute – a 20-minute drive to Witham Railway Station, 50-ish minute train journey into Liverpool Street Station and, for me, a further tube journey to Farringdon Road (having moved offices from High Holborn) – became a bit of a nightmare.

Angela, a neighbour who lived with local butcher and Quay Sports teammate Eddie, worked in Chelmsford and kindly delivered us to the station there each morning we were without our own transport, courtesy of her little mini which was so old that she needed to declutch, or double clutch, each time she changed gear. As Chelmsford is closer to London than Witham, and on the same route, we simply picked the train up further along the line, though with less chance of a seat for our £100+ per month ticket (a lot of money in the mid 1980s). The real challenge was getting home in the evening, as the journey concluded with a slowly meandering bus journey from Witham to Heybridge, or occasionally from Chelmsford to Maldon, and then a final walk home.

You will understand then that it was an even greater relief than we'd initially anticipated, when we picked up our second car. A dark green Ford Escort

MKII which we bought from a workmate of San's brother Tom. Manual choke, same as the Allegro and, to be honest, ultimately pretty naff. It had a tiny engine, about 1.0 litre if I remember correctly, and slow-moving lorries – the ones about which warning signs are posted on mountainous routes and which often even have their own dedicated lanes so as not to hold up everyone else - would overtake us driving across the Pennines on the M62. Which we did a fair bit as, for our visits home to Liverpool, our preferred route took us across country to the M11 and then, via the A1, rather counter-intuitively further north than our ultimate destination, picking up the M62 at Pontefract for the final leg of our journey.

As much as we didn't particularly like the old Escort, it did us a turn for a couple of years during one of the most important and precious periods of our marriage. In the spring of 1985, we discovered San was expecting our first child, due towards the end of October. As unlikely as it sounds these days, back then San had to phone the doctors from work to get the results of a pregnancy test and then phone me at work with the verdict. Excitement abounded. As we didn't have a phone at home, once the pregnancy was more established and we felt more confident of letting our parents in on our happy tidings, the office phones were put to good use again (pending the installation of, for obvious reasons, our newly ordered landline).

As San's pregnancy progressed, she suffered badly with morning sickness and then with the uncomfortable heat of the summer months. Then of course there was also the start of the new football season to contend with. Though Liverpool were enjoying the most successful decade in our long and already highly decorated history, a huge cloud hung over the club following the Heysel disaster a few months earlier in May. Despite that, and the potentially risky appointment of club legend with no managerial experience whatsoever, Kenny Dalglish as player-manager, we'd made a decent start.

Approaching the end of September, we'd lost just one of our first eight league games and sat in second place in the table, albeit a long way off United at the top who still had a 100% record, and with the first derby of the season, at Goodison Park against the reigning champions, next on the horizon. The derby weekend coincided with the weekend we'd decided to decorate the nursery (primarily a delicate lemon hue for those interested, with the sex of the baby still unknown). San had started her maternity leave the previous month and, with a month now until the baby was due and nursery furniture soon to arrive, it was all hands to the pump. Well, that is until Everton reduced a first-half three-goal deficit to just one, late in the second half.

I suffer from a particularly nervous disposition when Liverpool are playing important football matches which I can't attend, and listening to the game on the radio is my least favoured way of following the match. These days I never do it. San on the other hand quite enjoys listening to it. So, with five minutes to go and Gary Lineker having just scored Everton's second, I cheerfully announced to San, eight months pregnant and precariously perched on a stepladder with a paint roller in her hands, "I'm off!".

San knew exactly what I meant. The year before, as the final whistle blew at the end of extra-time in the Stadio Olimpico in Rome, confirming the need for a penalty shoot-out to decide the destination of the European Cup, I'd made the same exclamation and marched out to wander the streets of our estate in the dark, not returning until San called me in after the drama was over. We'd won our fourth European Cup that night and there was a similarly happy ending this time, with Liverpool holding out for the win and Dalglish, who had scored in the first minute to set us on our way, actually missing two relative sitters in the final few minutes which otherwise would have saved a few fingernails. Not mine of course.

So, we won the derby, completed decorating the nursery and continued preparations for the new arrival with the due date now only a month away. It came and went without any sign of baby gracing us with its presence. San visited the doctors on 5 November to be informed that her labour would now need to be induced, and consequently she wouldn't be able to give birth in St Peters, the local hospital in Maldon, but would need to go to St Johns in Chelmsford instead, which was more geared up for deliveries which were not going to be straightforward. I was expecting fireworks (badum-tish), but San took the news in her stride and her labour was induced that evening and continued throughout the next day.

As the morning of Thursday 7 November dawned, San was at least having contractions, but there was still little sign of the baby appearing of its own volition. San was clearly in some distress, mitigated only slightly by the gas and air combination she greedily sucked in, and the longer it went on the more worried, not to say angry, I became. Not at San you understand, but with this offspring of ours who appeared determined to delay its entrance into the world for as long as possible and never mind the consequences for anyone else.

Eventually, an obstetrician and his forceps arrived (rather San than me) and, once in place (the forceps not the obstetrician), our first born was, at last, quickly delivered at ten to nine in the morning. Thomas Leslie, a beautiful son named for both of his grandfathers. Long and lanky he may have been, and undeniably noisy. But 8lb 2oz of perfection in every way. San was exhausted, I was besotted, we were both overjoyed, all misplaced anger forgotten.

Within a couple of days San and Tom were transferred to the maternity ward at St Peters in Maldon, where they stayed until being discharged ten days after the birth, having been wonderfully cared for during that time. And much needed too. (Hard to imagine now when pressure on NHS resources reduces that time by as much as 90%).

My time off work as a new father – no paternity leave then – had to be taken from annual leave, and I needed much of what remained of that for the Christmas break, which was six weeks away and, with us living 250 miles from Liverpool, would be the first time our families had a chance to meet the latest addition to each clan. So, I was at work in London during that immediate post-natal period, rushing home each evening to be able to spend no more than an hour or so with my new family. At least I had work colleagues for company during the day though. Apart from the maternity ward staff and one or two other mothers and babies, San had no-one. When the time came, she was more than ready to bring Tom home.

Before travelling home to Liverpool for Christmas, we arranged for Tom to be christened while we were there, in the same church we'd been married in, and by the same vicar. It was great to have our two families and friends together to celebrate the occasion.

I like to think Tom's arrival somehow had an immediate impact on our football team's fortunes too. On the day of Tom's birth, bitter rivals United were undefeated at the top of the table with a ten-point lead over second placed Liverpool. Two days later they lost for the first time, and by the end of November had lost again, with the lead reduced to just two points. Though Liverpool would go on to have their own wobble in the ensuing couple of months, falling further behind United again, as well as new leaders Everton, all was not lost.

When Everton established an eight-point lead over now fourth placed Liverpool towards the end of February with a 2-0 revenge victory in the Anfield derby, the mountainous gap did look almost unsurmountable with just 12 league games remaining. But 11 wins and a draw saw us clinch the league title with a 1-0 victory over Chelsea at Stamford Bridge in our final league game of the season, a victory made even sweeter – if that was possible - by the fact that the winning goal was scored by much revered player-manager Kenny Dalglish. A week later, the first all-Merseyside FA Cup Final beckoned and, having been second best for much of the first hour and falling behind to a Gary Lineker prod, a couple of goals from Ian Rush and another from Craig Johnstone added the cup to the season's trophy haul. We'd won the double in Tom's first season!

We set off on our first family holiday - a week in a cosy Somerset cottage the perfect base to explore that part of the world - a few weeks after the Cup Final. The cottage was a short distance from Shepton Mallet, in the region of 180 miles from our Essex home. These days, a sizeable chunk of that journey is serviced by the M25 and it's not unreasonable to suggest that, even with a couple of comfort breaks, it should take no more than five hours or so. Back in 1986, the M25 was still being built, and the world and his dog seemed to be going in the same direction as us. We set off early enough, leaving before 10.00 am so that we'd have time to unload the car and do a spot of grocery shopping before settling down to watch the opening game of the World Cup between the holders Italy and unfancied Bulgaria. Or so we thought.

We actually arrived, after a fraught and exhausting journey – I can only assume Chris Rea, the gravel-voiced singer-songwriter and guitarist, was making the same trip, it would certainly have provided more than enough inspiration for his 'Road to Hell' hit - shortly after the game, an evening kick-off, had started. And without anything to eat or drink. This was in the days before the law was changed to allow shops to open on a Sunday, and as much as I've never been a fan of the change, on this particular occasion it would have been a godsend. Fortunately, we did at least have Tom's baby food with us and the cottage landlord, who lived in an adjoining property, kindly provided some basic foodstuffs – bread, milk and the like – which kept us going until the shops opened. Other than that, an enjoyable week passed without incident, the journey home proving far less troublesome than the journey out.

Back in Essex, summer turned quickly to autumn and winter. We enjoyed a shortened Christmas break in Liverpool again, staying with San's mum and dad as usual, but returning home before the new year dawned, prompted to do so by the inclement weather and the more severe conditions which were forecast. It was for that reason that we decided to give the trans-Pennine route a miss, and travelled back to Essex via the more conventional, and slightly shorter, route which took us south via the M58, M6 and M1 as far as St. Albans and then cross country via Chelmsford.

Plenty of yuletide travellers appeared to have the same idea, but perversely, the snowy conditions on the motorways, while having the obvious and desired effect of keeping speeds down, also seemed to help keep the traffic flowing. We certainly enjoyed a more straightforward journey than we'd expected and in spite of the treacherous conditions we arrived home safely and enjoyed a quiet New Year's Eve in front of the TV. Well, apart that is from Tom screaming his lungs out from his cot mid-evening, and not for the first time. We'd both already been up to comfort him, and we looked exasperatedly at each other. Time for a change of tack. I stood at the bottom of the stairs and shouted, "Shut up you little bastard" (lovingly of course!). To our amazement we never heard another peep from him. It's not a parenting strategy I'd recommend on a regular basis, but clearly tough love is sometimes the answer!

Back at work in the new year, the weather showed little sign of improvement, and on more than one occasion I struggled to get into the office, arriving late, leaving early and getting home even later than usual. Eventually

I just had to stay at home and phone in my absence. Enough became enough. After discussing it with San – the mere formality I knew it would be - it wasn't long before I requested a transfer to the company's office in Alderley Edge in the Cheshire countryside. We were going home.

* * *

When we put our house on the market, the estate agent in Maldon asked us why we were moving. In response to hearing that I was moving offices to Cheshire, he offered to put us in touch with an estate agent in the area that was loosely affiliated to them. Which is how we ended up with a bunch of properties to look at in Congleton.

Following an exploratory visit to the Alderley Edge office and a chat with my new HR manager, I took the opportunity to visit the old mill town in South Cheshire, thirteen miles further south on the A34, for the first time – we'd never heard of it before we decided to move – and I saw enough to consider it worthy of consideration for our next home. Of course, I was on my own, so I popped in to 'Raymond Dingle Estate Agents' on the corner of Swan Bank and West Street and picked up details on about half a dozen properties for me and San to mull over.

We viewed five properties in different parts of Congleton. Two in Buglawton, one in the town centre, and two in West Heath. We favoured one of the properties in West Heath and immediately arranged a further visit the following weekend. It meant round trips of circa 500 miles on successive weekends, but once we'd decided to move it became a simple matter of getting the job done as quickly as possible.

In the end, despite not knowing the area at all, we didn't look anywhere else. As is our wont, another big decision made at the drop of a metaphorical hat. Our offer was accepted, they threw in the blinds in the bathroom and we were on our way, our Essex home having sold quickly and fetching the full asking price. Our new home was half an hour or so from the Alderley Edge office (though ironically, I ended up hardly ever working there and spent the first 12 months and more at one of our clients, Royal Insurance, in Liverpool), and less than an hour from our families on Merseyside. Close enough to visit friends and family at our leisure, distant enough to discourage too many unannounced visits in the opposite direction. And, of course, Anfield beckoned.

We moved in on Friday 24 April 1987, a beautiful spring day, after an arduous journey made so by a seemingly never-ending series of roadworks and traffic incidents. At one stage we had to leave the M1 and divert through Towcester, a pleasant enough little town (in fact it has appeared quite charming on the numerous occasions I've driven through it since), but not built with the need to cater for heavy traffic in mind. I thought we'd never get out.

We eventually did of course and arrived at our current home in Penrith Court only a short time after most of our belongings, the removal men having suffered an equally frustrating journey. Tom and Gladys - San's mum and dad - along with Tom and Carol, her brother and sister-in-law, were also there to greet us and help with the initial unpacking, for which we were very grateful.

I treated us all to a chippie tea, once me and Tom had eventually located the fish and chip shop in West Heath shopping centre, and we retired that evening, exhausted after a long day but content. We'd already rationalised our big decision to move here with the idea that if it didn't work out, we could simply sell up and move even closer again to Liverpool. But for now, we were looking forward to seeing what the future held. And the future started tomorrow.

Which, coincidentally, was the day of the Anfield derby. During the 1980's, the first signs of spring would normally include birdsong, buds on trees, early spring flowers and, more often than not, Liverpool disappearing over the horizon at the top of the league. And for a while this year had appeared to be no different. In mid-March Liverpool held a nine-point lead over second placed Everton, albeit having played a couple of games more. Just over a month later, when the two teams prepared to clash at Anfield, that situation had completely reversed.

Following four defeats in five games, Liverpool's quest for the title had pretty much evaporated, with Everton now holding a six-point lead over the reds with a game in hand. Dropping another three points to our near neighbours now would give them a nine-point lead with only nine points left for Liverpool to play for. All expectations of us winning the league had gone, but the thought of allowing our blue brethren to all but clinch it at Anfield? Not to be entertained.

And thankfully, it wasn't.

Although ex-red Kevin Sheedy quickly equalised Liverpool's early opening goal, scored by ex-blue Steve McMahon, a brace by childhood blue Ian Rush gave the reds a 3-1 victory. The blue's title celebrations would have to wait, if not for long. Everton eventually clinched the league just over a week later with victory by the only goal of the game at Norwich. At the time of writing 33 years on, they haven't won it since.

As the summer months beckoned two things happened. We booked our first foreign family holiday, which would see the three of us spend the first two weeks of September in Mar Menor, close to La Manga on Spain's Costa Calida. And San, as the saying quaintly goes, fell pregnant again. Our second child was due in February which meant we could still look forward to our holiday without worrying about whether we'd be able to fly. Oh, and the new football season started too.

Following the disappointing end to the previous season, Liverpool had bolstered the squad with two top quality signings. Peter Beardsley and John Barnes arrived from Newcastle and Watford respectively, though I was personally a little surprised when Digger Barnes signed on the dotted line. Watford had accepted a bid from Liverpool midway through the previous season, but Barnes commitment to the move hadn't been forthcoming at the time, and rumours persisted that he fancied playing abroad next, preferably in Italy.

In one of those twists of happenstance often thrown up by the fixture list, Liverpool's final home game of the season had been against Watford, a narrow anti-climactic 1-0 win in Ian Rush's last game at Anfield before his own move to the Italian giants Juventus, and Barnes had been the target of crowd abuse throughout the game. Sadly, some of that abuse centred on the fact that he was black. Standing on The Kop that day, I turned to my dad and declared "No way he'll be signing for us after this".

When more rumours appeared in the press that, in the absence of interest from Italy he would prefer a move to London-based Arsenal over Anfield, the club issued a statement retracting their interest in the player. It took a firm denial from Digger about the veracity of the rumours to get the move back on.

Around the time we'd first registered an interest in Barnesy, we also signed John Aldridge, Oxford's scouse centre forward, in anticipation of Rushie's pending move to Italy, and shortly after the new season started, we returned to Oxford for their creative attacking midfielder Ray Houghton. What promised to be an enjoyable season ahead started with an impressive win at Arsenal, where Barnes and Beardsley combined to set up Aldridge for the opening goal in a 2-1 win, with Stevie Nicol heading a late winner from the edge of the penalty area. Beardsley scored his first for the club a week later in a 4-1 stroll at Coventry City, a game my brother Alan attended and was so gushing in his praise over the performance that I knew something special was starting to happen.

Before the season started a sewer had collapsed under The Kop and with repairs ongoing, our first home game of the season was still a couple of weeks away, by which time we were enjoying the sun, sand and sea in Spain. Actually, more accurately that would be sun, sand and saltwater lagoon.

Although the Mediterranean Sea was little more than a 5-minute walk away, our accommodation – the Hotel Doblemar Casino – was situated on the banks of the Mar Menor lagoon itself. The difference in water temperature between the two expanses of water was not insignificant, the lagoon being, and noticeably so, a few degrees warmer. It was also very shallow, which provided an ideal paddling area for Tom, who was not yet two years old, and with sunbeds and parasols available, we'd found the perfect spot for our daily sunbathing.

That's not to suggest it was the perfect holiday, as enjoyable as it was. Tom was teething and, with the food on offer with our half-board package aimed primarily at satisfying the culinary expectations of the hotel's Spanish guests, was finding little to tickle his taste buds. And typically, he wasn't backwards at letting us know he wasn't completely happy. It was also, not unexpectedly, very warm, which was particularly uncomfortable for his now four-month pregnant mum. So, we were ready for our return trip home when departure day arrived. Ready but unprepared.

We were due to fly from Alicante, a two-hour coach ride away, to Manchester. On the way out, though the journey was long, the coach had been only half full and we'd spread out a bit, allowing us all to have our own seats, Tom taking it in turns to sit next to me or his mum. On the return trip the coach was bursting at the seams and was running late to boot. We were the last coach load of passengers to arrive for our flight, which had already been called, and we were last off the coach. As a result, we were also pretty much last to check-in and, with the flight being full, predictably there wasn't two seats together left for us. Being under two years old, Tom wasn't entitled to a seat of his own, so he sat on my lap towards the rear of the plane, with San on her own near the front. Have I mentioned Tom was teething!

From the time we took off from Alicante to the time we landed in Manchester, Tom let everyone on the plane, many of whom ended up wishing they hadn't been I'd wager, know that he was teething. My thoughts oscillated between regretting that the windows on the plane didn't open to being thankful that was the case, so tempted might I have been to 'stop the noise'. As we queued to disembark after the plane had taxied to a stop, a chap behind me whispered "Just as well we weren't coming from Australia mate". I had to concur.

And as soon as we were on terra firma Tom brightened up. Obviously, having access to his mum again helped enormously. But it was an evening flight and, repairs to the sewer under the Kop having been completed a couple of weeks earlier, Liverpool had played their second home game of the season while we were in the air, coming from behind to beat Charlton 3-2. And Tom was now happy again. Coincidence? Okay, of course it was. Probably.

We arrived back home and as we struggled in with the luggage, I noticed a few black specks on Tom's face, and then on my feet, which were still in sockless holiday mode. To my horror, it quickly became apparent that the specks were in fact fleas. The previous owners had owned a Golden Retriever and, as the council workman who came out a couple of days later to treat the infestation explained to me, our (okay, San's) regular vacuuming would have kept them at bay, but flea eggs from the Retriever would have been buried deep in the carpet, and hatched while we were on holiday. Thankfully the treatment did the trick, and the horror receded.

* * *

Both my brothers were enthusiastic followers of the reds, home and abroad. John had emigrated to Australia shortly before we moved, and me and our Alan decided to get Kop season tickets. It was a lot easier then than now, with demand having somewhat dissipated following the Heysel disaster two years earlier. There was certainly no waiting list, for Kop tickets anyway, and we paid somewhere in the region of £70 - £75 for the privilege of being able to stand on the famous terrace for that season. And what a privilege indeed it turned out to be.

Two weeks after we returned from holiday, I watched my first match at Anfield since we'd moved home. As if to welcome me back, the opposition provided comforting echoes of my first ever game against Leicester City getting on for 20 years earlier. Derby County were the unfortunate lambs from the East Midlands this time round, also lining up with Peter Shilton in goal as Leicester had previously and, if not for the England goalkeeper, the slaughter would have been even greater than the 4-0 score line suggested. Liverpool were imperious, John Barnes unplayable, John Aldridge on target for the ninth consecutive league game.

Although I'd lived 'out of range' for much of the last five years, I'd still managed to get to a handful of games each season by ensuring as far as possible that visits home to the family coincided with one or more games at Anfield, and we were enjoying our most successful decade as far as trophy winning was concerned. But this felt different.

Without doubt we were playing the most exciting football I'd witnessed to date (and I'd watched the 1978-79 Championship winning team which had won 30 of its 42 league games, conceding only 16 goals in the process and only conceding more than once in a single game, a 3-1 loss at Aston Villa on the Easter Monday. Satisfyingly, three weeks after that we'd clinched the league at Anfield by walloping Villa 3-0 in the return fixture, though I missed that game as I was on the wrong end of my own walloping, Collegiate Old Boys suffering a disappointing 5-1 loss to St Andrew's in the I-Zingari League Challenge Cup Final, played at the Police grounds in Fairfield). The season turned into a procession as plaudits rained in, superlatives abounding, hyperbole impossible.

At the same time, our family cup overflowed as our second child, another beautiful son, Daniel James, blessed us with his presence – late in the season and while we were still unbeaten - his arrival and demeanour as quiet and reverential as his brother's had been loud and boisterous. As with Tom, San's labour hadn't been completely straightforward, with another induction required, though no forceps this time, and culminating at five to one in the morning on 2 March 1988, a week past her due date. Dan weighed in at a very healthy 8Ib 13oz, lording it over his elder brother by 11oz. We thought he might grow up to be a rugby player (spoiler alert: he didn't).

Liverpool immediately triumphed at Loftus Road on Queens Park Rangers artificial pitch, and a couple of games later we equalled Leeds United's record of 14 years earlier by remaining undefeated in our first 29 games, a 1-1 draw at Derby County doing the trick. Next up? Everton in the Goodison derby.

With Goodison a ferment, Wayne Clarke, younger brother of Alan who had been an integral member of that record-breaking Leeds side, scored early for them and a mixture of bad luck, bad finishing and backs to the wall defending by Everton ensured there'd be no records broken on their watch thank you very much. I'd watched from the middle tier of the triple decker Goodison Road stand and had struck a rapport of convenience with the chap sitting next to me, an Evertonian as desperate to win as I was not to lose.

We would have made a fascinating case study, I'm sure, on the application of the laws of relativity during the game. Certainly after the 14th minute when the only goal was scored. From that moment on his every utterance reflected how torturously slowly the time appeared to be passing. I, on the other hand, couldn't believe where the time had gone. But gone it had, along with thoughts of a record and hopes of a season unbeaten. Before the season ended, we lost just one other league game, 2-1 at Nottingham Forest and, as with Aston Villa in 1979, exacted a speedy and compelling revenge. Twice.

A week after our second and final league defeat, Forest were our opponents in the FA Cup Semi-Final, played at Hillsborough. Liverpool took a two-goal lead through John Aldridge, one a penalty, and though future red Nigel Clough pulled one back for Forest, Liverpool triumphed to confirm a Wembley final date with Wimbledon, the score line hardly reflecting our superiority. Worse was to follow for Forest just a few days later at Anfield.

With a performance hailed by the great Tom Finney – Preston and England legendary winger in his hey-day and a hero of one-time Preston teammate Bill Shankly – as the best he'd ever seen, Liverpool were in celebratory mood after reaching the cup final, a mood that offered little respite for their beleaguered opponents. Any thoughts of a consolation league double for Forest never lasted beyond Ray Houghton's early opening goal. Aldridge belatedly added another before half-time (it could have been six already) and added the fifth and final goal after Gary Gillespie and Peter Beardsley had also waded in with second half goals. It was the consummate team performance.

Ten days later, a single goal by Peter Beardsley was enough to defeat Tottenham Hotspur at Anfield and clinch the league title with four games still to play. (Interestingly, for the third time in seven seasons Spurs had shared the occasion as Liverpool were confirmed as Champions. Although, having been defeated at Anfield in 1982 and now again in 1988, a Spurs victory at White Hart Lane was not enough to prolong our wait for the title in 1983 with three games to spare, as our closest challengers United dropped points at Carrow Road against Norwich on the same day). With the league done and dusted, the coveted league and cup double beckoned for the second time in three seasons. Only one team could stop us now.

And stop us Wimbledon did.

Liverpool may have been the heaviest ever favourites in a two-horse race for this cup final and, with our massive fan base and Wimbledon's relatively tiny one, reds fans must have filled three quarters of the ground. But hats off to our opponents who, predictably, battled ferociously from the start and did enough to win the day, a first half Lawrie Sanchez header the difference.

In the ground I was beyond disappointed. And so too, at home, was San. But the fact that we'd had another child and not won the double this time round? I can't help but wonder if, as I made my way home from Wembley that day, alone with my dark thoughts and sulking on the coach, she at least found the time to enjoy a small sigh of relief. I wouldn't blame her if she did!

The following month, we took three-month-old Daniel on his first family holiday. Two-and-a-half-year-old Tom was also with us of course, enjoying the third such holiday of his young life, and San's mum and dad joined us for the week in a cottage in the Cotswolds. San's brother Tom was a prison officer at Long Lartin at the time and lived with his wife Carol and five-year-old son Christopher close to the prison in Evesham, and so we also managed to catch up with them during the course of the holiday.

The Cotswolds are another beautiful part of the world. Comprising the rolling Cotswold Hills, they are indeed the largest designated Area of Outstanding Natural Beauty in England. Very green. Of course, their verdant beauty owes much to the climate and during the week we spent there we came to appreciate just why it really was *so* beautiful. I mean, wherever and whenever you travel in the UK, the chances are at some stage you'll get wet. But on this holiday, we learned to really appreciate the few times we managed to stay dry. From biblical downpours to simply constant drizzle, let's just say it was a character-building experience. Still, it was nice to get away again, and with Tom and Gladys being there to help, me and San did manage to spend a bit of time together without the kids. I don't think anyone was too unhappy when it was time to return home though.

It was the only time we managed to go away with both San's parents. A few months later, and six years after Tom's cancer had gone into remission, it returned with a vengeance. A few days after he was taken into Fazakerley Hospital in North Liverpool, I received a call at work from a heartbroken San. Her dad had passed away that morning. The news was hardly a surprise, but still had the capacity to shock. It was a cruel prequel to the festive period, with Christmas, and the feelings and memories it is always prone to evoke, less than a month away, and Gladys took it particularly badly. They'd been married for over 40 years and were clearly devoted to each other. I could hardly imagine the magnitude of her loss.

San's own grief was exacerbated with the added worry of her mum's resultant depression, which lasted throughout the following year. Indeed, just over a year after Tom had died, Christmas of the following year was a particularly worrying time, especially for San, as her mum's state of mind seemed to worsen considerably. As usual, we'd spent a few days with her over the holiday period, her grandchildren at least helping to raise her spirits for a while, and returned home to Congleton around teatime on New Year's Eve - we did need some time to ourselves after all. No sooner had we opened the front door than the phone rang.

Tom and Elsie Kirkman were long-standing friends and neighbours of Tom and Gladys, having lived next door in Clent Road since before the family had moved there in the early 1960s. Indeed, their friends and neighbours on the other side, Les and Alma Fawcett, had also lived there longer than Tom and Gladys, as had Len and Lena Steele who lived on the other side of the cul-de-sac, as well as a number of their other neighbours. It was a typically tight-nit, friendly scouse community where everyone looked out for each other. Len had passed away a few years earlier and it was his wife Lena on the other end of the phone, calling with yet more sad news.

In neighbourly fashion, Tom Kirkman had been doing a bit of garden tidying for Gladys and had suffered a stroke, collapsing alone in the garden with no-one any the wiser until Elsie wondered what was taking him so long and came to look for him. An ambulance had been called, but in vain, with Tom passing away on what was his birthday. It was shocking news for everyone, and again Gladys was understandably distraught, hence the call from Lena.

San managed to find something for the kids to eat before we all jumped in the car again and headed back to Maghull. Having consoled Gladys and put the kids to bed, and with a dearth of provisions in the house, we drove around Maghull and its environs looking for somewhere to eat. A takeaway would do. It's hard to believe these days, but we couldn't find anywhere open, and ended the evening with a very early night and very empty stomachs. We've never been big fans of New Year's Eve, (though we've enjoyed a good few celebrations with close friends in later years), but this one really scraped the barrel.

That evening did prove to be a turning point for San's mum though. She very quickly rallied round Tom's wife Elsie, finding new purpose in comforting and helping her friend of many years to start to come to terms with her own loss. Elsie still had her own family, which included a couple of grandchildren, and obviously these provided her main source of comfort and support. But it must have been a great help having her friend next door who had very recently been through the same heart-breaking experience. Viewed from a familial distance, it certainly appeared to help Gladys.

On the pitch, the record books reveal that the 1988-89 season can be remembered for Liverpool winning the Cup and Arsenal denying us another league title, but they are simply the cold basic statistics of a season over-whelmingly defined by the Hillsborough disaster which claimed the lives of 96 of my fellow supporters. Suffice to say, the loss in the final game of the season to Arsenal at Anfield, with its painful but ultimately unimportant consequences, barely scratched the emotional surface.

The following 1989-90 season started well enough, a tepid revenge of sorts over Arsenal in the pre-season Charity Shield and remaining unbeaten until suffering a 4-1 drubbing at Southampton in late October. The preceding run of games had included an even bigger drubbing for opponents Crystal Palace, this time by nine goals to nil at Anfield, and Swansea City were on the receiving end of an 8-0 score line at the same venue in a cup replay early in 1990.

With dreams of another league and couple double (again) becoming less nebulous as the season wore on, we completed a league double over Palace with a 2-0 win at Selhurst Park and were then drawn against them in the FA Cup semi-final, to be played at Villa Park. Understandably, Liverpool were clear favourites to progress to the final again, with odds that appeared particularly generous after a one-sided first half saw the dominant reds lead through a single Ian Rush goal. As we settled back for a second half repeat, Liverpool kicked off, gave the ball away and conceded the equaliser all within

20 seconds.

Worse was to follow as Palace took the lead, but sanity appeared to have been restored when Liverpool scored twice again inside the last 10 minutes, through Steve McMahon and a John Barnes penalty. Incredulously (to me at least), Palace managed an even later equaliser to take the game into extra-time and won it 4-3 through an Alan Pardew (he continues to be an irritant to this day) header with 10 minutes to go. (Fun fact: In the other semi-final, Manchester United and Oldham Athletic played out a 3-3 draw, with United winning the ensuing replay 2-1, meaning that across the two semi-finals 16 goals were scored in total, each one by a different player. It'd make a great quiz question).

With seven league games to go slight concerns were whispered that the impact of this shock defeat might lead to a collapse in the league, with Aston Villa ready to take full advantage. But we won five of those, drawing the other two and, following a 2-1 win over QPR at Anfield, we were confirmed as Champions with two games remaining, Villa having failed to beat Norwich at home on the same day.

A 6-1 victory at Coventry City on the final day of the season a week later had the league table showing us finishing nine points clear, and with 20 goals scored and only six conceded in that seven-game run in, rumours of our demise, which had surfaced briefly after the Palace debacle, appeared to have been put to bed.

After all, this was our 11th title win in 18 seasons and our 18th in total, that being twice as many as next-most-prolific Arsenal. In six of those other seven seasons during that time we finished in second place, our lowest finish being fifth in 1981. Even then, we'd heavily compensated by winning the League Cup (for the first time) and the European Cup (for the third time in five years) that season. As Ronny Rosenthal rounded off the scoring with his second goal at Highfield Road, supplementing yet another by Ian Rush and a Johnny Barnes hat trick, who would believe we wouldn't win it again for 30 years? Certainly not me.

* * *

As the 1980s turned into the 1990s, my work started to have an increasing impact on our family life. Following our move back north, and a very convenient, and indeed enjoyable, assignment at Royal Insurance in Liverpool, I was put on assignment at the Midland Bank IT Centre in Sheffield, coincidentally starting there a few days before the Hillsborough tragedy in April 1989.

Congleton is fairly equidistant from Liverpool and Sheffield, but the road journeys are completely different. My trips to Sheffield took me through the Peak District and, beautiful though much of that journey is, it takes longer than half as much again as the journey to Liverpool, though I was at least still able to commute on a daily basis throughout the six-month assignment. My next assignment took me much further afield.

To Avon & Somerset Constabulary in fact, where the offices were based near Portishead just outside Bristol, and I stayed for the duration at the charming Rodney Hotel within Clifton Village on the Bristol side of the Clifton Suspension Bridge. Travelling long distances during the Monday morning and Friday afternoon rush hours, which has become commonplace for many people as the nation's working culture has changed over the years (and not for the better in my opinion), is far from enjoyable, and I wouldn't recommend it. But as difficult as I found it, it was worse for San who was basically having to bring up two very active under five-year-old boys by herself during the week.

A few months after that assignment finished, and following a welcome spell in the relatively nearby Alderley Edge office, I was assigned to a new client, a government department with offices based in Lytham St. Annes on the North West Fylde coast. For the next seven years, barring a few short months in the blisteringly hot summer of 1995 when I was based in London for another government department, my life increasingly centred around this leafy, sleepy resort just a few miles down the coast from the brighter, somewhat seedier, lights of its brasher neighbour Blackpool.

It was a round trip of more than 160 miles on a daily basis to start with, the novelty of which soon wore off. As the project progressed and the timescale for completion became increasingly tight, there was an 'expectation' (read 'unwritten demand') that project members would work a minimum 20 percent overtime – effectively a six-day week, usually crammed into five. The daily commute soon became impossible to maintain for five days every week and most of my colleagues who travelled similar distances to me soon developed the habit of staying in nearby hotels on at least one of those days.

That being the case, it wasn't long before Thursday evening became the new Friday night and an ever-evolving group of us would often work late then go for our evening meal and a few drinks. We were spending more time with each other than with our families, and while that was good for team morale, it had the opposite effect on many relationships.

I would also regularly spend the Monday evening in a hotel, often the Dalmeny in St. Annes (the green hotel as our kids called it after we'd spent a couple of nights there as a family, and which had everything to do with its verdant façade and nothing to do with any environmental policies it may have had in place at the time), some welcome respite from the seemingly interminable grind. It was during this period in the early 90s when mine and San's relationship suffered its most challenging time, and I will always be grateful that we came through it.

Early in 1992, San's mum sold up and moved in with us, using some of the proceeds of her sale to help pay for an extension to our three-bed detached home. This provided her own living space to a large extent, with an ensuite bathroom and stairs leading from her bedroom to her own small kitchen, with access to the back garden from there. It was an arrangement which worked very well while it lasted. Gladys still had her pension, the remains of the proceeds from the sale of her house, and no expenses other than for her subsistence requirements. Gone were the worries of heating her home on a meagre widow's pension and living and looking after herself on her own, with all the stress that entails for a vulnerable pensioner.

For us, it meant peace of mind knowing she was a visit up or down the stairs away, less compulsion to visit Liverpool absolutely *every* weekend (though even now, nearly 30 years later, we still do it more often than not) and a live-in babysitter (Gladys and the kids adored each other so there was no problem on that score). And of course, we ended up with a more spacious home without having to move.

Sadly, Gladys died in September 1993, not much more than twelve months after moving in with us. She was diagnosed with cancer in the spring, and died in late summer, a couple of days after San's birthday. Once she knew her prognosis, she was determined to take the kids (and us) to Disneyland Paris but wanted it to be a surprise for them. And so, we concocted a story whereby she wanted to visit the battlefields in France (as a member of the Women's Auxiliary Territorial Service she'd driven a tank around the streets of Edinburgh at the end of the second World War, so she had that as a back story for them).

Having flown into Charles de Gaulle airport we jumped on a shuttle bus bound for the Disney resort, and were immediately bombarded with adverts for it, via the onboard television sets, all the way there. Fearing the game was up, I was both amused and relieved, almost proud of their innocence even, when after a whispered conversation between the boys, Tom asked me if one day in the future we might take them to Euro Disney, as it was called then. I said I'd think about, and even put them on their best behaviour for this holiday as a pre-requisite.

We then queued for over half an hour to check-in to our Disney Hotel (Davy Crockett Ranch, not the *obvious* Disneyland Hotel) and they remained innocently oblivious until Chip and Dale turned up. Even then, we managed to delay their gratification slightly by hinting at a possible visit to the theme park later in the week.

It was such a wonderful moment when, having dropped our luggage in the rooms, we all 'went for a walk', eventually rounding a corner to be met by the magnificent sight of the Disneyland Hotel, unmistakably the gateway to Disneyland itself. The boys were beside themselves with glee, I'd rarely seen them so happy. Liv was less enthusiastic. But she was also less than six months old and stuck in a pushchair, so perhaps understandably so. (Having said that, she has been a self-confessed Disney Princess for as long as I can remember, so maybe she was celebrating on the inside even at that young age).

We had a great few days there, Gladys even managing to enjoy a few of the rides with us. In fact, her wheelchair got us to the front of many a queue. It was a lovely final gesture by her, and I think she enjoyed every minute.

Did the stress of moving home contribute to her illness? We'll never know. What we do know is that she was delighted and grateful when we invited her to come and live with us, she was able to eat well and stay warm without worrying about the pennies, and she spent a lot more precious time with her family, especially her grandchildren, than she otherwise would have done. I think she was content.

It was also around this time that seven-year-old Tom was diagnosed with dermatomyositis, a potentially life-threatening illness. A rash of sorts developed on his face and while we immediately suspected eczema, Tom's doctor was far from certain that was the cause. In fact he was pretty sure it wasn't. As the inflammation spread to Tom's joints, he was subjected to a series of examinations and underwent an electromyogram test which involved needle electrodes being inserted into his thighs and arms. San was with him for that, I simply couldn't face it. Poor from me I know.

I remember Tom and I seated in a specialist's office to discuss the results of one test and, before answering my query about his condition, the specialist asked Tom to leave the room. My heart sank. Up to this point, although we'd come to realise Tom's condition probably wasn't eczema, we hadn't seriously considered a debilitating illness. The specialist explained the diagnosis, that there was no cure as such, and that the consequences were potentially very serious, though certainly not set in stone. One silver lining was that Tom wasn't a middle-aged woman, for whom the consequences of the condition were believed to be most dire.

San was understandably distraught on hearing the news. It was difficult to take in. Tom had always been tall for his age, as active as any of his friends, and even at that young age was showing signs of sporting prowess, particularly with a football at his feet. His only symptoms related to the 'derm', or 'skin', element of the condition - the rash, or 'blush' as we'd been corrected into calling it, which became a little more prevalent on his knuckles, elbows, knees and ankles. There'd been no signs of the 'myo', or 'muscle', element to date. We could only hope and pray that remained the case.

And thankfully, it did. He grew to be over six foot tall, supported by a far from delicate frame. As a young teenager he could outsprint me, which may not sound too surprising but bear in mind I kept myself reasonably fit with regular games of 5-a-side and squash, so was no slouch. On our family holidays he enjoyed a swim as much as anyone, and during the summer months was a keen tennis player, cricketer and athlete.

Football was his first and true love though, and he excelled as a ball playing centre-half for a number of local teams, although any thoughts of staying competitive into his adult years were dashed by problems with his knees, which may have been a legacy of his condition, but just as likely were the result of playing so often while he was still growing. Like many people he also suffered with chest infections, particularly during the winter months. But I think it's fair to say that, after the initial shock of his diagnosis and a short period when we treated every minor ailment with suspicion, Tom's overall physical health never gave us any more cause for serious concern.

* * *

San's third pregnancy, which thankfully bore fruit in time for her mum to have a few months with our new arrival, is memorable for a few reasons. Of course, sadly and inevitably, there are a couple of football related markers for me.

With the baby due in early December, a water infection meant San had to spend three or four days in hospital under observation. This coincided with the start of the new season in August – the first of the Premiership / Premier League era. At the time Liverpool were still relatively recent winners of the League Championship, having triumphed two years earlier, and as fans we were still in that self-deceiving, if somewhat comforting, phase of denial which meant we still harboured hopes of reclaiming our crown at the dawn of each new season.

Although Leeds United were the reigning champions, Arsenal, who had won the other two of the previous four championships were still the team to beat as far as I was concerned and, while San was in hospital, suffered a shock 4-2 home drubbing at the hands of unfancied Norwich City in their opening game of the season. (It augured well for the season I thought, and indeed we did eventually finish above Arsenal, who ended up in ninth place. However, our fifth-place finish was nothing to write home about either, Norwich having the last laugh by finishing third above us both).

Then, on 19 December, two days before San's labour was again to be induced, Coventry City thrashed Liverpool 5-1 at their Highfield Road home, a result and performance which left us in tenth-place, eleven points behind surprise leaders Norwich, and which confirmed our newly acquired mediocre status.

It was as grim as I'd known since I attended my first game nearly 25 years before, but worse was to follow: that evening we attended a barn dance with friends. With San well past her due date and me avoiding alcohol 'just in case', I ended up doing the 'dozey-doe' in a state of complete sobriety. The things we do!

Happily, things started to brighten up a couple of days later. The maternity setup had changed a little in Macclesfield General Hospital since Dan had been born nearly five years earlier. There was now a new maternity wing which housed a much more spacious and comfortable birthing room. We were also encouraged to bring our own music, our own soundtrack to the labour if you like, and so we made a tape recording of a few easy listens.

We had already decided on names – Joe for a boy and Olivia for a girl – but while we were happy to share the boy's name with friends and family, San wanted to keep the girl's name quiet. Superstitiously, she was afraid of tempting fate in that respect and I must admit to secretly hoping for a little girl, being slightly concerned about how San would react to having another boy. I mean, I'm sure she'd have been fine, but I knew she was very keen for a daughter.

As the labour progressed San was moved into the birthing room, taking full advantage of the gas and air on offer again. We started to get a few signs then. Our midwife's name was 'Jo' Almonte, obviously a mere coincidence. Tiny disposable nappies were readied in anticipation of the new arrival and were all patterned in blue. Not a single pink one.

Similarly, the first tiny gown our new baby would wear was blue. The omens were stacking up. We were a few songs into our tape when the baby's head appeared to "Here Comes the Sun" (the Beatles version, naturally). Even the midwife laughed. By now, I was convinced we were having another boy and San was at the stage where she just wanted 'it' to be out.

Ultimately of course, we just wanted a healthy baby, and for a few seconds after she was born – for it was a 'she' despite all the 'signs' – I was slightly worried as she was a darkly unhealthy colour (to my inexperienced eye), but moreover she was noticeably silent. That lasted until they sucked her airwaves clear, at which point she let out the most wonderfully healthy scream. And to be honest, we've hardly had a quiet day since. And just like her brothers before her, she has been a joy.

Our family was complete.

4

HILLSBOROUGH

12 April 1980

I always associated Hillsborough, the home of Sheffield Wednesday Football Club, with FA Cup Semi-Finals and beautiful spring days, and in April 1980 I visited it for the first time for Liverpool's cup semi-final against Arsenal.

Five of us set off from Wedgewood Street in 'Frank's van'. Frankie Wheeler was one of my dad's best mates, having been a work colleague as a telephone engineer with the GPO before leaving to join 'Bolton Gate' – a company which, unsurprisingly, made and installed automatic industrial and commercial doors and gates. Frank had use of the firm's van outside of working hours and he'd used it to take us to away games on numerous previous occasions.

On this particular occasion, Frank, my dad and me were joined by a mate of mine – George Brash, a guy I worked with at Alexander Howden's Insurance Brokers and who had been on Liverpool's books as a schoolboy, and a mate of his, called Alan I think, who I'd never met before. We set off about 9.30 in the morning, well in time for the 3.00 pm kick off, and arrived in Sheffield just before noon, without incident. The weather had been glorious since the start of the day and was ideal 'beer garden' weather when we arrived in Sheffield.

The Hillsborough ground itself lies in the Don valley at the bottom of a long steep hill, and we parked up at a working men's club which was maybe halfway down this hill, about three miles northwest of the city centre. There were already quite a few scousers similarly parked up and milling around ('out of town' followers of Liverpool were a little less prevalent, though no less fanatical, in those days), although it was proving difficult to get access to the club (and hence the bar and beer!). None of us were 'affiliated' you see, as the doorman was keen to point out repeatedly, and he wasn't letting any non-affiliates in thank you very much – something to do with the rules! Eventually however, Frank managed to convince one of the locals to sign him in, promising that he alone would go to the bar and bring the drinks out to join the rest of us who would remain outdoors enjoying the sunshine.

Of course, once Frank had been signed in the dam burst and before long the grounds of the club were full of Liverpool fans enjoying the weather, the beer and the camaraderie which was always evident when the red army was on the road. On signing in – for a fee of a few pence - Frank was given a receipt to be shown each time entry to the club was required. As soon as he arrived back with our first round of drinks – two pints each – the receipt was 'loaned out' to a fellow fan who used it to gain entry to the club, and the process was repeated ad infinitum after that.

Unfortunately, with only a single receipt to go around, and more fans arriving by the minute, this was proving an increasingly inefficient way of getting sufficient beer for the thirsty hoards. A couple of lads turned up, assessed the situation, and one of them disappeared around the back of the car they'd just arrived in. A few seconds later he reappeared with a pair of dirty, oily hands and went up to the doorman with his mate.

"Just had a problem with me car, mate, and need to wash me hands. Okay if I just use your toilets?" he enquired.

"Shouldn't really, you're not affiliated" the doorman replied, half-heartedly rejecting the request.

"Oh go on mate, I'll only be a minute, me hands are filthy" the scouser pressed, sensing the argument was about to be won.

"Aye, go on then, but don't be long" the doorman again replied, bowing to the inevitable.

"I'll just show him where the bogs are then" his relatively clean-handed mate piped up – and they were in!

Subsequently, new arrivals would simply collect a couple of empty beer glasses and use these as a 'rite of passage' to the bar. The doorman eventually gave up trying to stop 'non-affiliates' getting in, his enthusiasm for the task no doubt diminished by the huge and unexpected takings the club was obviously enjoying. I take no pride in saying it, but I did have rather a lot to drink in the couple of hours before kick-off. As we all did, with Frank the driver drinking the most (not that I'm condoning this type of behaviour!).

We set off for the ground at about 2.15pm I guess, and were all inside in plenty of time for kick off. Unusually for me in those days, I had a ticket for a seat in the North Stand while the others would all be standing on the Leppings Lane terrace. To my left was the massive Kop end – roofless, lucky with the weather then – which, if I remember correctly, had been allocated to the Arsenal fans. The game itself was a bore draw, the only incident of note being when the Arse's Brian Talbot broke through the Liverpool back four with a couple of minutes to go and lobbed the ball over our advancing keeper, the late great Ray Clemence, and onto the bar.

The near miss had the effect of accelerating the sobering up process for me, and I was pretty much clear headed when I arrived back at the van. Thankfully, so was Frank the driver, though looking back he must have still been over the limit as we hit the trail home. He was certainly well over the speed limit on the way back to Merseyside, prompting George to wonder aloud if Frank had qualified for his pilot's licence yet!

Back home, I was immediately on the phone to San. We were still just friends and work colleagues at this stage, notwithstanding a couple of 'half-dates' we'd had up to that point. I wanted a ticket for the replay at Villa Park and San had a season ticket for Anfield, and so would highly likely qualify for said ticket. Did she want it and, if not, could I have it? Fortunately, she did qualify for a ticket – cup replays were played a few days after the original game in those days, and consequently ticket arrangements for potential replays were published well in advance - and was more than happy for me to have it.

The tie was eventually completed after three replays – two at Villa Park and the ultimate decider at Highfield Road, home of Coventry City, where a Brian Talbot header following a mistake by ex-gooner Ray Kennedy put the north Londoners through to a Wembley date with, and eventual loss to, second division east Londoners West Ham, who had needed just the one replay to account for Everton in the other semi-final. I was accompanied to the last two games of the semi-final quartet by San – we were now officially dating – for me at least a silver lining to the cloud of bitter disappointment following our cup exit.

Notwithstanding the eventual outcome of the tie, the second replay at Villa Park provided one of the most intensely engrossing match-going experiences I'd had up to that point. Arsenal kicked off and were ahead through Alan Sunderland after about ten seconds – certainly no more than 15. It then seemed to me that for virtually all the remaining 89 minutes and 50 seconds, plus injury time of course, Arsenal were simply unable to progress much beyond the edge of their own penalty area, much less their own half, such was Liverpool's furious response. It was as long a period of domination as it's possible to enjoy in a 90 minute game too, as Liverpool's equalizer, swept home by club legend Kenny Dalglish, only arrived deep into injury time at the end of the 90 minutes.

Celebrations in our half of the 'split down the middle' Holte End were appropriately delirious and the euphoria lasted throughout extra-time, where Liverpool, bolstered by the return to the action of a heavily head bandaged David Johnson, who had left the pitch with what looked like a serious head injury a few minutes before the equalizer, continued to dominate without managing to find a winner. And all to no avail given what was to follow in the final replay a week or so later. The life of a football fan eh?

* * *

9 April 1988

It was eight years almost to the day before I set off for Hillsborough again. Saturday, 9 April 1988 was another glorious spring day, and the occasion was another cup semi-final, this time against Nottingham Forest, who were no longer quite the same bitter rivals they'd been a decade earlier. Much had happened since my last visit. For starters, San and I were now married with a couple of children – Tom aged two (and nearly a half!) and Daniel who was just over a month old. We had moved back 'up north' a year previously after over four years living and working in London and the South East, before which we'd also spent six fairly uneventful months in New York.

I could drive now, having passed my test on my return from the States in 1982, and so four of us set off in my Nissan Stanza. My brother Alan claimed the front passenger seat with my mum and dad in the back. Off we went, along Edge Lane, onto the M62 and up to the M1 before again dropping down into Sheffield. The lovely weather had followed us into Yorkshire and, as in 1980, we were in plenty of time for a beer or two before kick-off. Our pub of choice wasn't quite close enough to the ground to walk from, but we only planned to have a couple before finding somewhere to park closer to the ground (the name of the pub escapes me, but I'm pretty sure it included the name of an animal - 'Bear' or 'Bull' I think, or perhaps I'm getting confused with the Stock Exchange!).

By the end of the day it had panned out pretty much as expected. After a couple of drinks we parked up closer to the ground, following the example of numerous other supporters by claiming a place on a grass verge which, though closer to Hillsborough, still left us with a reasonable walk. Again, we encountered the long hill down into Hillsborough, and it was noticeable that, before we reached the ground, we had to navigate a number of ticket checks by the police before we were allowed to proceed. This time, my mum was the odd one out with a ticket for the stands, while the three males in the party had tickets for the Leppings Lane terraces. One of the first things I'd done when we moved back north was, along with my brother Alan, to buy a season ticket for The Kop – my first one. These entitled us to semi-final tickets on the terraces.

By the time we got in the ground it must have been about a quarter to three, with kick-off fast approaching. I remember being slightly confused at first because, once through the turnstiles, we appeared to be in a sort of concourse area and faced by another large blue gate which was closed and thus barring our way in. A couple of policemen stood in front of the gate, I assumed wanting to check our tickets in the belief that we were in the wrong part of the ground. But they were simply redirecting fans away from the central pens – which were already full and had been sealed off to newcomers by the simple mechanism of closing the large blue gate which now faced us – to the pens at either side of the terrace. We chose to veer right and watched a memorable Liverpool victory from the pen beneath the police control room.

The Liverpool team at this time was in its pomp, arguably the most pleasing on the eye of all the great teams Liverpool fielded during the 60's, 70's and 80's. John Aldridge had taken over the goal scoring mantle of the previously thought irreplaceable Ian Rush – who had left Anfield for his Italian job with Juventus at the end of the previous season – and with the further additions of Peter Beardsley, Ray Houghton and the at times unplayable John Barnes, the team regularly embarrassed the opposition – home or away – with their flowing football.

In this game, two goals from John Aldridge (one from the penalty spot, the second a sweet volley into the Leppings Lane goal doing justice to a precise cross from Barnes after great work down the left wing between him and Beardsley) were enough to see off Forest who replied with a solitary goal from Nigel Clough.

We made our way back to Liverpool in jubilant mood – and with the windows open, our Alan having removed his shoes and thus allowed the rest of us the dubious pleasure of experiencing the full force of his (ob)noxious foot odour!

Liverpool went on to suffer a shock 1-0 defeat at the hands of unfancied Wimbledon in the final the following month. Having wrapped up the title with four games to spare following a routine 1-0 home win over Spurs when Beardsley scored, this rare defeat – we suffered only two in the league – which prevented us completing the double for the second time in three seasons, was particularly difficult to take in. Still, after the season we'd just had, Liverpool fans everywhere had every reason to hope, maybe even expect, that we could right that wrong the following season. How close we were to come, and perhaps how fitting that ultimately we would fail again, after the most harrowing end to a season in the history of our, or any other, English club.

* * *

15 April 1989

After the performance heights of the previous season, Liverpool unexpectedly made a relatively slow start to the 1988-89 season, with Arsenal making all the early running and establishing themselves as favourites to win the league title for the first time since 1971 (when, incidentally, they also became only the second team to 'do the double' that century, beating Liverpool 2-1 in the Cup Final after extra time).

However, cometh the spring, cometh the redmen. In fact, long before the clocks sprung forward Liverpool had picked up the pace – as we were wont to do in those days – and Arsenal suffered a slight wobble, dropping unexpected points in the league and suffering an early exit in the FA Cup to fellow Londoners West Ham.

Following defeat by the press monikered 'Fergie's Fledglings' at Old Trafford on New Year's Day, the following 13 league games harvested 35 of a possible 39 points. It was a run which suggested hopes of retaining our title might be far more realistic than the pipe dream they'd appeared to be when the final whistle had blown to end the debacle against the red half of Manchester. And of course, as well as resuming normal service in the league campaign, Liverpool had also progressed to the semi-final of the FA Cup and, as in the previous season, were drawn against Nottingham Forest. The tie was again to be played at Hillsborough.

In the years since the disaster which unfolded at Hillsborough on that day, I've often looked back at the ties we came through to reach the semi-final and wondered, if not wished, if somewhere en route the wheels might have come off and saved us all from the anguish, heartbreak and grief that awaited so many. However, in spite of the first three ties (rounds three to five) being held away from home – at Carlisle, Millwall and Hull City respectively – only

Hull City in the fifth round offered more than token resistance.

Two goals from Steve McMahon following an opener by John Barnes meant that Carlisle United, our third-round opponents, were comfortably dispatched 3-0 at Brunton Park on a typically miserable January day. The family – me, San, the kids and San's mother – spent most of that Saturday afternoon visiting various dog's homes in the Cheshire and Merseyside countryside, looking for a suitable pet for my mother-in-law. San's dad had passed away at the end of the previous November and her mum was now living on her own in Maghull, just north of Liverpool. A pet dog would serve the dual purpose of providing much needed company and added security, and anyway, I've never enjoyed listening to the match on the radio and was happy for any excuse to get out of the house while the match was being played.

In round 4 early second half goals from John Aldridge and Ian Rush – who had returned from his brief sojourn with Juventus after just a season – put paid to Millwall's ambitions at The Den, in a game we were able to watch on TV, to set up a fifth-round tie against Hull City at Boothferry Park. With the dawn of the home team's first competitive season in England's top division still nearly 20 years away, opportunities for the local fans to watch the country's elite sides were few and far between, and in spite of Hull's relatively low average match attendance at the time the game was a sell-out, with only a small allocation of tickets made available to Liverpool's huge away support.

In response to the high demand for, and low supply of tickets, Liverpool obtained agreement to relay live television pictures of the game to a big screen erected at Prenton Park, the home of Tranmere Rovers on the other side of the Mersey. Me and my mum duly attended this viewing, thereby mirroring my dad's experience of watching Liverpool take on Everton in the fifth round at Goodison Park in 1967 via the 'magic' of the big screens set up at Anfield to cope with the demand for tickets (a capacity crowd of nearly 65,000 packed into Goodison that night, with in excess of a further 40,000 watching on the big screens at Anfield – a combined 'live' attendance of over 100,000).

Against Hull, we watched Liverpool take control from the start, with an early goal from John Barnes only adding weight to the sense of inevitability of our expected progress to the quarter final. Completely against the run of play however, Hull scored twice in the ten minutes before half time, and for a short while the prospect of an embarrassing exit from the cup loomed large on the horizon. If only...

By the end, two early second half goals from Aldo proved enough to book a sixth-round home tie against Brentford, who performed well at Anfield. In front of over 42,000 fans, including 7,000 of their own visiting from the capital, they threatened more than once during the early stages of the game, but were ultimately steam-rollered in impressive fashion by a Barnes inspired Liverpool, who racked up four goals without reply through McMahon, Barnes himself and a late Beardsley double. The season was now shaping up very nicely, thank you very much, and we couldn't wait for the semi-final. Little did we know ...

At the start of this season, me and our Alan had swapped our Kop season tickets for seats at the back of the Kemlyn Road stand, more or less in line with the six-yard box at the Kop end of the ground. This meant that for this year's semi-final at Hillsborough we qualified for stand tickets – seats in the North Stand – rather than terrace tickets in the Leppings Lane. Our Alan had been suffering with a nasty back problem for quite a while and was recovering from an operation – a disc removed I think – when the semi-final dawned. His mobility was severely restricted, and he'd consequently foregone the option of a ticket for the match. With my dad also deciding his time would be better spent looking after Alan – who really couldn't get out of bed – our travelling party this time numbered just two. Mum and me.

As for the previous season, we set off in the Stanza on another beautiful spring day, taking the same route as a year ago. Just after we hit the orbital motorway on the west side of Manchester – the M60 now, but still part of the M62 then – traffic slowed to a halt, the result of what looked like a nasty traffic accident. As we crawled past the scene, I noticed a body – I presumed to be still alive – lying in the recovery position, an ambulance in close attendance. (At the time, my thoughts went back to another semi-final game, a replay against Leicester City at Villa Park in 1974, which we won 3-1. On the way home we were delayed for a long time because of an accident ahead of us. We eventually passed the scene of the accident about a mile

– less than a minute – from where we'd stopped, to find the cars involved completely burned out. It was a sobering moment after a great win, made even more so because word had already spread through the queuing traffic that fellow Liverpool fans had died in the pile up. A few months later I started college where one of the girls on the same course – Paula Burke – revealed that her boyfriend had been one of the victims that night. It's a small world).

Back on the M62 on route to our latest semi-final appearance, the Police were still clearing the site of debris and, as you can imagine, the traffic build up was huge with a large proportion of Liverpool's support for the day sure to be using this route. We'd set off pretty early as usual, so weren't too worried about the delay, but for fans leaving closer to kick off time, this would potentially have quite an impact on their plans for the day.

We eventually arrived in Sheffield later than expected, but still in plenty of time for a spot of lunch – a sandwich and a couple of drinks at the same pub we'd found the previous year. There were a few other reds in the bar – mainly young lads having a few pints and a good old singsong in anticipation of another famous victory en route to another Wembley day out. I seem to remember "Who put the ball in the Forest net?...Super Johnnie Aldridge" getting quite an airing. As the events of later in the day sank in, and in the years that followed, I often wondered about those young lads. Did they all make it home okay? Or were their number cruelly reduced in the mayhem that followed? I'll never know of course, so I'll always wonder.

Having left the pub early to park closer to the ground, we found a space in a residential street and walked the rest of the way. Unlike the previous season there were no ticket checks on the way to the ground this time, although police were stopping fans to relieve them of any alcohol they may have been carrying. As a consequence of the lack of ticket checks, I guess, there were also one or two fans who were there 'on spec' and on the approach to the ground were asking for 'any spares?'. Only a handful, if that, but it certainly hadn't been the case the year before.

We must have arrived at the ground sometime between 2pm and 2.15pm I would guess, because we know from reports since that by the time 2.30pm arrived the crowd situation outside the Leppings Lane end of the ground was already dangerously chaotic. In stark contrast, when we arrived there were hardly any fans queuing to get in. Although we had stand tickets, my mum's seat in the West Stand and mine in the North Stand, the approach to the turnstiles for both was the same as that for the many thousands who would also have tickets to the Leppings Lane terrace.

Fans, and the police we encountered, were all in good humour at this stage, and I recall a lad in front of us, when about to be frisked before passing through the turnstiles, jokingly asking to be searched by one of the WPCs in the vicinity rather than her male colleague. We all giggled, though she politely declined his request. At this point my mum and I separated towards our respective destinations, and I made my way unhurriedly to my seat in the North Stand, mum heading to hers in the West Stand directly above the Leppings Lane terrace.

My seat was a lot closer to the Nottingham Forest fans who were quickly filling up the Hillsborough Kop to my left – rather more quickly than the North Stand appeared to be getting filled – with the West Stand and Leppings Lane terrace further away to my right. The terrace was starting to look very full in parts, though curiously there appeared to be a lot more space available at either end of it.

I never really gave that situation more than a moment's thought though. I had no doubt the terrace, and indeed the currently empty seats around me, would fill up pretty quickly now with kick-off fast approaching, and I settled back to enjoy the building atmosphere – a lot of it admittedly being generated by the Forest fans at the moment – in anticipation of a great game and a result that would see us return to Wembley after our shock defeat there the previous season.

The slight air of abnormality heightened when a fan clambered out of the Leppings Lane end – a feat in itself given the presence of the spiked railings at the front of the terrace which were commonplace at grounds up and down the country, designed to prevent any such intrusions onto the pitch – and proceeded to remonstrate with the Forest fans from the vicinity of the halfway line. For the life of me I couldn't understand why he was doing it.

It could hardly be categorised as a pitch invasion – it was a single guy, there was no history of significant rancour between the opposing sets of supporters, and no history of angry pitch invasions by Liverpool supporters at all – and I rationalised it as the effects of a pre-match pint over the eight combined with too much sun. Still, it was something we could do without and which was likely to lead to ramifications for the club in the days that followed.

As kick-off time approached, I remained an island in a sea of empty seats, which weren't filling anywhere near as quickly as I'd thought they would, and certainly in my opinion wouldn't be fully occupied before the game started. Perhaps that accident on the M62 had indeed had the delaying impact I'd thought it might? A couple of lads of a similar age to me did eventually take their seats nearby, looking flustered and bringing tales of chaos outside the ground and not needing to show a ticket to get in, their ticket stubs still attached. They were clearly angry.

Nevertheless, with the teams now entering the pitch to raucous applause from all sides of the stadium and with playing conditions firmly in the 'glorious' bracket, my thoughts and attention quickly turned back to the game in prospect, passing their frustrations off as an overreaction to the usual mild to middling disarray often experienced whenever attending otherwise seldomly visited, and consequently 'unused to', stadiums in great numbers. As fans of Liverpool – the most successful British team of the era - attendance at semi-finals and Finals on neutral grounds had become commonplace, but still occurred only once or twice in a season at most.

Liverpool, with elegant club captain Alan Hansen starting his first game of the season after dislocating his knee in a pre-season friendly against Atletico Madrid, dominated the early stages, culminating in Peter Beardsley firing against the bar after six minutes. It was the final action of the game. Referee Ray Lewis brought the match to a halt on the advice of the police match commander Roger Greenwood, the teams left the pitch, and the extent of the disaster started to emerge in front of us.

For a short while confusion reigned around me as many of us, as yet still unaware of the scale of the tragedy, thought that the game might eventually restart. Forest fans briefly taunted the Liverpool supporters but, as the nature and magnitude of what had happened became clearer, that quickly petered out, as did any thoughts of the game being completed, and opposing fans became unlikely helpmates in the chaos which followed.

I recall seeing the first body carried out on a makeshift stretcher with a jumper pulled up to cover the face. That's when I realised that I was witnessing a disaster and I still remember the shock and feeling of helplessness. To be fair, many fans were proving themselves to be far from helpless, putting the emergency services to shame with their heroic efforts in the wake of the unfolding events.

After about half an hour or so I started to make my way out of the ground, passing a youngster who appeared to be being worked on by a couple of policemen attempting to administer oxygen. I remember almost screaming at the coppers to "Save Him" before arguing with another one who wanted me to calm down. To be honest, I wasn't doing anyone any good and returned to the car in a fog of confusion. Looking back, I was obviously in a mild state of shock at this stage.

Mum arrived back at the car a few minutes after me, and a resident of the house I had parked outside kindly offered me the use of their phone to call home – mobile phones were still largely accessories of the rich, the flash or the businessman at the time – and as soon as I'd let San know we were safe and asked her to pass the message on to my dad, we started the sombre journey back across the Pennines to Liverpool, kept up to date with the steadily rising death toll by the BBC on the way. Family had never felt so important. Football never less so.

The following day San and I visited Anfield to lay flowers on the pitch after the club opened the ground to the public because of the number of fans in mourning who had turned up, plenty who were fans of other clubs and many who simply didn't know what else to do in the wake of the previous day's events. By sheer coincidence, the previous week I had started an assignment at Griffin House, Midland Bank's computer centre in Sheffield city centre, and so returned to the city on Monday morning, and the ground during Monday lunchtime, to lay some more flowers. Dozens of people had the same idea, the atmosphere understandably solemn.

It wasn't long before the smear campaign started in the media, particularly in the written press, with the biggest, vilest culprits, though certainly not the only ones, being the Sun newspaper which, under a front-page banner headline of 'The Truth', formulated personally by the editor Kelvin Mackenzie, accused Liverpool fans of urinating on policemen trying to help victims and of pick-pocketing the dead and dying.

I have no desire to waste anyone's time here debating Mackenzie's motives, but I do recommend the book 'Hillsborough - The Truth', written by Professor Phil Scraton, as a must-read for anyone who wants to really understand the truth about what happened that day, and the cover up which followed and continued until the Hillsborough Report, the result of an investigation based on the 'paper trail' around the disaster and its aftermath by the Hillsborough Independent Panel, was published in 2012, more than 23 years after the tragedy occurred.

Suffice to say that the stance taken by that rag heaped more pain and anguish on the people of a city already on its knees in deep communal distress. From being the best-selling daily newspaper on Merseyside, sales of it almost completely disappeared overnight and have never recovered. Nearly a quarter of a century later the fans, who had never stopped fighting for justice, were finally exonerated and responsibility placed firmly at the door of South Yorkshire Police Constabulary where it clearly belonged.

I also recall that when the disaster occurred, the consensus amongst match going football fans across the country was that this was a disaster which could have happened to any of them, given the way football fans were viewed and treated by those in authority, and few were surprised at the blame deflection which quickly gathered pace before even the last fans had left the ground on that fateful day.

'When Saturday Comes' is a long-standing non-partisan football fanzine, a medium which was really taking off in the mid to late 1980's, and the front page of its first issue following the disaster contained a quartet of pictures featuring Graham Kelly, the Chief Executive of the FA at the time, Peter Wright, the Chief Constable of South Yorkshire Police, Prime Minister Margaret Thatcher and a stock photo of an unidentified football crowd. Speech bubbles from Kelly, Wright and Thatcher declared that "It wasn't our fault" with another from the crowd responding "Oh well, it must be our fault again", absolutely nailing the contempt in which all football fans appeared to be held by the chattering classes, and the helplessness many of us felt in combatting that perception.

In the days and weeks that followed, the only mild rebuke I received was from a work colleague who professed to being non-plussed at the club's unwillingness to start playing football games again as soon as possible. Andy (I'm omitting his surname to spare him any potential further embarrassment) was a fan of Manchester United and argued that following the Munich air disaster in 1958 United were back playing almost immediately, and crowds queued for hours to get into the games.

"We lost a *team*" he argued, quite vehemently actually, as if that should be considered of greater import than the loss of mere fans.

I explained my understanding that fans needed to show their support for the team under those circumstances, but at the moment our club needed to show empathy and support for the fans, which they were doing – and much more - by not rushing back. Many fans just didn't have the stomach for watching football again so quickly. That argument fell on deaf ears, but there was certainly no criticism of Liverpool fans by Andy or those of other clubs at the time.

It is saddening then that, as time has progressed, some fans of rival clubs – primarily, though not entirely, the younger generations – have had little compunction about taunting Liverpool fans as authors of our own misfortune, blaming us for the deaths of 96 of our own. Shame on them.

The season concluded, fittingly I think, with Liverpool as cup winners after defeating Everton 3-2 on an emotional occasion at Wembley. Everton deserve credit for equalising twice, but starkly, during the 120 minutes of the game, which included extra-time, the scores were level for just 18 of them, Liverpool having led early then regained the lead quickly after each Everton equaliser.

Me and my mum watched the game from the very back row behind the goal Liverpool defended in the first half, unable to see half the pitch when we stood up such was the outward reach of the sloping Wembley roof. Poignantly, the chap sat next to us was an Evertonian who'd lost his brother in the disaster and confessed he'd wanted Liverpool to win for that reason, appearing almost as pleased as we were with the result.

The following Tuesday Liverpool beat West Ham 5-1 at Anfield, relegating the Londoners and setting us up for the final game of the season a few days later on the Friday evening, where avoiding defeat by two goals or more to our closest rivals Arsenal would deliver the League Championship trophy. It would be our eighth game in 24 days since returning to action on 3 May, 18 days after the tragedy occurred. All vitally important in our quest for the league and cup double, which had taken on an almost holy grail like importance now, and apart from the first game, a scoreless draw at our Goodison neighbours, Liverpool victorious in all of them.

It was a game, perhaps just a minute, too far. With Arsenal leading 1-0 and requiring another goal to capture the league themselves, Liverpool's Steve McMahon urged his team mates to see out the final embers of the game, raising a single digit to emphasise the time remaining. Perhaps that was the trigger for Arsenal's young midfielder, and future red, Michael Thomas to chance one last throw of the dice, making the most of a favourable bounce of the ball to surge past Steve Nicol and place the ball beyond Liverpool's keeper Bruce Grobbelaar.

And that was that. It was one of the few times I've heard San, sitting beside me in the Kemlyn Road stand, swear.

"Bastard" she uttered.

Quite.

As Arsenal fans in the Anfield Road End of the stadium deliriously rejoiced, Liverpool fans saluted their team and filed out of the ground in near silence. It was surreal. On the way out someone remarked "ah well, at least no-one died".

Nobody argued.

5

OUR CONGLETON CLAN

"**I**f anybody really must watch the football, we've set up a television in one of the classrooms. For anyone else who just wants to know the score, it's nil-nil at half time".

Tom would be starting at the Quinta Primary School, a five-minute walk from home, when the new school year commenced in September and we, along with parents of other newbies as well as those of now more seasoned pupils, had been invited to the Summer Barbecue, arranged by the PTA, which heralded the end of the current school year. The 'football' in question was England's group game against Holland during the 1990 World Cup in Italy, and neither option presented by the now public enemy number one PTA committee member suited me.

England had drawn their opening group game 1-1 with the Republic of Ireland and needed a positive result in this game and I, a big fan of the World Cup despite my antipathy towards international football generally, had decided to record the game, avoid any mention of the score, and then watch it when we returned home. Plan A was ruined. I had no plan B.

To be honest, I don't remember too much else about that pleasant summer evening. (England performed very well but the game remained goalless and they needed to beat Egypt, which they did by the game's only goal, in the final group game to progress, on their way to a very creditable semi-final appearance and fourth place finish). But in my mind now, over 30 years later, after having been in situ for just over three years at the time, and despite being blessed with lovely neighbours on either side of us – Ray & Marlene and Graham & Mary with their slightly older families - this was the beginning of a period when the family really started to settle.

With two young children and me already starting to work long hours and long distances away, we'd decided that living closer to our Liverpool based families actually made more sense for us than being out 'in the sticks' (when compared to my inner-city upbringing). We reasoned it would give us the benefit of an extended friend and family support network as well as easy access to the Liverpool conurbation which we knew well and was well served by public transport, an important consideration with San not being a driver. We'd already had an offer accepted on a lovely three-bed semi in the Calderstones area of South Liverpool, just around the corner from beautiful Calderstones Park, but had to withdraw it as we couldn't sell our Congleton home. The housing market in South Cheshire had slumped, and once Tom started school the decision to remain was made for us.

Ullswater Road meanders through our estate, running across the top of Penrith Court, where we live, on its way from the Sandbach Road to Padgbury Lane. Three adjacent homes on it, which are part of a spread of semi-detached properties almost immediately opposite our cosy little cul-de-sac, housed – and still do - the Nash, O'Rawe and Glover families.

Starting school at the same time as Tom was Adam Glover, a couple of weeks older than Tom, and after Christmas Jamie Nash, who was a few months younger would also start his education at Quinta. James Byrne also lived close by, less than a ten-minute walk away on Padgbury Lane, and started school at the same time as Jamie.

In the ensuing years, first their parents, then their siblings, themselves and their partners became our firm friends, the support network we needed if you like, and it is difficult now to imagine what our lives would have been like without them. That circle of friends has obviously evolved over time, though ironically virtually no-one in it is a native Congletonian. Not that anyone would take offence I'm sure, but purely in alphabetical order of surname, the group included Ged and Jayne Byrne, Graham and Janet Glover, Alan and

Heather Kemball, Steve and Angie Nash, Charlie and Carol O'Rawe and Nigel and Sandra Poole, of whom I think only Carol hails from Congleton.

When the kids were growing up, the three sets of neighbours would often remove some of the fence panels which separated their back gardens so that the expanded space became a wonderful play area for their children and their friends, including our two boys. With Jamie's younger brother Daniel, Adam's younger sister Rachael, Christopher O'Rawe who was a bit older than the other boys, James's younger sister Hannah and our own youngest Olivia adding to the mix, during the summer months those gardens always resonated with the sounds of children's happiness (and indeed still do as grandchildren have started appearing on the scene).

The Kemball family also lived next door to the Nash's before moving when their growing family demanded more space, and were always welcome visitors with children Anna, Sarah and David simply adding to the revelry. Not forgetting the Poole's with their daughters Sarah Jane and Louise. The list goes on, but you get my drift I'm sure. And it wasn't just the kids enjoying themselves either.

Many a long summer evening was spent enjoying a barbecue expertly tended by Steve or Graham, sometimes Alan, on occasion Ged or Charlie. Not me though, for which they can all be thankful. I could boil you an egg, or heat up a bowl of tinned soup (hurrah for microwave ovens) but I never really got the hang of proper cooking. Or even barbecuing. In later years when I worked away from home and lodged in private houses, I expanded my repertoire slightly to making large amounts of Chilli or casseroles which provided multiple portions to be frozen and reheated when needed, but neither really cut it for a warm midsummer evening.

If it wasn't a summer evening, it might be a birthday celebration – child or adult, it didn't matter. Or maybe a festive occasion, a cup final, an England match – football or rugby, it made no difference. And it wasn't *always* at one of those three homes, but I think it's fair to say that far more often than not it was. They were the centre of our social existence, certainly throughout the final decade of the 20th century and well into the first two decades of the 21st. Today it's still a great thrill when the phone rings, or a text arrives, and we've been invited to join these lifelong friends for a get-together. A meal or just a chat maybe. Not forgetting the drinks, of course.

I'm not a big or regular drinker, but I do enjoy a pint of the right stuff at the right time and of course the drinks always flowed when we were all celebrating something together, even if it was just each other's company. Beer, wine, gin and tonic, perhaps a Pimm's and lemonade for the ladies, all helped oil the wheels of these special occasions, not to mention the vocal chords, mine included. I'd say spare a thought for my largely non-drinking wife, but I'm rather envious of the fact that she can enjoy the occasion as much as me without having to suffer the eventual consequences of too many over-the-eight the following day. And though my memories of these get togethers are overwhelmingly fond, I must admit I've let myself down on the odd occasion. Indeed, it would be remiss of me not to mention one evening in particular.

That said, I have no desire to attempt to recount the whole sorry episode here (not least because that would have been impossible on the following day, let alone nearly 20 years later). But even now, on occasion when the drinks are flowing, a mischievous mate might ponder if we're on for another 'Basle night'. The answer, my friends, will always be no.

Suffice to say, the red wine had flowed in Steve and Angie's kitchen that night and I'd had more than my fair share of it. In fact, I remember Ged being particularly impressed (but mostly amused) and metaphorically adorning me with, in Tour de France parlance, the yellow jersey. The following day, after spending the night on our sofa, we suddenly were in desperate need of a new carpet, regurgitated red wine not being a particularly good look, and, having apologised to San, I struggled up the street to apologise to our friends, and Janet in particular.

And I am happy here to confirm that apology in writing (I remain less than proud of some particularly 'industrial' language I may have used in her direction. Fortunately, she saw the funny side of it. I think).

And though in 2016, me and my Dan did actually get to Basle on the occasion of Liverpool's Europa League Final defeat to Sevilla, it wasn't what I'd had in mind on that memorable, though not entirely so, evening 14 years earlier.

And that's all I'm saying on the subject. Those who know, know (probably more than me!). And those who don't, don't need to.

* * *

You'll also be happy to hear, or at least I hope it won't come as a surprise, that there's a lot more to our friendships than the occasional boozy night, and a lot more sober occasions that our families have shared.

Adam, Tom, Jamie, James and Sarah-Jane were all eldest siblings, all in the same school year, and all graduated from Quinta to Heathfield (now Congleton High School) at the same time. As our children matured, so did our relationships with the friends we'd made through them, and in 2003 we arranged to go on holiday with the Byrne family. San had actually known Jayne since before the boys started school, meeting when Tom and James joined the same mother and toddler group, we'd met Ged not long after that and the kids all got on famously.

Our last flying holiday had been back in 1997, to the beautiful family friendly Balearic island of Menorca, one of our favourite destinations, after which San's aversion to flying – of being cooped up in an enclosed space as much as being several miles off the ground - had racked up several notches to the extent that air travel was no longer an option for us. The previous couple of summers we'd enjoyed package holidays, which included return coach travel, in the popular Spanish resort of Salou on the Costa Dorada, and this year we were contemplating driving to the continent.

Having driven to and holidayed in various parts of France already, when Ged and Jayne suggested a joint family holiday in Italy we excitedly agreed, and a beautiful villa in the Tuscan countryside, close to the town of Monte San Savino, with plenty of space for the nine of us, was booked in pretty short order. The holiday couldn't come quickly enough.

We crossed the channel via 'Le Shuttle'. It was the first time we'd used the Euro Tunnel - which immediately became our preferred method of getting over to Europe - and the train deposited us, without having to leave the comfort of our own vehicles, in Calais just thirty-five minutes after leaving

Folkestone. From there we drove on to our first overnight stop, just outside Dijon. It was a long and tiring journey, just over 350 miles, and even longer for the Byrnes who had travelled directly from Congleton that day to catch the shuttle, while we'd travelled the day before, stopping overnight at Ashford.

The hotel was basic, lacking air-conditioning which was a problem for sleeping in the current heat wave, but it was clean and tidy, and we soon relaxed over dinner and a few drinks. A journey of similar length the following day took us into Italy and our final overnight stop in Acqui Terme, known for its winemaking and hot sulphur springs.

Here, our hotel accommodation was in stark contrast to the previous evening. Luxuriously modern, spacious and air-conditioned, they'd allocated us five double rooms between the nine of us which meant the adults had their own rooms, the girls shared, the two eldest boys shared, and Dan had his own room. Everyone was happy with the arrangements and, after availing ourselves of the ubiquitous pasta and pizza on offer at a nearby eatery, slept well, and were bright-eyed and bushy-tailed the next morning, looking forward to the final leg of our outward journey.

The most direct route from Acqui Terme to Monte San Savino is just under 240 miles, a journey of about four and a half hours with a fair wind. Adding another 30 miles to that, and maybe an extra couple of hours touring time, allowed us to take in a couple of popular tourist destinations en route. Portofino is a fishing village on the Italian Riviera coastline, famous for its pastel-coloured houses which overlook the picturesque harbour, and a popular haunt of celebrities and artists alike. We spent an hour there strolling round the harbour, taking pictures, drinking coffee and, for some reason bizarrely memorable, making our acquaintance with the Italian bread, Focaccia. The kids drooled over it.

Ninety minutes, maybe a bit more, further along the same coastline is the resort of Viareggio, which we largely ignored, and slightly inland from there is Pisa, of Leaning Tower fame, which we didn't. It was a flying visit which enabled us to take a few more pictures, the results of which failed miserably to showcase any of us preventing the tilting tower from collapsing (at best, once developed, they appeared to show some of us languidly waving at it while assuming clearly unnatural positions to do so), and treat ourselves to tubs of Italian gelato. In truth, initial impressions of Pisa were less than favourable with it being predictably commercialised around the tower area. San and I have visited since, and found it a lot more appealing away from the tower.

A couple of hours after leaving Pisa we arrived at 'Bar Madison', on the edge of Monte San Savino, to collect the keys to our home for the next two weeks from the owners, as instructed. Time to relax.

And relax we did.

Both families were pretty good at it actually, which was just as well as the European heatwave continued throughout the holiday, making physical exertion of any kind something to be avoided when at all possible. The villa came with its own mole – which we never actually spied, but saw plenty of evidence of its presence around the garden - and a glorious swimming pool, so welcome under the circumstances, serving the dual purpose of enabling us to cool off during the hottest parts of the day and to assuage any guilty conscience over lack of exercise by getting a few lazy lengths in. Table tennis was available for the rare occasions more strenuous activity was called for, the boys making best use of that, though I proudly recall having an unbeaten record myself at the end of our stay.

Not that we confined ourselves to the grounds of the villa of course. Florence is a very beautiful and photogenic city, about an hour's drive from where we were staying, and the panoramic views of it from the Piazzale Michelangelo, which sits atop a hill on the south bank of the Arno River, are worthy of any visit. It must be one of the most photographed vistas in the world, and we certainly took our fair share, though the one Liv took of me and San, ostensibly with Florence's world-famous Duomo – the Cathedral of Santa Maria del Fiore – providing a stunning backdrop, turned out to be the pair of us blocking the view of the Duomo almost completely (though we've remedied that since). San and I have returned to Florence more than once over the years, and never fail to make that steep stepped climb to the top in anticipation of the stunning reward which awaits. The less said about the traffic and Italian drivers the better mind you.

Siena, home of the famous Palio horse race which takes place twice each year, in July and August, around the Piazza del Campo, a massive fan-shaped central square, was also on our itinerary and slightly closer than Florence, though our visit never coincided with either edition of the races. Much smaller than Florence, but with its own beautiful Duomo, it's another place we've returned to since, and still never witnessed a horse race.

Evening meals out, and not just pizza or pasta though they featured heavily, were regularly enjoyed in nearby Arezzo, where we rounded off the evenings with a stroll around the medieval town centre and a visit to our favourite gelato shop which offered a myriad of Italian ice cream flavours, and who can forget 'Il Riccio's', a lovely restaurant situated in the countryside between the villa and Arezzo, where we had a chance encounter with a feral rat and named him 'Basil' (fans of the 1970's TV comedy 'Fawlty Towers' will get the connection).

I recall a day trip to the pretty walled medieval hill town of San Gimignano as well. It was predictably very popular with tourists (and after all that's what we were), but I remember it most for San losing her sunglasses there when we stopped for an iced-coffee break, and the temperature in the car when we returned to it showing 104 degrees Fahrenheit in the shade. It was hot.

Cortona, in the Val di Chiana, and featured in the book 'Under the Tuscan Sun' and film of the same name, was another beautiful walled medieval town we visited for the first time and have returned to several times since, sitting atop another hill offering yet more fantastic views across the Tuscan landscape.

On different days during our fortnight at the villa, first San and I and then Jayne and Ged managed to have a day out on our own, in turn keeping our eye on each other's family back at the villa. I can't remember exactly where we went on our day out, but we'd noticed a sign for an off the beaten track 'Ristorante Belvedere' on the way and thought we'd check it out on the way back for a potential evening meal venue. It was quite a way from the main road along not much more than a dirt track, but it turned out to be a lovely restaurant with yet more stunning views of Tuscany to be had from its terrace. We decided to book tables for the nine of us that evening and, feeling pleased with ourselves, we navigated the dirt track back to the main road which, as in much of Tuscany, snaked around a hillside.

With no traffic coming in either direction, we turned towards our holiday home, chatting contentedly away to each other as we approached the next bend in the road. To our horror, a stream of traffic raced towards us on the same side of the road, held back only by the presence of a slow-moving tractor at the front of the queue. While San questioned the parentage and intellect of the oncoming drivers in a less than civilised manner, I braked sharply and swerved over to the other side of the road, heart hammering in my chest. I instantly realised my error.

With no other vehicles on the road to reference as I exited the dirt track, my driving head was immediately back on the roads I was used to back home and I was driving on the wrong side. Thankfully no lasting damage was done, but it was a scary few moments and a while before either of us could laugh about it. It never stopped us returning to the restaurant though, where we got to enjoy our supper from the terrace to the backdrop of a couple of hill fires in the distance being tackled from the air by what I assumed to be a couple of military helicopters. It all added to the holiday experience.

Our time at the villa was over all too soon. We'd had a great holiday and now had the mammoth return trip home to round it off. The first leg of our journey ended in the picturesque city of Bourge-en-Bresse in South Eastern France, nearly 500 miles from the villa, but it was a subdued evening for us, San having developed a migraine early in the day and taking to her bed immediately on arrival at the hotel. Thankfully, she was much more with it the following day, a Sunday, when another lengthy trip of nearly 450 miles took us to a thankfully air-conditioned Ibis hotel in Calais, ahead of our morning channel crossing.

After travelling almost non-stop through northern Italy and the length of France in the previous 36 hours, I think it's fair to say we were all ready to relax over our final holiday repast, complete with a few drinks for us over 18s of course. A very pleasant way to end a very enjoyable holiday. The following day, our two families said our goodbyes just before disembarking from the train in Folkestone, where due to the time difference we arrived on home soil about 25 minutes before we'd left France, and an uneventful few hours later we were firmly ensconced back home.

Aside from the many wonderful memories of our Tuscan adventure with the Byrne family, one other thing that has stayed with me is Ged's penchant for a long afternoon nap on any day we stayed around the villa. Jayne had mentioned this trait of Ged's before the holiday, and we thought nothing of it. Some of us need, and indeed have earned, their rest more than others, and Ged was always on the go – a committed husband and father and a very successful and well-respected business owner who was also a keen and talented golfer in what little spare time he had. He'd been the life and soul of more than one party in the years we'd known him as well.

Hardly a month after we returned, Ged was diagnosed with cancer and, despite a gallant fight, died a year later. It was a massive shock to us all, and obviously devastating for Jayne, James and Hannah. As a group of friends, our 'Congleton Clan' had rallied round Ged and his family as best we could during that year, initially with hope and belief that he would recover, finally with acceptance and a determination to be strong for each other, with Jayne and the kids obviously the main focus in that respect. When I look back on that holiday, I sometimes wonder if the disease was already having an effect then - I suppose it must have been to some extent - and am grateful we got to spend that quality time together. God bless mate.

* * *

Both before and after that holiday we've spent many happy times with our neighbourhood friends, from dads and lads weekends spent climbing mountains to cycling across the UK from coast to coast to our uniquely (but hilariously enjoyable) 'shit' golf, and I could probably fill a book entirely dedicated to our Congleton family.

But, without wishing to diminish the importance of our friendship with anyone else, or our appreciation of it, I'd just like to give an extra special mention for the Nash's. I doubt we're the only members of our circle to hold such views in respect of their own relationship with Steve and Angie, but from our perspective, their unflinching friendship has always meant we've never felt without the love and support we've needed, even in our darkest hours. In fact, especially then.

We love you guys!

6

ISTANBUL

One thing we've rarely shared with our friends is our football viewing when Liverpool are involved. My aversion to watching Liverpool with non-Liverpool supporters – not always possible to avoid when working away from home, where watching in a pub is often a necessity, for example – dovetails neatly with San's superstitious dread of receiving visitors at any time on a day Liverpool are playing. Which is how San came to watch the 2005 Champions League final at home with just our son Dan for company.

In the same hotel restaurant in Calais on the final evening of our continental holiday with the Byrnes, there'd been a couple of families from Liverpool, a number of Liverpool fans clearly amongst them. They were just at the start of their own continental road-trip and so up to date with the football news back home. It being pre-season, I'd been keen to know how Liverpool had fared in a friendly match the previous day against Spanish side Valencia, managed by a certain Rafael Benitez. We'd lost 2-0 they reported, a score line which apparently flattered us as we were soundly beaten. It had been a marker for the season to come.

Coincidentally, Liverpool and Valencia were subsequently drawn in the same Champions League group and would play each other on matchday 1 at Valencia's Mestalla Stadium. I booked a day trip with the now defunct 'Anfield Travel Club', travelling alone this time much to Tom's chagrin, and enjoyed a pleasant late summer's day on the Valencian coast, spoilt only by the absolute drubbing we received in the evening.

The 2-0 score line hardly did justice to Valencia's superiority and, with the mercurial Argentinian Pablo Aimar pulling the strings, at one stage I feared we might be on the end of our biggest European defeat. In the return game at Anfield they completed the double over us, just 1-0 this time but no less superior in performance. Liverpool failed to qualify from the group while Valencia won it and went on to claim the Spanish La Liga title with Liverpool qualifying for the following season's Champions League by the skin of their teeth.

At the season's end the Liverpool board would demonstrate unusually sound judgement by relieving Gerard Houllier of his managerial duties and replacing him with Rafa. Gerard had served us well for nearly six years, the highlight being a marvellous cup treble in 2001, but his powers had clearly been on the wane since returning to the role after a major heart operation and, in my opinion, should have left his position at the club 12 months earlier. And now, less than 12 months later Liverpool were playing in a Champions League final against the Italian champions of the previous season and widely proclaimed best team in Europe, AC Milan.

Although our league form had been inconsistent, dire in a 2-0 defeat at Middlesbrough one week, brilliant at home to reigning champions Arsenal in a 2-1 victory the next for example, we had progressed to the semi-finals of the League Cup following a penalty shoot-out victory at White Hart Lane. Working in London at the time, that was a game I managed to attend and witnessed an uplifting performance by a young Liverpool second string against a much stronger Spurs outfit, and the following Saturday I was at Villa Park with Tom for a disappointing - because we'd led - 1-1 draw in the league. Next up, Champions League.

Previous results in the group, along with Monaco's likely comfortable passage against the group whipping boys Deportivo La Coruna in a game that would kick-off at the same time as ours, meant that our final game, at home to Olympiacos, was effectively a winner takes all affair. In fact, Liverpool needed to win 1-0, or by at least two goals. Any other score line would see the Greek team going through to the knock-out rounds at our expense.

Being in London during the week also meant that I couldn't be at Anfield with Tom, a friend of his using my ticket instead. I rushed back from the City office to my digs in Victoria, changed and then jumped on the underground at Victoria Station, having treated myself to dinner on-the-go – a satisfying steak and ale Cornish pasty from the West Cornwall Pasty Co on the station concourse – before jumping off at Covent Garden.

My destination was 'The Sun Tavern' where I'd watched a few of our mid-week games already this season, including our previous home group game, a 0-0 draw with Deportivo, though not our opening 2-0 home win against last season's beaten finalists Monaco, which I'd managed to attend at Anfield with Tom, and I quickly settled myself at the bar with a pint. There was perhaps half a dozen or so regulars who I recognised as Liverpool fans from my previous visits, but the bar was far from crowded as the game kicked off, the atmosphere more a hubbub of after work chit chat than anticipation of a gladiatorial battle under the lights.

By half-time I was on my third pint and wondering if now was the time to start drowning my sorrows in it. Olympiacos led with the first goal they'd ever scored on English soil, with Liverpool's hopes of progressing seemingly receding by the minute. If that wasn't bad enough, club captain and talisman Steven Gerrard had hinted strongly that his future may lie away from the club were we to falter at this stage and, ignoring his complicity in this particular game, it was difficult to blame him.

Within a couple of minutes of the restart, our half-time French substitute Florent Sinama-Pongolle had equalised and, mirroring the Anfield crowd, the atmosphere in the bar notched up several levels. Liverpool attacked in waves, Olympiacos only occasionally threatening on the break, but with less than 10 minutes to go we still needed two more goals to qualify. Neil Mellor, another substitute, then scored within a couple of minutes of coming on and, with less than five minutes remaining, Steven Gerrard confirmed his immediate future at the club and ensured Liverpool got the victory they needed with a stunning effort from outside the area.

My pint remained on the bar as I ran the length of it to join the other reds who were celebrating just as manically as I intended to. I had no delusions about winning the competition – surely anyone who'd watched us that season shared similarly rational thoughts – but qualifying from the group stages, and in the manner that we had, was an achievement in itself, no matter how small it may have appeared to those without a Liverpool perspective, and the feel-good factor which accompanied it was almost tangible.

The Christmas period delivered our season's first three consecutive victories, the highlight being a 5-0 victory over West Brom at the Hawthorns on Boxing day. Even the temperature at the country's highest stadium, as cold as you would expect in the depths of winter given its location, couldn't dampen the festive spirit in the away end, Tom and I included, as the goals flew in. Unfortunately, the new year didn't start quite as brightly. A promising display against eventual champions Chelsea was ruined by a Joe Cole deflected shot for the visitors being the only goal, and a season threatening injury to Xabi Alonso courtesy of a reckless challenge by Frank Lampard.

We also exited the FA Cup at the first time of asking. Drawn away against lower league Burnley, the game was due to be played on the first Friday evening of January and I caught an early train from London to give me plenty of time to drive me and Tom to the game. It was a filthy afternoon in the North West. As we took the M65 exit for Burnley, and with barely 30 minutes until kick-off, news of the game's postponement came through. Never believe for one moment that broadcasters have the best interests of match-going fans at heart. The game should have been postponed hours earlier such was the weather's inclemency, but of course, the TV barons knew better.

A comical own goal by our bambi-like full back Djimi Traore settled the tie in Burnley's favour when it was eventually played, a game I watched back in The Sun Tavern. No manic celebrations this time. In fact, I was so amused by the goal that I phoned our Alan immediately from the bar and in reply to his greeting simply said, "What the fuck was that?". We both fell about laughing.

Which, considering we were on the verge of being on the end of a giant killing should give you some indication of how comical the goal was. (The only other time I've reacted with such mirth when Liverpool conceded a goal, I was actually at the game. Our hapless centre-back Phil Babb had just rapped his nether regions around an Anfield goalpost in an unsuccessful attempt to prevent Pierluigi Casiraghi scoring his first and only goal for Chelsea a few years earlier. I was in parent and child seats with Dan at the time, front row of the top tier of the Anfield Road end, just above the away fans, in line with the six-yard box and no more than 25 yards away from the incident. It was a great spec, probably the best we've ever had. Another dad with his lad, two seats away from me, glanced in my direction, I glanced back, and neither of us could hold back. We dissolved into fits of laughter, hands having reflexively adopted the shielding position innately beloved of all postpubescent males).

By the end of the month though, we'd qualified for the League Cup final, beating Watford home and away in the semi-final. Ironically, I missed the home leg but managed to get to the away leg at Vicarage Road, that being my final day working in the London office.

We were consistently inconsistent. In February we built a 3-1 first leg lead at home in the first leg of our Champions League round of 16 game against Germany's Bayer Leverkusen and then lost to Chelsea in the League Cup final by three goals to two after extra time. Steven Gerrard had been linked with a move to Chelsea since before the season started, with some fans still questioning his commitment to the club, and his unfortunate own goal, doubly so under the circumstances, equalised a first minute volley from John Arne Riise to give Chelsea a lifeline and take the game into extra time. A long and miserable journey home from Cardiff ensued.

Ten days later, and continuing the theme of inconsistency, we won the second leg in the Bay Arena against Bayer Leverkusen, 3-1 again, to progress to the quarter finals. The next draw covered both the quarter-final and semi-final rounds of the competition, and we were pitted against the Italian champions elect Juventus (though they would later be stripped of their title and relegated following their involvement in the calciopoli match fixing scandal) and should we emerge victorious against the Bianconeri, the possibility of a semi-final with Chelsea. Bloody Chelsea again.

Though our league form was giving most cause for concern, we were unbelievably still in with a shout for a top four place to give us another chance of Champions League football the following season, and our main rivals for that fourth spot were also our city rivals Everton. While they were losing at home to Chelsea, we failed to take advantage in a 2-0 defeat at Birmingham City. We were so disillusioned with the performance on the day, San and I were back in the car before the final whistle blew.

On the same weekend Everton lost at home to Blackburn Rovers, Liverpool were falling to a 1-0 defeat at Newcastle. Another long and miserable trip home beckoned, this time on one of the many supporters' coaches that had made the trip to the north east. A bit of light relief on the way home involved a young lad, certainly compared to me, lamenting his hunger – no doubt exacerbated by the amount of ale he'd obviously consumed – but declining the offer of a chicken sandwich on the basis that he had no way of knowing if the chicken had been corn fed. It made me and the majority of the assembled company laugh anyway, I guess you had to be there.

In the Anfield derby towards the end of March, our 2-1 victory in a game we finished with only 10 men following the dismissal of Czech forward Milan Baros, promised to breathe new life into our league campaign, and a hard fought 1-0 win over Bolton at Anfield in our next game closed the gap to a single point, with Everton losing at West Brom the following day. But all eyes were now on the next fixture, Juventus in the Champions League, at Anfield under the lights.

In the first meeting of the two clubs since the Heysel disaster nearly 20 years earlier, a memorial ceremony of sorts in honour of those who had perished took place before the game started. Plenty, certainly a large minority, of Juventus fans refused to acknowledge the olive branch of apology which had been offered, and of course that was entirely their right. Whether that contributed to the atmosphere or not is difficult to say, but Anfield was electric that night, the atmosphere seldom bettered.

Juventus, strong favourites to progress and one of the strongest favourites for the competition itself, were clearly shaken and found themselves two goals behind with barely a quarter of the game gone. They did rally and pull a goal back in the second half, but at the final whistle the feeling of elation, the sense of achievement, was only slightly tempered by thoughts that an opportunity may have been missed. Certainly, as Tom and I left the stadium that night, there was no talk of inevitable failure to come, although the Italian catenaccio masters would be very confident of scoring in front of their own fans in Turin and keeping their own back door bolted. All they needed was a 1-0 win.

They never got it.

Eight days later, Liverpool welcomed back Spanish metronome Xabi Alonso, missing since New Year's Day with a broken ankle, but took to the field at the Stadio delle Alpi without the freshly injured Steven Gerrard. An already difficult task appeared to have become almost impossible. But, after Zlatan Ibrahimovic missed a golden opportunity to give Juve the lead early in the game, we enjoyed a pretty plain sail to a scoreless draw. Cannavaro, who had scored the Italian's reply in the first leg did head against the post as the game neared its conclusion, but Liverpool had arguably better chances to score and, superbly marshalled by Alonso, comfortably held out for the result which took us into our first European Cup semi-final for 20 years.

I say 'comfortably' advisedly and after watching the game again in an emotionless state already knowing the outcome. During the build-up to, and the game itself, our stress levels were off the charts. Liverpool fans revelled in our storied history, as well as more recent successes which most other clubs would eye enviously and, as the great Bill Shankly made clear, our bread and butter was the league championship, which we longed for again with a passion. But the jewels in our crown were indisputably the four European Cup successes we enjoyed in the late seventies and early eighties. With another final now potentially just 180 minutes away, the scent of a possible fifth was intoxicating. And, after their own narrow, if high-scoring, 6-5 aggregate victory over Bayern Munich, Chelsea again beckoned.

In between the two games against Juventus, Liverpool had again stumbled in the league, losing at Manchester City to the only goal of the game, scored in the last minute by 'Kiki' Musampa. A journeyman player, his goal had unforeseen consequences for his brother 'Kris', whose own commercial activities included the sale and distribution of festive food packages at Christmas. They took a hit as reds fans everywhere rushed to find an alternative supplier for their yuletide goodies, in an admittedly somewhat childish overreaction to his brother's late winner.

After the high of the result and performance against Juve just a few days earlier, Tom and I had left that game even more fearful of our chances in the second leg. What did we know?

The next three league games brought just four points. A home draw to Spurs was followed by a victory over Portsmouth at Fratton Park, with relegation threatened Crystal Palace up next at Selhurst Park on the Saturday afternoon. Everton, themselves struggling for consistency in the race (perhaps that should be 'plod') for fourth place, had unexpectedly dropped two points at home to Birmingham City in the early televised kick-off. Consensus among the travelling reds congregated alongside the pitch in South London was that this was our last chance to put a run together and some pressure on Everton for that final Champions League qualifying place.

But, with the first leg of our semi-final tie with Chelsea looming, and despite the fillip of Everton's dropped points, Rafa rested a few regulars and fielded a weakened side, with future bluenose Andy Johnson scoring the only goal of the game for Palace in the first half. With three games remaining we sat four points adrift of fourth placed Everton, who still had a game in hand, with Bolton Wanderers now immediately below us only on goal difference. We were all but done.

On the train back into Victoria Station, me and San and a few other Liverpool fans chatted with a few Crystal Palace cohorts. Talk turned from our chances of top four and theirs of avoiding relegation (spoiler alert: they went down) to the Champions League, and the first leg of the semi-final just four days away. In tones, if not words, that suggested they didn't rate our chances of progressing very highly, the Palace fans asked who we thought would end up winning the trophy. Immediately, and to a man (and woman), we replied somewhat bemusedly "Us!", indignant that they would suggest we might countenance any other outcome. They almost offered us their sympathies for our childlike optimism, while continuing to wish us well against the country's new 'most hated' team and fans.

The first leg against Chelsea was to be played at Stamford Bridge with the return a week later at Anfield. I was working in Birmingham when the first leg came around and watched the game, a tense scoreless draw, at home. As expected, Chelsea were the dominant force, but failed to turn that into goals, Liverpool defending stoutly and attacking on the break when possible. In the last couple of minutes Xabi Alonso was shown a yellow card following a theatrical collapse to the turf by Chelsea's Eidur Gudjohnsen, which meant he was out of the second leg. A huge blow to our chances of making the final.

I wasn't one of the 99 percent of Liverpool supporters who Chelsea's manager Jose Mourinho claimed thought Liverpool were already in the final. I doubt many of us were actually. No away goal scored, Chelsea clearly a superior side, and now no Alonso. We needed something special.

Six days later, Chelsea arrived at Anfield as newly crowned champions with games to spare following their victory at Bolton the previous weekend. When I'd first started going to the match back in the late 1960s you could often hear the crowd singing on the approach to the ground, but it had been a while since that had been the case. As Tom and I walked to Anfield from our usual parking spot about 20 minutes away, it was clear that tonight, that was back. As soon as we opened the car doors, the noise wafted across Oakfield Road and up and over Breckfield Road North, softly welcoming at first, then with increasingly urgent calls to arms the nearer we got to the ground. The air was alive. The feeling that we may have that 'something special' necessary to get us over the line after all was growing.

In the ground itself the noise was deafening a good half an hour before kick-off, probably longer, and once Luis Garcia scored within five minutes to put us ahead on aggregate (I'd have preferred a penalty and for Petr Cech, the Chelsea keeper, to have been sent off, rather than a 'ghost' goal, for anyone asking), the decibel level rose again. It hardly abated. Even at half time as the crowd drew breath, the atmosphere continued to sizzle.

Defending the Kop end, Liverpool were on the backfoot throughout the second half, Chelsea almost irresistible, but resist them we did. Dudek made important saves, Carragher last-ditch tackles until, deep into six minutes of added time, it looked to have all been in vain.

Chasing the equaliser they needed to go through to the final on away goals scored, the ball broke kindly just yards from goal for Chelsea's Gudjohnsen, villain of the piece in the first leg. Time stood still for all of a red persuasion, but unbelievably his shot flew across the face of goal, somehow avoiding myriad limbs of players from both sides, and went out for a goal kick. It felt like a wrong had been righted, and when moments later the final whistle blew, the explosion of noise from all parts of the ground, save the small pocket of Chelsea fans, threatened to burst the ear drums.

Against all the odds, we were going to contest another European Cup final, 21 years after we'd last won it. Okay, it was called the Champions League these days, but it was the same competition, the same trophy, and we'd get to keep it for good if we won it for the fifth time in Istanbul in just over three weeks.

Coincidentally I was due to start work back in London the following day (I'd taken holiday from the start of the week so I could go to the game), and the late Brian Woolnough, senior football writer for one of the big daily's and presenter of Sky's Sunday Supplement flagship programme for discussing all matters football related at the time, was in front of me in the ticket queue at Euston Square underground station. He'd obviously just got off the same train as me.

"What did you think of that last night, Brian?" I chanced a question.

He turned to me, smiling.

"It's all about the passion isn't it?" he replied. "I've never known anything like Anfield last night".

That was good enough for me.

The league season ended two games later for Liverpool. The following Sunday I was on an early train from Crewe to Euston to enable me to take in our final away game against Arsenal at Highbury. The train I caught just happened to have started its journey at Liverpool's Lime Street, and Steve Hothersall, Radio City's regular commentator on Liverpool matches was sitting just across the aisle from me (as it was a Sunday, I'd treated myself to first class for a few quid extra), making his own way to the game.

We chatted (quietly I thought, though on reaching Euston Station a fellow passenger complimented us on our passion for a sport she freely admitted she had no interest in) about the semi-final just gone, our chances in the final, and the many 'omens' Liverpool fans had found pointing to our ultimate success in the competition. Things like the date – 25 May – which was the same date we'd won our first European Cup in 1977; in both 1981, when we won it for the third time, and 2005: Ken & Deidre got married in Coronation Street (the great northern soap opera), Prince Charles got married (though not to the same woman!), a new actor was cast to play Doctor Who, both Norwich City and Crystal Palace were relegated from the top division.

The list went on.

We were also, strangely given our own illustrious European history, playing one of the European giants for the first time. In 1981 it had been Spanish behemoth Real Madrid, this time it would be the Italian aristocrats AC Milan. The fly in the omen ointment was that in 1981 Real Madrid were a faded force – it was 15 years since they'd last triumphed in the competition, and it would be another 17 until they did it again – and Liverpool were winning it for the third time in five seasons. Now, in 2005, 21 years had passed since Liverpool last picked up the trophy, and just two since our opponents had done it for the sixth time. Omens Schmomens.

At Highbury, needing a win to keep our faint Champions League qualification hopes alive, at least through our league position, Liverpool were always second best to an Arsenal side not far off their peak (though, with hindsight, now on the downward side of it). The gunners 3-1 victory meant that Everton were now certain to finish fourth and claim a place in the next Champions League qualifying rounds. Fair play to the blues though for still managing to give us our biggest laugh of the season. A few days after our loss, they visited Highbury to play their game in hand. I watched from a pub in Kensington (the West London version), enthralled as Arsenal scored seven without reply. Everton became the first, and to date only, team to claim a coveted place in the Champions League qualifying rounds and end the season with a negative goal difference.

More laughs would follow at the start of the following season as they lost their qualifying tie with Spanish side Villareal (the decisive second leg on my birthday, which was nice), and then proceeded to be knocked out in the first round of the UEFA Cup, the consolation prize for failed Champions League qualification. But that was for our future entertainment. Our own qualification for next season's Champions League competition now depended on winning it at the end of this one.

Aston Villa were our final opponents as we signed off the league season at Anfield with a fairly regulation 2-1 victory, the crowd understandably in celebratory mood during the final home game of the season, the first home game since we'd qualified for the Champions League final, and with the final itself just 10 days away. All roads now led to Istanbul.

Tom and I qualified for tickets to the final by virtue of our season tickets and having attended all our home games in the Champions League during the season. Personally, I'd missed a couple of them due to my working away, but the ticket had been gladly received by friends of Tom for those games and I had no qualms about taking the ticket for the final. I was at the end of the 37th full season since my first game, my 18th as a season ticket holder, and I'd missed out on all our previous finals, primarily due to a lack of funds. I was now in the fortunate position of having a decent regular income and, let's be honest, our appearance in the final this year was an unexpected bonus. Who knew when we'd reach another?

We booked a flight plus a night's accommodation with one of the myriad of companies offering such packages, which would see us leaving Liverpool's John Lennon airport early on the morning of the match and staying in a hotel a few minutes from Taksim Square after the game, returning home the following day. It was far from cheap, but it meant I could work the two days before the game, an important consideration given my self-employed status. From the start of match week, tales and footage of Liverpool supporters in Istanbul, particularly around Taksim Square, which had been identified as an official congregating area for reds fans, flooded our numerous fan forums and told of days and nights of non-stop joyous revelry. Wednesday couldn't come soon enough for me and Tom.

In fact, Tom couldn't sleep the night before the game (I managed forty winks), and we set off at some ungodly early hour. Peter Kenyon, Chelsea's CEO and former CEO of Manchester United – more than enough black marks there for him to be held forever in low esteem by any self-respecting Liverpool fan – owned a Cheshire mansion about five minutes' drive from us and on our route to the airport. I must belatedly apologise to any residents of the sleepy Somerford and Brereton Heath area on the A54 who may have been awakened by my childishly joyous and exaggerated use of the car horn as we sped past his home in the darkness. Pointlessly as well as he was already in Istanbul as a guest of UEFA. But in my defence, at 46 years of age I was feeling like a kid at Christmas again.

Left at home behind us were San, Dan & Liv. They were all invited to watch the game at the Glovers', along with the Nash's, the Kemballs' and the Byrnes (and maybe one or two others). Liv, 12 years old at the time, happily grabbed the opportunity, and it was a surprise to no-one when San politely declined it. Dan, being the dutiful son he has always been, opted to watch the game with his mum. And that's where they stayed until the final whistle.

* * *

In the fifteen plus years since, the tale of the 'Miracle of Istanbul' has been recounted countless times, millions of words written covering the occasion, the build-up and the outcome. Istanbul, the great historic metropolis which straddles two continents; Taksim Square before and after the game; gridlocked traffic on the way to the Ataturk Stadium; a sea of yellow taxis and free buses; the biblical traipse across a barren landscape to a stadium seemingly built in the middle of nowhere; Milan fans outnumbered four or five to one. It's all been brilliantly captured elsewhere, so I won't attempt to force my inferior version upon you. But the story of the game itself surely deserves one more retelling.

We got in the ground about 45 minutes before kick-off, the organisation outside the stadium best described as chaotic. Not so much a queue as a crowd of fans with very few stadium officials, one of whom took my ticket, tore off the stub, then returned the ticket to me. The crowd shifted before I managed to proceed and when I eventually showed my ticket again to the same official, he appeared aghast that my ticket had no stub.

Having come this far and got this close, I was in no mood to be denied entry and told him so in as many words. Whether he understood what I'd said, or simply took stock of my demeanour was unclear but, brooking no further argument, a few seconds later I was in the ground with Tom. The atmosphere was bubbling nicely, the Milan fans impressively choreographed at the opposite end of the stadium, the Liverpool fans impressively off-the-cuff.

When I say the opposite end of the stadium, I refer to their proximity to me and Tom. The length of the stadium away. It soon became apparent that apart from that end of the stadium, the rest of it was populated almost entirely with Liverpool fans. As the teams took to the field to a cacophony of tribal rivalry, the uniqueness and enormity of the occasion really hit home, the feeling of utter privilege at simply being there almost tangible. Twenty years after our last such final, Liverpool were back at European football's top table.

That feeling lasted for as long as it took Milan to take the lead, less than a minute into the ninety. The captain's shook hands, the game kicked off and Milan scored. In echoes of the start of the second half of the 1990 FA Cup semi-final against Crystal Palace, Liverpool had kicked off and immediately ceded possession. Seconds later, Milan's left back and captain Paolo Maldini, hardly noted for his goal-scoring prowess, powered home Andrea Pirlo's precise cross from a free kick. We still had 89 minutes to respond of course, but Milan's strong pre-game favourite tag was already looking well deserved. By half-time, it looked like a no-brainer.

Two further goals from striker Hernan Crespo, a world class striker on loan from Liverpool's semi-final victims Chelsea, in the six minutes before the break, appeared to have made a difficult task nigh on impossible. In truth, as well as Milan had played, sitting off Liverpool and hitting us on the break each time we courteously returned the ball to them, Liverpool showed all the signs of suffering from stage fright. We'd had plenty of possession but little cutting edge and no midfield shield to speak of for our vulnerable defence either.

As the whistle blew for half-time, a minute after Crespo's second goal, jubilation poured from the Milan fans behind the goal defended, poorly, by Liverpool. Our end of the ground could best be described as deflated. Tom was almost inconsolable, his phone pinging incessantly with messages from the UK. Given where we lived, hardly any of his mates were Liverpool fans so I can only imagine that most of the texts he was receiving at this juncture would be far from supportive, indeed mocking in nature. I spent the first few minutes of the break trying to persuade him to put this down to experience, that we'd be back. I didn't believe a word of what I was telling him mind you, and I'm pretty sure neither did he.

"What a shit day" was his only response.

As the start of the second half neared a few wags started singing "we're gonna win 4-3", a prospect so outrageously unlikely that most of us genuinely laughed. It was followed by a rendition of 'You'll Never Walk Alone' which started as a murmur, almost mournfully, but was soon picked up by others in our support, the sound building until it became a crescendo of defiance. Personally, I was hoping for an improved showing in the second half, but not much more. Let's at least save some face.

Almost from the kick-off, Liverpool's keeper Jerzy Dudek was forced to make a fine save from Milan's other world class striker Andrei Shevchenko – himself destined for Chelsea 12 months down the line - tipping the ball round the post from a well struck free kick and, just for a moment, with Milan seemingly picking up where they'd left off at half-time, an embarrassing repeat of the first half, maybe a record-breaking cup final score line defeat, seemed an all too real possibility. Tom's 'shit' day was in danger of becoming all our worst nightmares. Less than 15 minutes later, it was promising to be our finest hour.

Spanish journalist Guillem Balague has written a book about this, Rafa's first season, called 'A Season on The Brink'. I highly recommend it. Between pages 142 and 143, an insert of glossy colour photographs is included, all related to the Champions League final, the first one of which is a full page shot of the scoreboard behind a section of our fans. Look closely, and you may spot me and Tom towards the bottom right-hand corner of the picture. On the other hand, you won't have to look too hard to find the most important pieces of information it presents. Fifty-one minutes and fifty-six seconds of the scheduled 90 minutes have been played, and AC Milan still lead Liverpool 3-0. There must be about 200-300 fans in the picture, each face telling its own similar story, and it's not a happy one.

About two minutes after that snap was taken, captain and talisman Steven Gerrard craned and twisted to score with a well-directed header from a John Arne Riise cross. Probably no more than a consolation, but at least my hope of a face saving second half performance was alive and well. A modicum of pride might yet be restored. Certainly, a few of those faces in the crowd had a bit more of a smile on them.

Two minutes further on and I was blurting out "Back in it", after Vladimir Smicer, a first half substitute for the injured Harry Kewell, had taken a short sideways pass from Didi Hamann, a half-time substitute for the injured Steve Finnan, and found the bottom left-hand corner of the net from outside the penalty area (though at the time I was convinced Luis Garcia had scored the goal). Face-saving was dropping down the agenda now. With more than half-an-hour to get an equaliser and, who knows, even win it, we had grander aspirations.

Less than five minute later, that agenda was in the bin. The Spanish referee, who had waived away our claims for a penalty in the first half, seconds before Milan's second goal, pointed to the spot after Milan's Gennaro Gattuso fouled Gerrard as he was running through on goal. With Gerrard about to shoot, the Italian clipped his heels and could consider himself fortunate not to be sent off.

Xabi Alonso stepped up to take the first penalty of his professional career, but was thwarted by a fine save from the Brazilian giant Dida in Milan's goal. As the ball spilled back out, a fan behind me needlessly pointed out that he'd "missed it", superfluous information that might have triggered an unprintable response from me given my immediate sense of deflation, a sense that a spell had been broken, if Xabi hadn't followed up a split second later by slamming the rebound into the roof of the net.

3-3.

Three quarters of the ground exploded into a frenzy of joyous disbelief.

Back home, as I would find out later, San's own joy was tempered (though only slightly I'm sure) by her annoyance at Milan Baros half-strangling Alonso in wild celebration. Unbelievably, we were level, all thoughts of hitherto certain acute embarrassment extinguished. Magic spell still in force, optimism reignited. Whatever happened now, we'd still be able to hold our heads up. Not that that was uppermost in my thoughts at the time. Or those of any Liverpool fan I'd have thought. Now we wanted to go on and win it. A couple of minutes later Dida saved a dipping long-range effort from Riise, and the spell was broken at last.

I don't recall another attempt on target from Liverpool, certainly not one worthy of the name. From having nothing to lose at the start of the second half such was our dire position, now everything was on the line. That sense was everywhere, on the pitch as well as in the stands. It was however accompanied with a new doggedness, a sense of determination and resolve to go the distance. Milan reasserted their dominance but were kept at bay by a resolute defensive performance, with scouser Jamie Carragher excelling throughout, ably assisted by fellow centre-back Sammy Hyypia and joined by Gerrard, switching from his marauding attacking midfield brief at the start of the second half to put in a sterling stint at right back when needed in extra time.

And it was much needed. Once extra time had started, it was clear Liverpool were pretty much spent as an attacking force. The fans did what we could, keeping the noise levels up, willing the team on, our raw support all we had to offer. With three minutes of the 120 left, for once Gerrard was unable to prevent a deep cross from Serginho, one of the Milan substitutes. It was a superb cross which dissected the Liverpool centre-backs and found Shevchenko moving onto it, unmarked just outside the six-yard box with only Dudek to beat. Behind the goal, as the cross arced onto the Ukrainian's forehead, the previous 117 minutes of the game flashed before my eyes.

We'd played our part in one of the great European finals, saved our reputation, restored our pride. Hands would be shaken, hugs shared, and a fully deserved lap of honour trudged by our gallant losers and acknowledged by fans of both sides. The journey home would probably be a lot less onerous than it was looking like at half time. But ultimately trophyless. Pride at our comeback from a hopeless position notwithstanding, the sense of impending loss – for that surely was imminent – was difficult to bear.

Shevchenko nodded downwards, the ball pitching just in front of Jerzy and giving him a chance to save which, though still difficult, he probably shouldn't have had. He managed to parry the ball but only straight back to Shevchenko, who surely couldn't miss the rebound. Miraculously, and it did feel like a miracle from my vantage point, a split second after the ball left the striker's foot, Dudek's hand reflexively reached up from his prone position and deflected it over the bar.

In that moment, as those with Milan tendencies held heads in hands as one, and the rest of us eventually exhaled our shared relief, I told myself we'd won it. I never voiced that opinion, not even a whisper to Tom standing next to me, but if ever a sign was given that was surely it. A few minutes later the referee's whistle signalled the end of extra time. Penalties it was.

A quirk of the game was that all six goals had been scored in the same goal, directly in front of the Milan fans, as far away from where me and Tom stood as it was possible to be. So naturally, the penalties would be taken at that same end.

My conviction that Shevchenko's miss was a sure sign our name was on the trophy did little to calm my nerves as we prepared for the penalty shoot-out, however. What did help was Milan, going first, missing their first two spot kicks taken by Serginho and Pirlo, and Liverpool scoring both theirs, through Hamann and Cissé.

2-0 and looking good.

Milan's third penalty, struck home by former Newcastle player Jon Dahl Tomasson, was their first success of the night, and was immediately followed by Liverpool's first failure, Riise the culprit, victim of another fine penalty save by Dida. The nerves were back, and I screamed my frustration at the Norwegian, much to Tom's amusement.

2-1. Still promising but the irony of Milan possibly staging their own penalty shoot-out comeback was not lost on me. The nerves cranked up another level.

The Brazilian Kaka was up next for Milan and netted with aplomb to level the scores, though they'd taken one more penalty than us. The noise level had hardly abated since the shoot-out started, and when Smicer then converted his, the sense of anticipation soared off the scales.

3-2. With both teams having taken four of their five penalties, the moment of truth was potentially seconds away. Shevchenko now needed to score to keep Milan in it.

I doubt there were many in the crowd of 72,000 who expected that the Ballon d'Or winner, Milan legend and widely regarded world superstar, who had scored the deciding penalty in Milan's shoot-out victory over Juventus to lift the same trophy two years earlier, would do anything other than score from the spot, thereby ensuring that Liverpool's Steven Gerrard would need to convert his penalty, his team's fifth, to complete a remarkable turnround.

Maybe one or two Milan fans, shaken by their reverse in fortunes during the game and now considering the consequences of ultimate failure when they returned home, would have watched him place the ball on the spot with some little dread. I certainly had no doubt he would score. Even as he scuffed his effort directly down the middle, I envisioned Dudek diving to one side and the ball nestling in the net.

It didn't happen. Jerzy stood his ground and saved the admittedly dismal effort.

All over. Liverpool 3-2 winners on penalties and Champions of Europe for the fifth time after one of the most remarkable finals ever.

Pandemonium ensued. On the pitch, the Liverpool players celebrated, many of them seemingly in a daze. In the stands, Liverpool fans laughed and cried, sang and danced and acclaimed their heroes. Me and Tom hugged each other, and anyone else within hugging distance. The Milan fans silently left. There wasn't much else for them to do. I know there were fireworks at the end as we collected the Cup because I've seen them on the recordings since. I don't recall them at all at the stadium.

Back home, San and Dan celebrated in the street as the Glover household emptied to meet them halfway.

As we left the ground, now well into the morning after the day the game had kicked off, the quietness was eerie. It had been a very long and tiring day, especially for those of us who'd travelled on the day of the game, and the game as emotionally draining as any I'd experienced. A surreal end to a surreal journey. In a good way.

I've watched the game many times since, the emotion of the occasion receding slightly as time passes, but always there just below the surface.

Me and Tom and Istanbul. I'll always have that.

7

ANNUS HORRIBILIS

23 June 2010. Mustard Bar, Smithdown Road, Liverpool

Actually, I'm not sure if it was still called the Mustard Bar then or if it had already reincarnated into one of its many successors, but let's stick with it for now. It was pretty packed for a Wednesday afternoon, but then again this wasn't a normal Wednesday afternoon. Not for me and not for pretty much anyone else in the bar I'd imagine.

To start with I'd normally be at the office of whichever client I was currently working for – The Co-operative Bank at Leek up in the Staffordshire Moorlands at the time – added to which England were playing Slovenia in a World Cup group game, needing to win to qualify for the first knock out round. I'm not a big fan of England, nor of international football generally, but I've always loved the World Cup. One of my football related party pieces is that I can tell you the winner of every World Cup since its inaugural tournament in 1930 (okay, I never said it was a wild party piece).

Liverpool fans have a bit of a reputation for being anti-England. That's certainly true of some, but probably not as many as social media might suggest, and I'm certainly not anti-England. I like to see them do well in international tournaments and am old enough to remember Geoff Hurst and 1966 (and let's not forget Sir Roger Hunt) and all that. Like many though, I reckon I've just been ground down over the years by the media fuelled hyperbole which seems to precede every tournament, followed by the subsequent scraping through to the knockout stages of whichever tournament in whichever country, and then the inevitable shocking / glorious / unlucky failure (depending on the performances and prevailing media narrative du jour) just as the country had started to 'believe' again.

And of course, there's the Neanderthals which seem to follow 'Ing-ur-land' to whichever corner of the globe (do globes have corners?) they're playing in, apparently hell bent on reminding the rest of the world about our largely lost empire and making them grateful that we'll never be in a position to build another one. That is not to say that everyone, or even the majority, of England followers fall into this category. But, you know, a few empty vessels making enough noise to spoil it for the majority is where we've been at for a long time.

Suffice to say, I can take or leave the English national team. But the patrons of the bar, myself included, were happy enough when Jermaine Defoe scored the only goal of the game to set up a knockout tie against old foes Germany. I was already looking forward to the media build-up to that one. Or perhaps not.

I knew pretty much everyone in the bar that afternoon, and those I didn't were known to my mum or siblings. My brother Alan, whose furniture reclamation & restoration business was located just on the other side of the road and who consequently knew the manager pretty well, had hired the bar and organised a buffet, and along with the rest of the family had split the cost between us. And it was nice to meet up with people we hadn't seen for a long time, you know, the weddings and funerals crowd. That's not a denigration by the way, I'm one of that crowd myself after all. But life does tend to get in the way of our best intentions a lot of the time and, thankfully, these celebrations of heartfelt commitments to a lifetime union, or of a life well lived, and loved, provide us all with a perfectly acceptable opportunity to catch up and congratulate or commiserate as appropriate.

In fact, the only thing spoiling this otherwise rather pleasant afternoon was the occasion. My dad's funeral.

* * *

Eight days earlier. 15 June. Britannia House, Leek

I'm at my desk at the aforementioned client's office, the building proudly reflecting the company's maiden name – Britannia Building Society – prior to its much publicised, in financial circles at least, marriage of convenience with the Co-op the previous year (although marriage of 'inconvenience' may better describe it, given the travails of the combined entity since, and that it needed a new Act of Parliament simply to allow it to happen, what with Britannia being a Building Society and the Co-op being, well, a Co-operative). I've just finished the morning's first coffee while preparing for the morning's first meeting when my mobile phone rings. A bit of a surprise in itself to be honest. My desk is on the lower ground floor - the basement area - of Britannia House, which is known for its poor cellular reception. It must be my lucky day.

That thought lasted as long as it took me to answer the call from our Alan, barely managing to say hello before he shouted down the line at me.

"Les, it's me mum's birthday and me dad's just died".

It seems almost comical now looking at those words written down – I mean, I didn't need telling it was my mum's birthday - but no-one was laughing.

My dad had been unwell and wheelchair bound for a while, maybe 12 – 18 months, and reliant on portable oxygen tanks to assist his breathing almost constantly. This was a legacy not of a lifetime of heavy smoking - he classed himself as a social smoker, enjoying an occasional cigarette with an occasional pint, and indeed was far outdone in the smoking stakes by my mum – but of, in his younger days, working in an environment laden with asbestos, before the deadly ramifications of exposure to its fibres were fully appreciated.

I hadn't lost anyone so close to me since great Auntie Nellie died in her sleep at the Little Sisters of the Poor Home for the Aged in St Augustine House, situated on Aigburth Road, in 1972 nearly 40 years before, having had her usual bottle of Guinness and a couple of sleeping tablets before retiring one last time. Nanny Jackson, my dad's mum, had died six or seven years earlier closely followed by Nanny Jones, my mum's mum. San's parents were born half a generation and more before mine and we had sadly long since said goodbye to them, and more than one set of close friends had lost one or both of theirs, and even a partner in one case.

While I had vicariously shared the pain of some of those losses, and in more recent times had started to try and prepare for my dad's passing, which was clearly approaching – after all, he was 78 years old and had only recently 'escaped' from Broadgreen Hospital when my mum had put her foot down and demanded he be allowed to return home when the medical staff pretty much insisted he wouldn't ever be leaving again – it still came as a massive, almost physical, shock when I heard those words. So much so in fact that I remember immediately starting to tremble as the full import of what I'd just heard took hold.

When Alan's name had appeared on the screen of my phone, I hadn't considered for a second that he would be calling with bad news. Maybe on some level I thought he might be calling in relation to it being my mum's birthday, and I was completely shaken. It was also disconcerting to hear the anguish in Alan's voice. He had lived with my mum and dad for a few years, initially moving in temporarily when his own home needed some major refurbishment, and then staying to help my mum with caring for dad. He would have been even more aware than I was of how poor my dad's prognosis was, and his obvious distress only added to my own.

I promised Alan I'd be there as soon as I could, grabbed my coat and bag and asked Nic Shaw, a co-worker, to close down my workstation – I really couldn't concentrate enough to do it myself. Leek is roughly a twenty-five-minute drive from our Congleton home which, luckily, is pretty much en-route to my parent's home in Liverpool and I called San on the way to give her the news. As Liv was at school, we decided that San would stay in Congleton and let Liv know about her grandad when she arrived home, and I would travel to Liverpool immediately.

* * *

Earlier the same morning. Mum & Dad's house, Mill Lane, Liverpool 15

Mum and dad had moved into a new property in the summer of 1996 after living in Wedgewood Street since getting married in December 1957, when they moved in with our much-loved Nanny Jackson and her equally loved sister Auntie Nellie (much loved by us kids that is. My mum's relationship with them was stereotypically in-lawish).

My dad had been resident there for many years before that, and had also previously lived in Adderley Street, literally 15 seconds walk away. So, my dad had lived over 50 of his 64 years (up to that point) in that house, and all of his life in the immediate vicinity, and had never given any indication that he would ever want to live anywhere else. When we were growing up, the terraced homes of Wedgewood Street and Adderley Street were part of a pretty tight knit community. All the houses had vestibules, which you entered immediately through the front door, with a vestibule door which led into the hall and the rest of the property. During the spring and summer months especially, this meant that front doors would be left open, often with a baby dozing in its pram in the vestibule or even on the front step, and everyone looked out for each other.

As kids we used to take turns in nipping to the corner shop for Florrie - Mrs Metcalfe who lived next door. She was deaf as a door post, couldn't walk without the aid of her walking stick (and couldn't walk very far with it) and she frightened the life out of us, and plenty of other kids in the neighbourhood too. She certainly knew how to bang on our vestibule door with that walking stick. The fear, of course, was actually borne out of respect, which was fostered by our parents, themselves a little bit frightened of her I think.

Our neighbours on the other side were Brenda and Tony who used to provide tremendous, if unintended, entertainment with their constant verbal battles which the party walls that separated our two homes struggled to shield us from. If their football allegiance had been as blue as the air during their many heated rows, then we were undoubtedly living next door to fervent Evertonians. Don't suggest that to Tony though, he was as big a red as they come.

Further up the street lived the Gaileys, all Evertonians, and in the top two houses the Andrews and the Sloanes. I'm not certain of their allegiances football wise – or even if they had any - but Pete and Barbara Andrews and Les and Lily Sloane were probably the closest friends of my mum and dad in the street. The Sweeney's, who lived in Adderley Street just across the way were all Liverpool fans and, if memory serves, always seemed to be at odds with the Gaileys. That could just be my memory playing tricks, although with the matriarchal Mrs Sweeney hailing from Germany anything is possible. I mean, the mid-60's wasn't *that* long after the end of the war, and some bitter memories linger I suppose.

Also in Adderley Street we had the Moretons, the Carters, their cousins the Haskells, and opposite them the Hanlons and the Gilmores. All with reasonably sized broods who must have lived within a 100 yard square and were by no means the only inhabitants of that space, and while there were always arguments and disagreements between neighbours, our sense of safety and security seldom, if ever, felt threatened.

However, over the years, lifelong neighbours had moved on (one way or another) and let's just say some of the newer, younger generation of neighbours didn't share the same values as my dad's (or even my) generation. Drugs were becoming more prevalent and when, during a short paternal visit to the dentist, the house was burgled – with the newest next-door neighbour the prime suspect as far as my dad was concerned – my parents decided the time was right to move, and their newly built home in Mill Lane, a short ten-minute drive up Edge Lane towards the start of the M62 motorway, beckoned.

As mum's 71st birthday dawned, my dad was pretty much using the oxygen tanks full time, even while sleeping, and my mum had developed an early morning routine whereby she got up, got herself ready and brought my dad a cup of tea in bed, before helping him with his ablutions. On this particular birthday morning, she followed the same routine but was interrupted by a phone call. It was from her youngest sibling, brother Bernard, or Benny as everyone knew him, who had called to wish her a happy birthday and they had spent a few minutes chatting.

It seems that during this time dad had needed to use the bathroom and must have decided he either couldn't, or wouldn't, wait any longer for mum to come back with his cup of tea. Sadly, in his attempts to get out of bed he had become detached from his oxygen and had collapsed onto the floor. When mum eventually returned to the bedroom it was too late.

When I arrived, the house was full. My brothers and sister were already there with other friends and relatives, and the doctor was just about to leave. It was over 52 years since my parents had tied the knot and it must have felt like mum's own world was ending as, inconsolable as she was, she took me upstairs to see dad – she was quite insistent actually - and left me to spend a couple of minutes with him privately, before an ambulance arrived to take him away.

Though bruised from his fall, he looked as peaceful as I'd seen him in a long time, finally free of the agonising pain which he'd recently confided to my brother he was in constantly. I kissed him on the forehead for the last time and left.

* * *

To be fair, 2010 wasn't completely awful. I mean, it really was, but it also did have the odd highlight. Hopefully I've remembered one or two before I finish writing the next few paragraphs, and you can pick them out. Good Luck!

On the football front Liverpool started the new year in seventh place following a last-minute Torres goal victory at Villa Park in our final game of 2009. Me and Dan attended the match on a bitterly cold December evening, making the round trip to Birmingham in my Ford Mondeo without a working heater, which became more of an irritant the further we got from home. As enthusiastically as the injury time winner was celebrated by the travelling reds, the performance did little to convince any of us that the season was likely to take a turn for the better anytime soon.

A poor start to the campaign had seen us lose seven league games already and fail to qualify for the Champions League knockout stages despite getting, at least what appeared to be at the time, a favourable group draw. The first two games of 2010 only served to underline the dearth of quality and entertainment on offer as mid-Championship side Reading knocked us out of the FA Cup, coming from behind to win 2-1 at Anfield, following a 1-1 draw at their Madjeski Stadium home.

It was all so disappointing after the previous season had seen us lose only two league games when finishing runners up, again, in the Premier League, and reaching the quarter finals of the Champions League following a resounding 5-0 aggregate victory over Spanish giants Real Madrid, with the second leg 4-0 drubbing handed out at Anfield immediately followed by a superb performance and 4-1 victory over Man United at Old Trafford in the league.

The revered Xabi Alonso had left the club to become a Madridista before the new season had started and had not been adequately replaced – which would have been difficult to be honest, not least in the hearts of the supporters. The cracks behind the scenes at the club which had started appearing within days of its ill-fated purchase by the American duo Tom Hicks and George Gillett – please do read 'An Epic Swindle / 44 Months With A Pair of Cowboys' by author Brian Reade for the gory details – had become fissures, and manager Rafael Benitez's attempts to navigate his way through the ensuing mess were clearly taking their toll on him. He had borne the brunt of the fallout from their failed ownership, managing to maintain his integrity throughout. I'm not ashamed to say I shed more than a few tears when he was eventually 'mutually consented' out of the club at the end of the season.

It ended up being the poor season it had promised to be, the 'highlight' being an undeserved loss to Atletico Madrid at the semi-final stage of the Europa League, Atleti's single extra-time goal at Anfield in a 2-1 defeat being sufficient to take them to the final against Roy Hodgson's Fulham having scored the only away goal in the tie following their 1-0 victory at the Vicente Calderon Stadium in Madrid. We may have missed out on the final in Hamburg and a day of destiny with Roy Hodgson as a result, but he was about to loom much larger on the club's horizon.

Christian Purslow, the club's serpentine Managing Director appointed to find a buyer for our absentee owners, decided that Uncle Roy was the perfect man to replace Rafa. Like many fans I was unconvinced but willing to give him a chance to prove us wrong. Sadly for Hodgson (though more so for us), every time he opened his mouth he further distanced himself from our affections, making no effort to harness, or even understand, the scouse psyche which, as far as our football team is concerned, brooks no wilting underdog sentiment, especially from our own manager who is expected to lead the club with integrity and, when called for, defiance.

Our season opened at Anfield with a simultaneously encouraging and disappointing 1-1 draw with Arsenal. Encouraging because the team had been reduced to ten men when new 'boy', the moribund Joe Cole, was sent off in the first half, yet still managed to take an early second half lead; disappointing because Arsenal had equalised in the last minute following one of a growing number of mistakes which had begun to creep into our goalkeeper Pepe Reina's game. In the build-up to our next game, away at Manchester City with their expensive and talented squad, assembled courtesy of Sheik Mansour who had bought the club a couple of years earlier, Hodgson's opinion of his own, relatively impoverished, charges was made plain by his assertion that he hoped "we don't lose 6-0".

He must have been delighted when we 'only' lost 3-0. Following another assertion that fourth tier Northampton Town would be formidable opponents after being drawn against them – at home – in the third round of the Carling Cup, he no doubt remained unsurprised when, in spite of taking an early lead in the game, we deservedly exited the competition on penalties. This followed a 3-2 defeat to Manchester United at Old Trafford the previous weekend where he failed to defend striker Fernando Torres when United manager Alex Ferguson accused our centre forward of diving to try and get their defender Jonny Evans sent off, the best he could offer being that he would neither agree nor disagree with 'Sir Alex'.

By now, less than two months into the season, Hodgson was already on a slippery slope with a majority of fans, and when he described the performance in a 2-0 derby defeat to Everton at Goodison Park as 'as good as we have played all season' further indicating that 'to get a result here would have been Utopia', the writing was well and truly on the wall.

This was the club's first game under our new owners New England Sports

Ventures (NESV) – soon to be rebadged Fenway Sports Group (FSG) – who had purchased the club from the Royal Bank of Scotland by taking on the previous owner's debt following a stressful, unedifying, court battle, with Hicks and Gillett ultimately relinquishing control without receiving a penny from the sale. They gave Hodgson a couple of more months in charge, and enough rope, before putting us all out of our misery by sacking him ahead of a third round FA Cup tie in early January.

Of course, the ownership issue had itself contributed to our unforgettably forgettable year. In fact, the increased paucity of entertainment and inspiration from the team's pitch side endeavours, which had seen match attendance becoming an increasingly unwelcome chore, was counter-balanced to an extent by the after-match protests of a hardcore of a few hundred fans, primarily situated on The Kop, but which me and San were proud to be a part of from our spec, with a few others, in The Kemlyn Road Stand.

I was one of the many 'internet terrorists', so labelled by previous owner Tom Hicks, who had sent stark fact laden emails to various financial institutions rumoured to be considering refinancing loans made to Hicks and Gillett. The emails, thousands of them, advised recipients of the depth of opposition amongst the club's worldwide fanbase to the continuation of the current ownership, and the resulting toxic publicity which would undeniably be unleashed should such financial support be forthcoming. The campaign appeared to work, with one such institution, US based private equity firm The Blackstone Group, announcing that it had ended talks with Hicks regarding a £280m two-year refinancing package, after receiving more than seven thousand emails from protesting Liverpool fans.

Less than a month later, on Wednesday 13 October, I was at the so-called 'best away' of the season, travelling on the Spirit of Shankly sponsored supporters' coach to wait on The Strand in London outside the Royal Courts of Justice for Mr Justice Floyd to rule that Hicks and Gillett had breached their contract with Royal Bank of Scotland, thus enabling the sale of the club to NESV to proceed. As it transpired, there were still a couple of days of shenanigans to get through, but the sale was duly completed before the weekend.

I'd started the year out of work, in the middle of a 10 in 13 months 'dry' period, no doubt due, in part at least, to the impact of the financial crisis which engulfed us in 2008. I was out of work again when the sale of the club took place, though my next contract was already signed and sealed and the financial pressure of not knowing when my income stream would start again had receded. Arriving back in Liverpool on the SOS coach, I popped in for a cup of tea with my mum and brother Alan before driving back to Congleton. We discussed the outcome of the court case, sharing each other's delight that we were about to see the end of Hicks and Gillett at our club.

The following week I was to enjoy a few days in Manhattan with daughter Liv, an early 18th birthday gift to her, booked earlier in the year during another period of gainful employment. An enjoyable trip which would provide one of the year's highlights, reviving memories, rose-tinted through the mists of time no doubt, of when San & I had lived there briefly in 1982. We even managed to take in a Liverpool win, 2-1 against Blackburn Rovers at Anfield, from the welcoming packed 11th St East Village Bar, home of the New York Liverpool Supporters Club. Were things starting to look up? As autumn beckoned, I looked back on the preceding nine or ten months and reasoned things could only get better from here.

Sadly, 2010 had one more massive kick in the crotch lined up for all of us.

* * *

20 November 2010. Anfield. Liverpool 3-0 West Ham

A rare bright spot in a dismal first half of the 2010/11 league campaign saw Liverpool take a 3-0 first half lead against East London's finest in the Saturday teatime kick-off. We never added to that score line in the second half, but thankfully neither did the cockneys, and in this dog of a season three goals and a clean sheet at any juncture was not to be sneezed at.

More importantly for me, following a fall out with Tom a couple of weeks earlier – the only time I can recall ever having a fall out with anyone that lasted longer than the argument itself – we were back on speaking terms, and to be honest I was overjoyed to be able to give both him and Dan a hug when we met up back at the car after the match. To be fair, during the time we hadn't spoken I'd been working in Swindon at the Head Office of Nationwide Building Society, my latest client, so it's not like we'd gone out of our way to avoid each other, but still, memories of the disagreement lingered, and I was glad the air was now clear.

The previous weekend me and San had been in the away end at the Britannia Stadium, home of Stoke City and the closest Premier League ground to our Congleton home, where we witnessed another in a seemingly never-ending stream of dreadful refereeing performances, this time given by Mark Halsey.

The only worst performers on the day were wearing the black shirts of Liverpool, and our disillusionment with the performance and the season to date led to us leaving the ground moments after Kenwyne Jones had underlined the home team's superiority at the start of injury time with their clinching goal in a 2-0 win, their first league victory over Liverpool in 26 years. Thankfully we missed the subsequent dismissal of our Brazilian midfielder Lucas Leiva and the braying, taunting celebrations of the Stoke faithful which must surely have followed. To add insult to injury, when we arrived back at the car, I discovered I'd lost my iPhone.

Subsequent half-hearted calls to the club and the local constabulary in search of the phone proved predictably fruitless and in a final desperate bid to recover it I posted a message on the Red And White Kop (RAWK) LFC forum, hoping against fading hope that I'd lost it somewhere either inside or just outside the away end and a kindly fellow scouser would own up to having retrieved it. Following some light-hearted banter on the forum, some of which suggested I might just be 'fishing' for a phone (as if I would), I was both amazed and delighted when a poster came forward with details of where I could pick it up. It was at an address in Kirkby, a few miles north east of Liverpool, and so I asked our Alan to get it for me during the week, in advance of my collecting it from him after the West Ham game the following weekend.

* * *

Just after the match. Mum & Dad's House, Mill Lane, Liverpool 15

Somewhat unexpectedly, my mum appeared to be in conversation with a couple of guys I didn't recognise outside her house when we arrived there to pick up my newly recovered phone. After we'd parked and approached the front door, it was clear she was actually on her way out with them. One of the men, yet another Les – who it transpired worked for our Alan – turned to me and asked who I was.

Having determined that I was Alan's brother, he told us that Alan had been taken to the Royal Liverpool Hospital in Prescot Street after being struck by a speeding car which had left the road outside Alan's business premises, the Liverpool Furniture Repair Centre on Smithdown Road, opposite the Mustard Bar. Worryingly he added "I think you should prepare yourselves for the worst".

During the course of the evening, most of the family, including Alan's daughters Sian and Sophie, converged on the Accident & Emergency department at the Royal awaiting news from the Emergency Room where Alan was being treated. A few of Alan's friends appeared as well.

In a meeting with a police officer shortly after we arrived at the hospital, I made the point that Alan looked after himself physically, and was a strong lad, not least through regular attendance at the gym where he enjoyed using the weights, eliciting a response to the effect that that "would stand him in good stead then". Looking back, he was obviously humouring me, as he will have known I was being recklessly optimistic. I mean, he'd been hit by a massive lump of speeding glass and metal for crying out loud.

Shortly before midnight, his immediate family – mum, me, brother John, sister Stephanie and Alan's daughters - were called into another meeting, this time with the doctor who had been treating him. There was to be no happy ending, Alan had died a few minutes earlier. Years before he'd told me "You'll never need to worry about me, Les. I'm a survivor" and I'd believed him wholeheartedly. Now my indestructible brother was gone.

The driver of the car - a 'boy-racer' who'd lost control, ironically while rushing home to watch the match on television, and a university drop-out according to the Liverpool Echo, though I'm not sure that had much relevance - was himself hospitalised for a while in the Walton Hospital neurology centre having suffered a number of brain traumas in the 'accident'.

Of more relevance I think, and the reason I would qualify describing it as an 'accident', was the discovery of videos on his phone which exposed his propensity for speeding and consistently ignoring the rules of the road, along with his general lack of thought and respect for the well-being of other road users. In legal terms it may have been an 'accident', but it was one waiting to happen and indeed could have been foreseen by his friends, himself and anyone who knew of his driving 'style'.

He was subsequently charged with 'Dangerous Driving' and prior to appearing at Liverpool Crown Court in October the following year, his Facebook posts bemoaned the fact that he was currently unable to drive following his brain injuries. His guilty plea and protestations of remorse, delivered through counsel – who also indicated, somewhat disingenuously I believe, that he'd voluntarily stopped driving pending the outcome of the trial - may well have impressed the judge enough to limit his sentence to 4 years and a few months in an open prison, and to ban him from driving for a further 5 years, but I don't believe for a second they were heartfelt or sincere. In fact, they were probably as genuine as the 'punishment' handed down which ended up being just over two years of incarceration given time off for good behaviour.

And that's if you can even call minimum supervision, minimum perimeter security, minimum cell time and weekends at home 'incarceration'. Sounded more like a holiday camp to me.

8

23 AUGUST

Nearly 8 months before. Teatime, UK. 5 January 2016.

Big game tonight. Well, big-*ish*. Stoke City will be entertaining Liverpool at the Britannia Stadium in the first leg of the League Cup semi-final, a competition we've already won a record eight times. It's an opportunity for Jurgen Klopp, our newly installed manager of just under three months, to reach a cup final in his first season and, given our dearth of success in recent years, it's an opportunity not to be sneezed at.

"Alright dad, I'm gonna watch the match in the Unicorn later. Having a few drinks with the lads as it's my last night. Fancy it?".

Tom would be starting his Australian 'adventure' the following day – spending a few days with Jamie and Claire in Bangkok on route – and was combining his farewell drinks with his farewell match.

"No thanks son. Have a good time!"

"Really? Thought you'd be well up for it" Tom expressed his surprise at my response.

"Nah. You know I don't like watching the reds with non-Liverpool fans if I can help it. And it's a Stoke pub too. Definitely not my cup of tea" I explained.

"Oh yeah, I forgot it'll be full of Stokies. You don't mind me going on my last night, do you?".

"No mate, you go and enjoy yourself. Don't forget we need to be at the airport early in the morning, so take it easy" I ended the conversation, slipping him a tenner to have a drink on me.

Long story short, Liverpool won 1-0 on their way to a final defeat against Manchester City, Tom returned home in plenty of time for a decent night's kip, and I delivered him to Terminal 1 at Manchester airport in the morning, having made sure he was in possession of his plane ticket, passport and what bit of currency he was taking with him. Rather than just drop him off, as I'd done on numerous occasions before - when he was off on a short vacation and not travelling to the other side of the world for example - I parked in the multi-storey car park and accompanied him to the check-in desk.

A few minutes later, bags checked in and boarding pass in hand, Tom was ready to head through security, our paths about to diverge. As we hovered on the edge of parting, I found myself unexpectedly tearful at the thought of Tom going so far away, for such a long time – at least two years if his plans came to fruition – and Tom clearly sensed my melancholy, indulging me with a long goodbye hug, before almost literally skipping through the security checks.

Other side of the world? It could have been another planet.

* * *

1 day before. Lunchtime, UK. Late evening, Queensland. 22 August 2016.

Replete after my sandwich and coffee fuelled lunch break, I've a few minutes to spare before my latest teleconference is due to start, when my phone pings. Not a text, but a Facebook message from Tom. He's just finished a FB conversation with his mum and now it's my turn. Our communications with Tom are far from regular so it's always great to hear from him, whatever the medium and whatever the time of day, but our digital chat is necessarily short due to my looming conference call.

After a few months struggling to find his feet, it's encouraging - indeed a relief - to hear that he's approaching the completion of his 88 days farm work, necessary for the 12-month visa extension he is keen to earn, and looking forward to visiting the Whitsunday Islands and Byron Bay before travelling back to Melbourne where he has already made friends and been promised more work. Before he can do any of that though, he needs to clear his debt with the hostel owner who, according to Tom, has confiscated his passport 'for safe-keeping', pending repayment of the debt.

All too soon our conversation is over:

"Anyway gotta go. Meeting in 2 mins. Stay in touch. Love you xx" I key into my Messenger app.

"Love you too, enjoy your teleconference x" replies Tom.

"As if!" says I.

Tom ended the exchange with a winking emoji.

* * *

The day itself

"That'll do me" I thought, draining my pint glass immediately after the wriggly armed dancing maestro that is Daniel Sturridge had taken a pass from our latest shiny new signing Sadio Mane, and drilled the ball into the bottom right corner of the net.

With less than ten of the 90 minutes left on the clock and Liverpool leading lower league Burton Albion 5-0 in the League Cup second round tie – a welcome, if not completely surprising response to a 2-0 defeat at Burnley in the previous weekend's Premier league fixture - I reasoned it was time to head home from the Fox & Hounds pub in Stony Stratford near Milton Keynes.

During the week, 'home' was a rented semi about half a mile 'up the hill' in Old Stratford, which had been my base for the last four or five months while working for Santander Bank in nearby Shenley Wood. Weekends when Liverpool were playing at home would find me with my wife Sandra at Anfield in our seats in the Lower Centenary (now Sir Kenny Dalglish) stand. Kop end, seven rows back, in line with the penalty spot. Great spec. My weekday evening routine when Liverpool were playing, and on the telly, consisted of getting home, getting changed and getting to the pub in time for something to eat before kick-off, and tonight had been no different.

The new season had only been underway for a couple of weeks, and towards the end of the previous season the Fox & Hounds had become a regular haunt when what promised to be a decent match was on the box. It offered a decent bar menu, decent pint and a couple of decent sized screens for the footy lover and I'd struck up a few conversations with the regulars over that time.

One such chap, a friendly enough native of Manchester and lukewarm City fan of a similar vintage to me, was there to watch the first leg of City's Champions League semi-final against Real Madrid, and had been moved to comment on the Hillsborough inquests which were ongoing at the time, suggesting that perhaps it was time for 'people to move on'. To be fair, he was suitably chagrined when I asked him how quickly he might 'move on' if he'd lost a loved one in similarly tragic and unresolved circumstances. Our paths never crossed again.

The following evening, another Champions League night, I overhead a conversation on the same subject between two locals, one of whom professed some, in my opinion unwarranted, sympathy for the police officers in charge on that fateful day, and Chief Superintendent David Duckenfield in particular, adamant as he was that Duckenfield 'hadn't woken up planning to kill anyone that morning'.

I pointed out, as politely as my simmering rage would allow, that I found such comments offensive as well as spectacularly missing the point, and that, as he was now speaking to someone who'd been in attendance that day, he might be a little more circumspect in the future when espousing such a point of view – after all, you never know who's listening, especially when you're hardly trying to keep a low profile.

Perhaps our paranoia that the rest of the country, or at least a sizeable chunk of it, really didn't have an issue with football fans – Liverpool fans – being 'unlawfully killed', or with the fact that the match commander had been found 'responsible for manslaughter by gross negligence', wasn't actually paranoia after all. Thankfully I never saw him again either.

A week prior to that I'd watched us demolish Everton 4-0 at Anfield in the same bar, where one of my drinking companions on the night was a fellow scouser, albeit an Evertonian. I think it's fair to say I enjoyed that evening rather more than he did.

But I digress.

The following day would dawn on my 58th birthday and, even though the mighty Burton had been vanquished, long gone were the days when I might have considered staying for a few more pints, perhaps to bask in the afterglow of a comprehensive victory. Besides, and with no disrespect intended, it was only Burton Albion and only the League Cup – or whatever it was actually called these days - and I was nearly 130 miles from the family home in Cheshire and 160 miles from our native and spiritual one in Liverpool. There were only a handful of fellow drinkers in the bar, and as far as I could tell none were Liverpool fans (or Burton Albion fans for that matter).

In days of yore, I'd have phoned my dad Les or brother Alan to discuss the match and we'd have berated or laughed along with each other depending on the performance, the result and whether our opinions on the match coincided or clashed, but sadly they were no longer with us. Most of the rest of the family – wife Sandra, home alone in Congleton during the week while I worked away, sons Tom and Dan, daughter Olivia, mum Jean and brother John - were all big reds, but for reasons I still can't articulate never fully replaced my dear departed dad or brother as suitable candidates for an immediate post-match phone rant or celebration.

San had actually suggested a while back that there was really no need for me to phone her after a match anymore, as if she didn't agree with my opinion we'd usually end up falling out. Not for the first time I could see she was right and I'd been happy to concur. So, I was mildly surprised that evening as I started my walk up the hill to my mid-week home in Mounthill Avenue, when my phone rang. It was San calling and I immediately assumed she'd been so impressed with our summary dispatch of Burton that a celebratory phone call was in order after all. If only that had been the case.

"Hi sweetie, how's it going? Decent win that, eh?" I greeted her.

"Yeah OK. Listen, there's no easy way to say this. Tom has been attacked and he's in intensive care in a critical condition" San responded.

"What? What's happened?"

"Not entirely sure at the moment, but another person was also attacked and has died. They've told us to prepare for the worst".

And there it was. My, our, world upside down in the space of a few seconds. My head was already spinning, my heart racing.

"Well, I'm coming home" I said into the phone, completely unnecessarily. Of course I was coming home. What else would I do? I was already fighting, in vain, to hold back the tears. We are blessed to have a number of very close friends who live nearby and one of them, Steve Nash, was with San when she made the call (it was only later when I checked my phone that I realised I'd had a few texts from Steve asking me to call either him or home. The Fox & Hounds was in a 'dead spot' cellular wise, at least for my network provider, and between them they'd been trying for a good few minutes to get hold of me, only managing to do so after I'd left the pub).

Looking back, San and Steve had to try and keep me calm as I faced a three-hour drive back to Congleton, when I felt San and I should really have been trying to comfort each other. Tom's brother Dan and sister Olivia were both in Liverpool, in fact Liv was still at work and Steve, God bless him, made the near hundred-mile round trip to collect them.

Having promised San I'd be home as soon as possible, while at the same time pledging to drive extra carefully, I ran up the hill in a state of some distress, sprinting into the house and quickly throwing a few things into my weekly bag. I was finding it difficult to think straight but for some reason recalled when my brother had died in the emergency room after being struck by that speeding car in Liverpool nearly six years before. I'm not a particularly religious person, but I remember thinking that perhaps I could have done more that night, in the way of prayer at least, to help give our Alan the best chance of survival.

It was no doubt with that in mind that I immediately called Heather Kemball, a close family friend and local minister. Heather immediately sensed my distress and after I'd put her in the picture, I beseeched her to pray for Tom. As I headed for home, I could not imagine what a rock of love and support Heather would be for us over the coming weeks and months.

About three hours later I pulled onto our drive in Congleton half an hour into my birthday, though that was the last thing on my mind. I'd hoped the journey would be quicker but, considering the time of night the traffic had been much heavier than I'd expected, and I was peering through moist and misty eyes much of the time, praying that there'd be no even worse news when I reached home. Thankfully there wasn't. San and the kids were there, Steve and the police having left a little earlier after Steve had dropped Dan and Liv off and ascertained that I was on my way home.

Tom had been backpacking and resident at a hostel in Queensland, Australia, and San had spoken to the Foreign and Commonwealth Office (FCO) for an update, as well as to doctors in the Intensive Care Unit (ICU) at Townsville Hospital, where Tom had been operated on, his life now hanging in the balance.

She had also somehow stayed calm enough to research flights to that part of the world and there was one leaving Manchester airport just after nine in the morning which would get me into Brisbane, via Abu Dhabi, just over 24 hours later. San is absolutely terrified of flying but had rightly assumed I'd want to be by Tom's side as soon as possible, so we booked a single ticket – one-way, who knew when I'd be ready to return? – and thankfully my online visa application was granted immediately, presumably because someone had been primed to expect it.

I headed off to Manchester airport at six in the morning, full of trepidation having said a tearful and emotional goodbye to San and Dan. Steve had very kindly offered to give me a lift, and Liv was accompanying me to the airport before returning home to be with her mum and brother. No-one had slept a wink. After another tearful goodbye with Liv and Steve I joined the queue at the Bureau de Change preparing to be fleeced for my couple of hundred Australian dollars, which would mean I'd at least have some local currency when I eventually arrived.

The journey from Manchester to Abu Dhabi and then from Abu Dhabi to Brisbane can best be described as torturous. While waiting to board the first flight at Manchester airport, I called my sister Stephanie and brother John to put them in the picture and asked them to let my mum know what had happened (my mum was 77 at the time and I reasoned eight o'clock in the morning was much too early for her to be woken up with such news, especially via a phone call), and also managed to catch my manager, Jackie, at work – a lot had happened since I'd left the office the previous evening.

Everything ran on time and the service from Etihad was as good as you would expect. But I was physically and emotionally shattered, frequently in tears, and absolutely dreading turning my phone on between flights. When I eventually arrived in Brisbane, the British Consulate had arranged for me to be the first person taken off the plane and met by local police and Laura Morgan, a member of the consulate itself, for which I was grateful. My suitcase was collected for me and I was rubber stamped through immigration in double-quick time.

The end of my journey beckoned, but not before another plane trip. Waiting for the two-hour flight up to Townsville, I was taken to a private room where I got to spend half an hour or so with Menna Rawlings, the then British High Commissioner to Australia. In more pleasurable circumstances I suppose I'd have relished this VIP treatment, but this was far from a happy visit. Menna was waiting for her connecting flight to Canberra having just visited the hostel in Home Hill where Tom had been attacked.

She was lovely, a proud welsh lady, very humble, understanding, sympathetic and genuinely concerned for my wellbeing and that of the rest of the family. Moreover, the half hour we had in that quiet, private room was a welcome departure from the head swirling chaos of the past 24 hours. She had no more specific update for me regarding Tom's condition, but assured me that the emergency services in Queensland had been quickly on the scene and that he was in the most capable hands in Townsville hospital.

As I mentioned previously, Tom hadn't been the only victim of the attack. He had actually been trying to help save the life of 20-year-old Mia Ayliffe-Chung, another young Briton, who had only been at the hostel for a few days (Tom had been there a few months), but tragically Mia had died at the scene.

We would get to know Mia's mum Rosie Ayliffe, and her partner Stewart, quite well over the next few months, as Rosie campaigned against the often shockingly negligent (at best) practices and customs which appeared to be commonplace amongst many of those employing or providing accommodation for young backpackers attempting to secure a second year working visa extension in Australia. (Her book, 'Far from Home', describes her devastating loss and her fight to protect others from suffering a similar tragedy).

Jamie Nash, Steve's eldest son and one of Tom's closest and longest standing childhood friends – they started school a term apart when they were both still four years old – lived and worked in Bangkok with his wife Claire, and Tom had visited them often during his travels around South East Asia. As soon as he heard of the attack on Tom, Jamie was on a plane to Brisbane and we met up in the departures hall shortly before taking off for Townsville. We hugged our hellos and boarded the flight for the final leg of our respective journeys. I was immensely grateful for his presence, and he would become a pillar of support for me over the ensuing days, starting with our arrival in Townsville a couple of hours later.

We were met by Megan Hunt, the British Vice Consul based in Queensland's capital, Brisbane, who earlier in the day had been on site at the hostel in Home Hill, sometimes known as 'Shelley's Backpackers', where Tom and Mia had been attacked, liaising with police and other young travellers at the scene, and generally providing consular support and assistance where at all possible. Jamie collected my suitcase while Megan escorted me to a waiting car, which proceeded to deliver us directly to Townsville hospital.

It was late in the evening in Queensland, approaching midnight I guess, and barely 48 hours had passed since the attack. It was still a massive news story, both here and at home, and a number of reporters were still present, wanting a comment on what had happened, while flash bulbs dazzled and disoriented in equal measure. But I was far too tired and emotional to contemplate speaking to any of them at that particular moment.

I just wanted to see and hold my eldest son, my first born, for the first time since we'd said our goodbyes in the departure hall at Manchester airport nearly nine months earlier. At the same time, unbeknown to me, back in the UK the rest of the family were starting to get their own taste of unwanted and unnecessarily intrusive media attention.

* * *

Townsville Hospital is big and clean and gleaming and as impressive in every way as a hospital can appear to the uneducated eye, and its ICU does not let it down in any respect. Its staff were ready for our arrival, and over the next week or so I would experience – and be grateful for - their professionalism, dedication, empathy and compassion.

I sincerely hope that they will forgive my inability to remember names (although 'Wayne' and maybe 'Kate' strike a chord). I certainly remember explaining the significance of a couple of of Tom's tattoos to them: "JFT96" alongside the 'Hillsborough flame', commemorating those who had died in that tragedy in 1989, and the band of five stars around one of his biceps, each identifying a year ("77", "78", "81", "84", "05") of one of Liverpool's successful European Cup campaigns (to date), and I do recall a young nurse dedicated solely to Tom's care who was on duty in his room when we arrived. A young doctor quickly joined us to give an update on Tom's condition, though the poor lad was as white as a sheet and had nothing really new to tell me.

Simply put, Tom might fully recover, might be mentally impaired, or might not recover at all. All possibilities were still on the table and only time would tell. By this time, I had also already met Vera Hemp from the hospital's Social Work service, and she would also provide tremendous support over the coming days. However, nothing and no-one could have prepared me for my first sight of Tom lying in his hospital bed.

He had been stabbed in his right eye, which was covered by a patch, and was attached to various apparatus which breathed for him and monitored his blood pressure, heart rate and the pressure inside his skull. Tom had also been stabbed at the base of his skull and was in a therapeutic coma, induced to force his brain to rest. The pressure inside his skull was being monitored to ensure that as little stress was put on his brain as possible, though this also meant that his brain activity couldn't be monitored at the same time (this is my recollection of how it was explained to me at the time, but in truth I can't be certain), and the doctors were clear with me that Tom's prognosis could not be determined until the swelling in his brain reduced enough to enable it to be examined via a scan.

I kissed Tom, held his hand and hugged him as best I could. And simply sobbed.

After a brief phone call to San back home to put her in the picture (there wasn't much to elaborate on, but I think we were both glad that I'd arrived at last, safely, and had at least managed to see Tom), I was allowed to spend that first night in one of a number of rooms which were available for just that purpose – that is, for close relatives visiting patients receiving intensive care. What stories – both sad and uplifting – previous occupants of this room would be able to tell I thought, hoping beyond hope that mine would fall into the latter category.

The room was antiseptically clean and sparsely furnished, with a single bed, toilet and walk-in shower. All very modern, but bloody freezing as I recall due to a combination of the air-conditioning and the scantiness of the bed linen. As tired as I was, and I was *so* tired after the best part of two days since I last got out of bed at my digs in Milton Keynes, I struggled to get more than a few hours of broken sleep and was grateful for the shower, long and hot, when I eventually decided to bite the bullet and give up trying to force myself to sleep.

While I'd stayed 30 yards along the corridor from Tom, Vera had checked Jamie in to the Australian Red Cross accommodation situated on the hospital campus. This was a short 5-minute walk from the main hospital and was to prove a godsend over the coming days. I would spend the rest of my time in Townsville there, initially sharing with Jamie until he returned to Bangkok and a semblance of normality with Claire, and my daughter Liv would also spend a few days there after flying out from the UK at the start of the following week. And all provided free of charge by the Australian Red Cross. They will always have my heartfelt thanks.

The chronology of the rest of my stay in Townsville is somewhat hazy to recall with utter certainty but if I remember correctly, Vera (the social worker) met me early on that first morning, as I was required to vacate the room after the first night, and transported me and my suitcase across to the accommodation I would be sharing with Jamie. Jamie meanwhile had already had a busy start to the day and informed me (or was that Vera?) that the detectives working on the case would be travelling down from Home Hill to meet us later that morning and bring us up to date with any progress they might have made.

Detective Inspector Kelly Harvey and Detective Constables Nick Bach and Gavin Neal introduced themselves as they joined us for a late breakfast at the popular little café situated on the hospital campus, where my toasted egg and bacon sandwich and café latte provided much needed sustenance. They explained to us what their enquiries had managed to uncover so far.

The simple cold facts were that Smail Ayad, a French backpacker who had been resident at the hostel for a number of months, appeared to have attacked and killed Mia with a large kitchen knife, and had subsequently attacked Tom with the same knife, leaving him in his current critical condition.

As the story unfolded it seems that Ayad, a trained UFC fighter who had fought professionally in Thailand, had been acting strangely throughout the day until he eventually started shouting and screaming unintelligibly before dragging Mia from her bed in a room they shared on the top floor of the hostel (there were only two levels, one of which was the ground floor) at knifepoint and stabbed her in the chest.

Mia had somehow managed to escape from him and stagger into the bathroom, before Ayad performed a swan dive from the first-floor balcony to the ground floor – possibly intending to end his own life? – but ultimately managed to perform a back flip before hitting the ground. He had injured his back and neck in the 'fall' and my Tom, who had been working on his laptop in the room he shared with five other backpackers and, having heard the commotion outside the room but unaware of what had just transpired, ran to Ayad's aid.

At this stage, another young backpacker Dan Richards, who had witnessed the attack on Mia and initially tried to calm Ayad down, called to Tom that Mia needed urgent assistance and Tom then immediately ran upstairs to provide what help he could in the bathroom. (It is a source of pride to us, though absolutely no surprise and indeed little comfort now, that Tom appeared to be the backpacker's 'go-to guy' in the circumstances).

171

As Tom and Dan were doing their best to help Mia, Ayad had picked himself up and run upstairs, confronting Tom at the door to the bathroom. Apparently, CCTV footage shows Tom attempting to calm Ayad at this point, asking that they be left to tend to the stricken Mia, before closing and locking the door. Ayad then kicked the door in and attacked Tom in a frenzy, stabbing him repeatedly in the head and torso, before turning on one of the hostel managers, stabbing him in the leg, and also fatally stabbing the owner's German Shepherd dog.

Mia's travelling companion, Chris Porter, had raised the alarm and warned fellow hostel dwellers to lock themselves in their rooms, before falling from a drainpipe and breaking both ankles. He narrowly escaped with his own life when a passing motorist stopped to help him as he was being chased by Ayad.

As all this was happening, the police had been called and pretty quickly arrived on the scene along with the paramedics. While the paramedics attended Tom and Mia – we later learned that Mia had initially been their priority as Tom appeared to have been a hopeless case, such was his loss of blood – Ayad was eventually apprehended after attacking and injuring a dozen or so police officers. (Nick Bach, the arresting officer, intimated that Ayad had demonstrated almost superhuman strength and aggression, and continued to display that same level of aggression in the days immediately following his arrest, to the extent that his initial court appearances – having been charged with Mia's murder and Tom's attempted murder – were facilitated via video link to avoid any possible risk to the general public and members of the court).

Other information regarding Ayad's state of mind – his obsession with Mia after only a few days of her being there, and his paranoia that members of the local farming community were planning to kill him, for example – and the effect of his long-time addiction to smoking marijuana, would come to light over the ensuing months, culminating in his appearance at the Mental Health Court in Brisbane in April 2018, nearly two years after the attacks took place.

But on that first morning in the little café on the Townsville hospital campus, my only concern was the condition and survival chances of my son. Jamie became my personal carer, assistant, secretary, general dogsbody and basically go-to man for everything during those first few days. It was now the Friday morning after Tom had been attacked on the Tuesday evening and, while we waited for the pressure in Tom's skull to subside enough for a definitive scan to be performed, we had to look after ourselves. More accurately perhaps, Jamie had to look after both of us.

Shopping lists were made and acted on – we had access to a kitchen in the Red Cross accommodation – local police were liaised with, and even my Aussie family members, half a dozen of whom travelled up from Melbourne to see Tom, engaged with. Just like his dad Steve, his mum Angie and his brother Daniel – what a great family to be able to call your friends – Jamie is a natural leader and took all of this in his stride despite the fact that Tom was one of his closest friends from childhood and was obviously dealing with his own feelings about what had happened.

Tom was taken to theatre on the Friday to be examined by one of Australia's leading ophthalmologists, as I was informed. After the procedure I was called to a meeting with the surgeon and his assistant who explained that they had assessed the injury to see if the eye could be saved. His sight in the eye had gone but they had been hoping they could at least avoid the need to replace it with a false one.

The news however was not good, and they were visibly upset when informing me they could do nothing to save it. It is perhaps an indication of my state of mind that the news barely affected me. I shrugged my shoulders as I told them that I didn't care if Tom wouldn't be able to see out of one of his eyes, I just wanted to be able to take him home with me at some stage. We could work through anything with him as long as he survived.

A consequence of this attempt to save his eye however, was that I reasoned they wouldn't even be trying to save it if his was a hopeless case. All things being equal, the following day Tom would be getting taken for the scan to assess the extent of the injury to his brain. My hope sprung eternal. Back home, they were ten or eleven hours behind Australia Eastern Standard Time, and I phoned to update the family with these latest developments. Their reaction was similar to mine. At this stage, nothing else mattered but Tom's survival.

The next day, Saturday 27 August, dawned. Back in the UK Tom Goodhew and Rachael Glover, contemporaries of Tom, Dan & Liv and who our relationship with over the years had matured from being friends of our children and children of our friends to simply being our friends, were getting married. We had all been invited and Liv was due to be one of Rachael's bridesmaids. At Townsville hospital in Queensland, I sent Rachael and Tom a message of goodwill for their wedding day and implored them to put Tom's situation out of their minds, while Tom was taken for the brain scan which would determine the extent of his head injury and his prognosis.

At some stage during the late afternoon or evening – I honestly cannot remember which – me and Jamie were called to a meeting with two of the doctors who had been looking after Tom. The meeting room was situated just outside the ICU, no more than five metres or so from its entrance, and was accessible only by entering the correct access code into a keypad attached to the door, a mechanism no doubt designed with more than a nod to the potential privacy needs of friends and relatives of ICU patients receiving news about their loved one's conditions.

It wasn't our first time in that room – the ophthalmologist and his assistant had delivered their assessment of Tom's injured eye to us there, we had greeted Tom's friends visiting from the hostel there, and we would go on to greet more of his friends in the days to come, not least Kay and Ryan, particularly close friends of Tom, to whom we would deliver the same news we were about to receive – but I still can't describe it in much detail. My hazy recollection is that it was small, no more than three or four metres square, sparsely furnished with a few reasonably comfortable chairs and perhaps a small coffee table, or similar, and with a muted colour scheme of maybe cream or grey. An unremarkable and easily forgettable room. Tragically, the news we received was neither unremarkable nor ever likely to be forgotten.

I sat with my head bowed, Jamie's arm protectively around my shoulders trying in vain to shield me from the pain of the medic's words, while at the same time providing what little comfort was possible, as Tom's future was laid out in front of me. In short, he didn't have one.

The scan had revealed that the knife wounds to the back of his head had severely damaged his brain stem and the senior doctor explained the best-case scenario was that he would be in a persistent vegetative state. Brain-dead to use the vernacular. Even with the ventilator continuing to breathe for him, ensuring that blood and oxygen continued to circulate around his stricken body, neither would be sustaining Tom's brain and it was very likely that his heart would eventually stop beating of its own accord.

I was heartbroken - devastated, distraught, grief-stricken, all the words you can think of that might be used to describe your emotions at times of loss and distress, but never come close to conveying the depth of your despair. However, Jamie and the doctors who delivered the news would be forgiven for not necessarily recognising those emotions in me, reacting as I did quietly with a resigned acceptance (as far as I am aware). Certainly, there was no wailing or outpouring of grief.

Looking back, I think I'd been preparing myself for losing Tom since San had first uttered "prepare for the worst", and certainly after I'd seen him for the first time in his hospital bed. Ever since I'd been deluding, perhaps protecting, myself with false hope based on little more than wishful thinking. Now I needed to let his mum know.

Like most other males with a family I guess, as a husband and father I have always felt an acute sense of responsibility for providing and maintaining the safety and wellbeing of my wife and children. As illogical as it may seem, that sense of responsibility does not diminish – or at least not for me – as our children mature into adults and leave home.

One TV show I have particularly enjoyed is 'The Good Doctor'. The title character is a young surgeon named Shaun, played by Freddie Highmore, who has suffered with autism from an early age and, after the death of his brother who he adored, and his rejection of his abusive Father, is pretty much brought up by Dr Aaron Glassman, played by Richard Schiff (who also plays Toby Ziegler, the White House Communications Director in 'The West Wing', another favourite show of mine).

In series 3, Shaun is persuaded to visit his dying Father and is accompanied by his friend Lea, played by Paige Spara, and Dr Glassman. Dr Glassman and Lea don't always see eye to eye, especially where Shaun's well-being is concerned, Lea believing Dr Glassman to be a little over-protective at times, while Dr Glassman, who had lost his only daughter, is a little wary of Lea's youth and slightly more care-free attitude.

Dr Glassman sits Lea down and asks her if she is planning to have any children of her own one day. To which she confirms that she'd like to, but, you know, who knows? It's then that Dr Glassman tells her that if she does have children, she is "...going to be responsible for another human being". Followed by...

"Your first job, Number One, is to keep them alive".

It matters not a jot that Tom was a fully responsible 30-year-old man who hadn't lived with us permanently since leaving for University 11 years earlier and, standing at 6 foot 3 inches tall in the prime of his life, was far more capable of physically looking after himself than I was. Although I didn't realise it at the time, my emotional state was undoubtedly exacerbated by the sense that I'd failed at my 'number one job'.

Now, in the space of less than a week I had been ten thousand miles away from my eldest when he received the wounds which would ultimately end his life, and the same distance from the rest of my family at a time when the only worthwhile thing we could do was comfort each other. I felt lost.

Using FaceTime on my iPhone, I called home as the rest of the family were getting ready for Tom and Rachael's wedding, so I guess late morning on Saturday 27 August in the UK. In a role reversal of the phone call I'd received from San just a few days earlier – though it seemed a lifetime ago – I did the hardest thing I've ever had to do. My heart broke again giving the news to Tom's mum and siblings, and at being pretty much as far away from them as it was possible to be. I needed them as much if not more than they needed me. San had sounded reasonably upbeat when answering the phone, at least under the circumstances, but my news quickly changed that, and her face crumpled as she sank to her knees sobbing.

Eventually, her voice cracking with emotion, she agreed with me that we simply couldn't leave Tom indefinitely on life support, even if that was an option, when there was no hope of recovery. The hospital had already broached the possibility of organ donation with me and the following day we quickly decided, after consulting Dan & Liv, that without any evidence that Tom had ever indicated he wouldn't want to donate his organs under such circumstances, we would give our consent for it to happen.

That was, is, us to a T. Big decision to make? No problem, bang, it's done. Ask me to choose between half a dozen parking spaces or San to decide where to eat and chances are we'll wander around for half an hour and end up falling out over it! We agreed that I'd give the hospital the go-ahead to do whatever preparations were required and we would sleep on our decision before confirming our consent. Not that we expected that decision to change, but there was plenty the medics needed to do before Tom's organs could be removed, and it made sense to use that bit of breathing space.

As it turned out, Tom had spent some time before he left for Australia working with his cousin Phil and for some reason – probably because they'd exhausted their football talk for the day – they had discussed organ donation and Tom had declared himself very much in favour. And so, the lives of six people in Australia were about to be prolonged or in some way enhanced as a result of receiving Tom's heart, liver, lungs and kidneys. It felt like the right thing to do, but it offered absolutely no immediate comfort, regardless of any public utterances to the contrary I may have made at the time.

Of course, as time has passed, and we have exchanged correspondence (anonymously of course) with some of the recipients of Tom's organs, we appreciate how important our decision was to so many people and we are happy that we made it. May they all live longer and happier lives.

* * *

San, Dan & Liv bravely attended the wedding, keeping our heart-breaking news to themselves so as not to dampen Tom and Rachael's big day celebrations, and I confirmed our consent to the doctors allowing the ensuing organ donation process to click smoothly into gear. Tom was given another scan a couple of days later on the morning of Monday 29 August which confirmed that he had actually died, probably on the day before although his official date of death would be recorded as the 29th.

Thankfully (small mercies) this avoided the need for any decision on my part to agree to turn off any of the equipment which had been keeping Tom alive, technically at least, though many of the news reports which covered his death insisted that I had indeed had to make that 'heart-breaking decision'.

Over the next two or three days Tom's sister Liv would arrive from the UK, god bless her, having gamely completed her duties as a bridesmaid; Tom's close friend Kay would arrive after a long and torturous journey from a work placement in India; Ryan, another close friend of Tom's and former work colleague on the Scilly Isle of Tresco, who had subsequently moved back to Australia and was about to start making a name for himself in the world of Real Estate, would arrive again having been turned away earlier by the hospital as he wasn't a relative; and a number of members of our Australian family – Sue, Ian, Sam, Pat, Chris and Tiff – would arrive from Melbourne. They were all able to visit Tom before he was taken for the surgery which would harvest his vital organs on the start of their transplant journeys.

As for me, by now I couldn't wait to leave Townsville. The hospital staff and local police had been fantastic, the people of Townsville wonderfully supportive – I received many messages of sympathy, tangible help including offers of lodgings for as long as I was there with lifts to the hospital as and when required, and gifts which included baskets of food, presents which had been hand made by young children, and even some cash donations (which I passed on to the Australian Red Cross hospital accommodation when we eventually left). But once Tom had gone the place held no allure for me.

I had turned down a number of requests for media interviews – both press and TV – since I'd arrived and had even been approached out of the blue by a reporter outside Townsville hospital on the morning after I'd learned of Tom's dire prognosis (but before the news had been released to the media).

I politely declined her request for a few words, and even thanked her for her interest before walking off. A few seconds later she was trotting alongside me and Jamie, filming us on her phone while professing her heartfelt apologies for doing so. "I'm so sorry, I'm so sorry" she kept repeating bizarrely, the footage subsequently appearing on the ABC news website. The whole thing was surreal.

Nevertheless, I didn't want to appear to sneak away from Townsville without conveying my thanks to the local community so arranged, through the hospital's Public Affairs department, to give an interview to The Townsville Bulletin, the local newspaper. They sent a reporter and photographer to interview me and Liv at the hospital, with Ryan Groube, the Public Affairs Manager, sitting in on it.

It was a perfectly reasonable interview during which we gave some background details about Tom and our family and his reasons for being in Australia, and after which we agreed to a few photographs being taken. The front page of the following day's edition of the paper was entirely dedicated to us with the headline 'OUR HERO FOREVER' sitting on top of what we considered a pretty inappropriate photo of us, with Liv almost draped across my shoulders.

I accept that we consented to have the photos taken, but we hadn't seen any of them before publication and let's just say we were a little disappointed, not to say embarrassed, with the one they selected. Worse still, a headline on the inside pages where the story was continued declared 'FATHER'S SYMPATHY FOR ACCUSED'.

During the interview I had professed a degree of sympathy for Ayad's family, his mother in particular, at the same time making it quite clear what my feelings towards Ayad himself were. Although the printed article was faithful to the interview – at least in that it never implied anything we didn't say, though it omitted much of what we did – the accompanying headline was a complete misrepresentation of what I'd said and caused our family further unnecessary distress.

As the article had not even conveyed any thanks from us to the people of Townsville, including the hospital and ICU staff in particular – my whole reason for offering to do the interview – on my return to the UK I sent a 'Thank You Townsville' letter, via email and with a note expressing my disappointment at the initial article and a request for my letter to be simply published in their letters section, to the journalist who had interviewed us.

I received a reply in turn thanking me, apologising for the omissions from the article they had printed, and indicating that the editors of the paper and its sister paper, the Burdekin Advocate which covers the Home Hill area where the hostel was situated, may wish to turn it into a story using quotes from my letter. I was gob smacked.

It was only after I replied with a strongly worded email directly to the editor of the Bulletin refusing them permission to use my letter other than in their letters section, that I then received an acknowledgement from the editor Ben English, and the letter was printed as intended in the letters section. The whole episode left a sour taste.

Liv and I spent a few more days in Townsville, completing formalities with a local funeral parlour for Tom's repatriation, accepting a kind invitation to visit the Billabong Sanctuary where we were able to hold and have our photographs taken with Koalas and Wombats as well as view some other rescued Australian wildlife like kangaroos and crocodiles, and visiting the hostel in Home Hill where the attacks had taken place. The local community there had already planted a couple of trees in honour of Tom and Mia, so it was nice to see them.

However, the Mayor of Burdekin had arranged to take the majority of the backpackers out on her boat on the same day our visit was organised by the local Ayr police department, so it was a quick visit.

(Coincidence or a convenient way to avoid my meeting them as a group? Mia's mum Rosie would shortly launch and run the 'Tom & Mias Legacy' campaign, which would raise questions at the highest levels of the Australian government about the abuse and exploitation of immigrant workers, including backpackers of all nationalities, and the Queensland farming community, which was served by workers from the Home Hill hostel was – and still is – heavily reliant on immigrant labour.

The dual attraction of keeping the backpackers sweet with a nice little jolly while at the same time ensuring the father of one of their murdered colleagues was kept at arm's length may have been a temptation easily succumbed to. Or I may just be indulging my paranoia, who knows?).

I did very briefly meet the hostel owner Shelley who was visibly upset and soon took her leave without saying anything more than hello, as well as half a dozen or so backpackers who hadn't gone on the trip. All had known Tom and relayed their solemn condolences to me and Liv before giving us a guided tour of the hostel, including Tom's room which he had shared with another five backpackers, the kitchen from which Ayad had obtained the knife he used in the attack, and the bathroom were Mia had died and Tom had received his ultimately fatal wounds. It wasn't an enjoyable visit.

We spent our last full day, a Saturday, in Townsville visiting Magnetic Island (Maggie Island to the locals), a popular holiday destination about five miles offshore from Townsville in Cleveland Bay. It was nice to visit and have a quick look around, but we really weren't in the right frame of mind to enjoy it properly and ended up getting a much earlier ferry back to the mainland than we had originally intended.

Back home in the UK, another of Tom's friends from his travels, Cameron Johnson, had made a call via Facebook for a 'Toast for Tom', which would entail anyone who knew Tom (and a few who didn't!), wherever they were in the world, raising a glass in his honour at nine o'clock on the Saturday evening, UK time. This would be six o'clock on the Sunday morning in Queensland and, along with Kay and Larissa (another of Tom's friends made during his travels) and her husband-to-be Peter, we made an early start and headed for the top of Castle Hill in Townsville, having spent a relatively enjoyable evening the night before with all three.

Kay and Larissa had made banners and brought vodka and cranberry juice – a favoured tipple of Tom's – and, in sync with hundreds of Tom's friends all around the world, we toasted Tom's life and mourned his loss again as the sun rose majestically over Maggie Island in the distance.

Even at that time of a Sunday morning however, we couldn't stay for long. The road to the top of Castle Hill would shortly be closed to accommodate a foot race which was due to start later that morning, so we said our goodbyes to Kay, Larissa and Peter and headed out of Townsville for the last time. Tom's friend Ryan, and his parents Russell and Paula, had invited us to spend a few days with them at their lovely home in Cairns, before returning to the UK, and so we pointed our hired car in that direction and started the two hundred mile plus journey which would see us arriving there, after a couple of comfort breaks, about six hours later.

Our stay in Cairns was uneventful, just what we needed. We spent a fascinating day in the tropical rainforest, walked on the beach at Palm Cove and cycled along the beach front with Ryan on bicycles borrowed from Russ and Paula. Russ is a fellow scouser who was brought up in the Old Swan area of Liverpool, just a few short miles from my family home in Kensington (if the affluence and grandeur of the West London area of the same name, with its stately Victorian buildings and embassies, its tourist attractions and its chic boutiques immediately spring to mind, you couldn't be further from the actuality, though having stayed briefly in the West London version when working in the capital, I'd recommend the company of the scousers any day of the week), and we reminisced over familiar landmarks. Russ was particularly amazed that Quinn Cycles on Edge Lane, the main drag from the end of the M62 into Liverpool city centre, which was going strong when we were both young lads, was still operating from the same premises.

Liv and Paula hit it off straight away too and it resulted in a welcome few days of relative calm before we finally returned to the UK where the new 'normal' for our reduced family would begin. In truth, over four years on we're still coming to terms with it. We probably never will.

* * *

The journey home was a lot more relaxed and comfortable than the outward journey had been. The most direct route from Cairns to the UK was via Hong Kong with Cathay Pacific, with whom coincidentally the British Consulate appeared to have a close working relationship, and I'd been happy to give my credit card details to Laura Morgan to enable her to book flights on our behalf. It was one less thing to worry about at the time.

Russ had jokingly apologised for the weather while we'd been in Cairns, as it had more resembled a changeable British summer than what they were used to enjoying (or enduring?) in their own little corner of the tropics, and I'd reciprocated by apologising for bringing the British weather with us. Apparently, the weather's a staple topic of conversation for us Brits wherever we may be in the world!

Typically though, the weather when we arrived at Cairns airport had reverted to seasonal type, as if mocking us for having the temerity to leave it in favour of colder climes. It was meltingly hot. Having dropped off the hire car and proceeded to the Cathay Pacific check-in desks we were delighted to be informed that our booking had been upgraded 'gratis' to business class for both legs of the homeward journey.

As we left the desk, we were approached by a Cathay Pacific stewardess who told us simply that "He was a true hero", which Tom always would be to us of course but it perhaps meant even more than I'd expected it to coming from a complete stranger, and we set off for the business class lounge with slightly more of a spring in our step. I'd used dedicated airport lounges before (without ever travelling in business class) but this was Liv's first time and she was thrilled with the oasis of air-conditioned calm and comfort, not to mention the food and drink! The captain of our flight to Hong Kong even introduced himself to us and commiserated with our loss. We thought it incredibly thoughtful and classy of Cathay Pacific and will always be grateful for their kindness.

If we'd been impressed with the service so far, the actual journey home was an experience both of us will remember, and perhaps aspire to repeat under happier circumstances, for a long time. From the seats which reclined into a fully flat single bed to the entertainment system to the amenity kit (sleeping mask, slipper socks, ear plugs and various toiletries) to the catering and cabin service, both flights, if not an absolute joy, were as far removed from the 'cattle class' economy flights we'd taken on our separate outward-bound journeys as it was possible for us to conceive.

At the end of our seven hours plus flight from Cairns, we descended into Hong Kong under cover of darkness, the island twinkling below us with its myriad sparkling lights - street, building, traffic - providing a bejewelled welcome, and were greeted off the plane by a member of Cathay Pacific's airport staff who escorted us to one of their very own luxurious business lounges to await our twelve and a half hour second leg flight to Manchester. The lounge must have been as long as the playing surface at Anfield, and almost as wide.

Our short stopover wasn't long enough to allow an impromptu trip into Hong Kong itself – I doubt we'd have been in the mood for that anyway – or to make use of the available sleeping quarters, but the luxury showers were very welcome as were the three or four individually styled restaurants catering for a plethora of different tastes from travellers of all nations. We even made use of the library-like working lounge with its comfortable armchairs, desks and internet access to the wider world.

Mind bogglingly, to us less-seasoned travellers at least, there was a separate first-class lounge, of apparently similar size, right next door to our business class lounge. How the other half (or maybe 1 percent) live! As keen as we were to complete the final leg of our journey home and our family reunion, we did linger as long as possible in the lounge when our flight was eventually called.

Just under 13 hours after boarding the flight for the final leg of our journey in Hong Kong we were back in the UK, landing at Manchester airport to be met by Mike Price, our Police Family Liaison Officer from Cheshire constabulary. Mike had been providing support for our family more or less since just after I'd left for Australia two weeks earlier and had met Liv a few times before she joined me there. They greeted each other like old friends as, again, we were taken off the plane first and whisked through immigration control and customs. We were again grateful to Cathay Pacific as one of their staff collected our luggage and arranged for a damaged suitcase to be replaced free of charge, before we left the airport with Mike via a little-used back-entrance.

After my arrival at Townsville had been greeted by what I'd imagined to be a media frenzy (but in reality was probably just a few reporters and cameramen with flashing light bulbs, albeit a few more than I'd anticipated) we had expressed some concern that a similar welcome from the British media might await us in Manchester, and Mike had consequently arranged for a more surreptitious departure.

A half hour drive through the Cheshire countryside had me reflecting on the previous two weeks as I mentally prepared for our reunion with San and Dan. In that short space of time San and I had lost our first-born child in horrific circumstances, our 35th wedding anniversary and both of our 58th birthdays had passed with us on opposite sides of the world to each other and, for a brief period at least, our family had been the centre of a lot of unwelcome, if understandable, media attention.

Dan had been staying with his mum during my absence and had dealt with a myriad of callers to the house, well-wishers and media alike, while also trying to start to come to terms with his own grief at the loss of Tom, his very close friend as well as his elder brother. Our family's mettle had been put to the test and would continue to be over the coming months and years.

Before the end of September Tom would be repatriated and we would visit him at rest at Alan Finneron's Funeral Directors in Congleton – harrowing for us all, but particularly so for San and Dan who had not seen him since he'd left for Australia at the start of the year – before attending his funeral at a packed St Mary's Church in Astbury near Congleton.

Dan, his cousin Phil, Tom's best mate Scott Richards (who had come late into Tom's life but the pair had developed a wonderful bromance in a few short years), Jamie and another two of Tom's childhood friends Adam Glover and Rob Nichol, sombrely carried Tom's coffin, all sporting an official LFC Club tie kindly provided by the club. Tom would definitely have approved and revelled in the obvious mischievousness, given that outside of Dan and Phil the pall bearers were fans of Arsenal, Everton, City and United.

I gave the eulogy on behalf of me and San, a task I far from relished but unexpectedly drew some comfort from as it at least offered me a final chance to sing Tom's praises to several hundred mourners. Dan and Liv and a number of Tom's friends, including Jamie and Claire who had flown in from Bangkok, paid their own heart-warming and heart-breaking tributes.

The church was packed and the congregation included one or two minor political dignitaries and, in anticipation of this and a possible unwelcome media presence (which never materialised), we had also decided to hold a separate service at the crematorium a few miles away in Macclesfield on the following day. This was a more private affair attended by family and close friends (ours and Tom's) only, which was again led by our ministerial friend Heather.

An emotional Dan Nash gave a reading and Tom's former fiancée Kay her own even more emotional eulogy, and the whole congregation sang You'll Never Walk Alone from their seats at the end. It was very moving.

Then we went home and watched Liverpool win 2-1 at Swansea on the box. Even Scott, an Evertonian, gave a quiet little air-punch when our goals went in. A week or so earlier, as a family we had also attended an emotional memorial service for Mia held in Derbyshire, where we met Rosie and Stewart for the first time at a packed all-faith service in St Mary's Church, Wirksworth.

Since then, the adjustment to our new family circumstances has continued, and I suspect will continue for the rest of our lives, helped greatly by our local community and a wonderful set of friends and neighbours – both ours and Tom's – who, without a single exception that I can recall, have stood beside us in our grief and loss and, lest we forget, their own grief and loss as well. Tom's actions on the evening he received his fatal injuries have been recognised by the posthumous award of the Queen's Gallantry Medal (QGM), presented to his mum at Buckingham Palace by the Prince William, Duke of Cambridge on what would have been Tom's 33rd birthday.

Even as late as the summer of 2020, the Court of Directors of The Royal Humane Society of Australasia bestowed on Tom the 'Clarke Posthumous Medal', awarded for the most outstanding case considered that year.

Immediately after Tom was attacked, the Queensland Premier Annastacia Palaszczuk stood up in the Queensland Parliament and praised Tom for his selfless act, declaring that she had personally nominated him for a bravery award, and followed that up with a private phone call to me, reiterating what she'd announced in Parliament. We remain hopeful that in 2021, nearly five years later, such an award will finally be confirmed.

Back home, local radio stations Silk FM and Signal Radio, at the behest of their listeners, made Tom the recipient of their annual 'Pride of Cheshire' and inaugural 'Bravery' awards respectively, and he has also been memorialised by Cheshire East Council (with an inscribed bench and tree at Tatton Park in Knutsford dedicated by the then Mayor Arthur Moran), creation of a 'Garden of Reflection' in Congleton by the Town council, introduction of the annual 'Tom Jackson Football Award' at Congleton High School, dedication of a memorial plaque at the entrance to Quinta Primary School in Congleton and, perhaps even most wonderfully, the commissioning and installation of a memorial bench on a local field by friends from Tom's schooldays.

'Newby field' is at the end of Newby Court on the same estate that Tom and many of his friends grew up on in Congleton and was where they spent most of their out-of-school hours playing football and living the dream. The inscription reads '*In Loving Memory of Tom 'Jacko' Jackson 1985-2016. This was his Wembley*'. Fantastic.

* * *

In the annals of 'memorials for Tom', the second weekend of May 2017 was a particularly memorable one for us and, we hope, for anyone who shared some or all of it with us. As part of a charity fund-raising weekend, we organised the 'Tom Jackson – Forever in Our Hearts' Ball, a black-tie event which took place on the Saturday evening.

Friends, a plethora of businesses – both local and further afield – and big names in the world of sport, donated countless prizes for the silent auction and raffle, both of which took place after an excellent three course meal for over one hundred paying guests, made up primarily of Tom's family and friends, at Congleton Town Hall.

The Town Hall is an impressive Victorian Gothic building, and its Grand Hall which hosted the ball impresses with its exposed beams and spectacular Minstrels Gallery. This was augmented on the night by the sterling work of Karen Swindells and her team of volunteer helpers who made a fantastic job of decorating it to a magnificent standard which contributed hugely to the special 'feel' of the evening.

Gentle sounds from an all-female string quartet welcomed guests as they arrived and accepted a glass of fizz or a beer while buying their raffle tickets, and continued to provide a soothing musical backdrop to the babble of excited conversation during the meal, made even more so by guests making their sealed bids on the prizes up for auction.

A group of magicians, led by local star of the genre Nick Barnes, who had happily made themselves available for the evening at Nick's request, wowed each table as dinner was being served, a memorable part of the event. After the auction, guests happily danced the night away to tunes from a local disco, continuing the vibe of the whole evening which reflected our stated wish for everyone to celebrate Tom's life by doing what he loved most – having a great time.

But the undoubted highlight of the evening was the silent auction. Angie Nash and Liv had opened the occasion by officially introducing the 'Sounds Interesting' string quartet, passing on our thanks to everyone involved and letting guests know the format of the evening which included plans for the auction. Towards the end of the meal the sealed bids were collected, and Angie then had the job of inspecting them and identifying the winners of the individual lots. Less than an hour after the meal was complete Angie was ready to reveal the winning bids, and I swear I could feel the tension in the room.

The star of the show was a boxing glove signed by British and soon to be World Heavyweight Champion Anthony Joshua, kindly donated by ITI Network Services, which attracted the highest bid of the night from Glenn Holmes, father of Tom's friend David, contributing to over £7000 raised in total along with more than £1300 profit from ticket sales for the event and over £1500 in cash donations.

Tom's friends had also organised a Charity football match to be played the following day at the Booth Street home of Congleton Town FC, our hometown team for the last 30 years. Me, at the ripe old age of 58, and Dan captained opposing teams made up of Tom's family and friends. Willie Stevenson, a Liverpool stalwart from the 1960's and one of my dad's favourite players presented the 'Tom Jackson Memorial Trophy' – kindly donated by Congleton Town Council – to the winning team (mine, obviously!) at the end of the game, with San and Liv presenting the medals – all winners, no losers – to players, managers and match officials (Nigel Poole and his youthful assistants) alike.

Donations from a crowd of several hundred people and a percentage of the takings from the bar – thanks again to Congleton Town FC who also let us use their ground and facilities free of charge – swelled the money raised over the weekend by a further £1800, giving a final total raised for charity approaching £12000, a fantastic amount and a worthy tribute to the many people who put in so much hard work to make it happen and ensure its success.

* * *

In April 2018, Liverpool FC were the talk of the football world again following their three-goal demolition of tournament favourites Manchester City in a Champions League first leg quarter final tie at Anfield. It was a game I missed as I was back in Australia to attend the Mental Health Court hearing in Brisbane the following day, at which Tom's attacker was scheduled to appear.

After more than 18 months being monitored and assessed by four different psychiatrists, Smail Ayad was adjudged to have been 'unsound of mind' when he committed the attacks and all criminal charges against him were dropped.

I understood the decision and said as much when interviewed the following day for the 'A Current Affair' Australian TV programme on the 9News channel. Not quite the same as believing the decision to be 'right', as the programme anchor reported I'd said when introducing the segment.

Who's to say if it was right? What would or could be deemed to be right under the circumstances? An eye for an eye? Not for me. But then again, should we simply turn the other cheek? What we did know was that due process had been followed, a group of independent, suitably qualified psychiatrists had assessed him and, from a legal perspective that was the end of the line. I understood and accepted that.

Ayad currently remains detained in a mental health facility in Queensland, where his condition continues to be assessed as he awaits deportation back to France, his homeland.

* * *

So, August 23rd. It'll be here again soon enough. The start of, as Dan has labelled it, our "annual festival of misery". Every. Fucking. Year.

9

TOM Q.G.M.

fter he blessed us with his arrival on 7 November 1985, Tom threw himself into the challenge of living his life to the full, cramming more adventures and experiences into it than many would manage in an eternity.

He was actually due a fortnight earlier, and his arrival two weeks late foretold an attitude towards punctuality from which, no matter how hard we tried, we could never dissuade him. Tom lived in, and for, the moment and that usually meant he arrived or got things done at the last 'moment' possible. Long term plans or arrangements were anathema to him.

San's labour lasted for 27 hours and towards the end of it she was exhausted and in no little pain as you can imagine. By this stage I had started to become increasingly angry at my yet to arrive first born. How dare he put his mum through this ordeal, two weeks late and still dragging it out. My concern for San increased as the labour went on – *and then Tom arrived.*

Well, of course, I immediately forgot all about my poor exhausted wife and was instantly besotted with this bawling, red-faced, stringy bundle of noise. It was a pattern in our relationship that hardly changed over the next 30 years – our cheeky, charming son often pushing the limits, and our patience, only for his charm offensive to win out in the end usually ending up with Tom's desired result.

When he was very young, he suffered badly with croup and so on occasions

I'd strip down to my waist and Tom down to his nappy and boil an open kettle in the bathroom to allow the steam to ease his breathing. It was 30 to 40 minutes of time together for just the two of us which I never appreciated enough at the time but is a treasured memory now

Bedtime was story time and amongst Tom's favourites was, naturally, Thomas the Tank Engine. We had all the ladybird books (still do in fact) and after a while Tom knew them all off by heart. One particular evening I remember I had a thumping headache and decided it would be a good idea to finish more quickly by skipping pages as I read that night's story to him. Bad move!

"No daddy, that's not what happens next. This is what happens ..."

and he'd go on to recite word perfectly the section I'd missed. My strategy proved to be entirely counterproductive as the telling of the story took twice as long as usual due to Tom constantly filling in the gaps!

When Tom was three, I took him to his first football match at Anfield. It was a reserve game between Liverpool and Everton, and we went with a friend, my old boss Alan Mason, and his young son Paul. Tom wasn't remotely interested in the football and spent a lot of his time running up and down the steps in the huge main stand which must have seemed never ending to him. This only stopped when a policeman stepped in and politely suggested he return to and remain in his seat. For one of the few times in his life he was very quiet for a while after that!

Nevertheless, it wasn't long before he was a regular at Anfield with me, and his young brain, seemingly insatiable, began to soak up an interminable supply of facts and knowledge about the game we loved. His knowledge quickly became encyclopaedic and I would often defer to him when challenged on facts and statistics about the club. He became a true football aficionado.

When he was 16 we decided to surprise him with a trip to Barcelona for an important Champions League game. The trip was booked secretly months in advance, and in the weeks leading up to the game I teased him with memories of a trip we'd made the previous season – also to Barcelona – and how we'd be missing out this time, but never mind I'm sure there'd be other opportunities in the future. On the morning of the game, I crept into his room to wake him up gently.

"Come on son" I said as his eyes fluttered open "we're off to Barcelona".

He looked at me incredulously for a moment and then sighed as he closed his eyes and said "I'm just dreaming aren't I?".

It was such a lovely moment when he realised it was for real and bounced out of bed – not something that Tom did very often!

A month or so later, one of Tom's teachers – who shall remain nameless to protect the guilty – suggested to Tom that the reason he failed to pass an exam by a couple of percent was because he 'took a day off to go to that football match'. Many of our teachers do a great, often underappreciated, job but I can tell you now that the shared memories we had of that trip will be one of many sources of joy and comfort to me for as long as I live. I know Tom loved every minute of it. There are many occasions I think I maybe should have done or said something different where Tom – or indeed Dan and Liv - are concerned. That trip isn't one of them.

No list of football memories would be complete of course without mention-ing the Miracle of Istanbul in 2005. Suffice to say that experience was *the* highlight of Tom's teenage years.

Tom also played football, with no little distinction for local sides Vale Juniors, Haslington Villa and Congleton Town Youth as well as supporting Liverpool up and down the country and across Europe – but there was so much more to him than that.

He loved his school days at Quinta and Congleton High, where he made so many good friends, and where I think it's fair to say that his achievements centred more around the sports field, especially in football and athletics, than in the classroom. Nevertheless, he went on to gain his BTEC in Sports and Exercise Science at South Cheshire College after which he tried a number of '9 to 5's which frankly weren't for him.

He soon acquired the travel bug, perhaps inspired by his brother Dan's earlier trips to Borneo, Thailand and South America, and got into the routine of working away in hospitality during the summer, first on the Scilly Isle of Tresco, followed by successive seasons on Herm, one of the Channel Islands (where he met his soul-mate Kay). During these times he would save to fund trips further afield between summer seasons, and always with new friends he had made during the summer. He visited India twice, as well as many other locations across South East Asia and he particularly enjoyed visiting his great friends Jamie and Claire in Bangkok.

Prior to Australia, his most recent trip had seen him spend well over a year in Phnom Penh in Cambodia where, to his great surprise and delight he discovered a passion for working with children at the Western International School, where he brought the English language to life for them in his own novel ways, even turning to 'rap' on one occasion to get his lesson across. The children he taught were devastated when he left the school and made a lovely tribute to 'Teacher Tom' on Facebook after he died – a true testament to the impact he made during his short time there.

Tom also loved to write and indeed aspired to be a journalist, planning to take a specialist course when he eventually returned from Australia. However, his travels had honed his developing sense of social and political awareness – being a scouser by heritage, if not by birth, he was naturally inclined to trumpet the cause of the downtrodden, and hated bullying, unfairness and injustice in any form - and he was very cynical about mainstream media and western politics.

He came home from Cambodia and promptly horrified us with his stated desire to become a war correspondent in Syria, where he wanted to bring to the world what he called the *true* story of what is happening there. 'News without Agenda' he called it. We suggested, hopefully, that perhaps for his next foray into journalism he might instead consider writing football match reports for the local paper (wherever that might be), and indeed we heard no more about his idea to be a war correspondent during the rest of the time he was with us.

However, just before he left, he confided in me that he did have some potential irons in the fire once he reached Australia to develop the idea of reporting 'News without Agenda', and if anything came of it, he might end up putting himself in harm's way.

The last time I saw him was as I said a tearful goodbye at Manchester airport (the tears were all mine, Tom was actually bouncing as he was stopping off with Jamie and Claire in Bangkok for a few days on the way!). On the one hand I didn't know when I'd see him again, but on the other I didn't think for a second that I never would.

It was a great, ultimately ironic, relief when Tom got in touch to say he'd finally started the farm work he needed to complete to qualify to extend his visa for an additional year in Australia. During our last conversation the day before he was attacked, he reiterated his plans to stay down under for as long as possible, saying he had just started to find his feet there after a difficult first few months, and aiming to find sponsorship for an even longer stay further down the line.

Tom wasn't perfect – who is? - but his heart was truly in the right place. As his mum often said, he was a beautiful, unique soul with a great sense of humour. Though many things to many people, above all Tom was a friend who valued friendships highest of all. To paraphrase a song title from a family favourite Disney film – 'You never had a friend like Tom'.

I haven't heard that unmistakable, infectious, high pitched laugh of his, which told you Tom was about and good times were being had, for such a long time now.

I am bereft.

10

HERE WE GO GATHERING CUPS – IN JUNE!

I t's approaching 7 o'clock on the morning of Saturday 27 June 2020 and I'm up early again after another restless night, the second in succession, a product of the stifling heat and humidity no doubt – but also something else.

Sitting in my favourite armchair, the conservatory pleasantly cool under a grey non-descript sky, my Apple weather app foretelling the imminent unwelcome arrival of stormy showers which are expected to be with us for the next week or so, it's not the fact that I am feeling ever so slightly regretful that our summer holiday – a cruise around the Mediterranean - which should have started today, was postponed some time ago because of the Corona virus pandemic which has swept over the planet since the start of the year.

Only slightly regretful mind you, aware as I am of my privileged position in being able to afford a regular annual holiday and indeed of the fact that for many people, this year has brought a lot more heartache than the relative triviality of re-scheduling a summer break.

That's what June normally means to me. Summer holidays and lazy weekends. Barbecues with good friends – their barbecues to be fair, as I've never really got the point of setting fire to a bag of charcoal and throwing some meat on it, when there's a perfectly good and serviceable kitchen appliance capable of providing a similar result in a much easier and more efficient manner sitting idly no more than ten yards away.

Father's Day, my mum's birthday (on a sadder note also the anniversary of the day my dad passed away), my father-in-law's birthday. Lots of birthdays, weddings and Summer balls. It's a month of recovery and rejuvenation, when spring showers turn into summer storms, and occasionally if we're really lucky, a rise in the mercury and a break in the clouds (yes, I am in the UK!). When batteries start to be recharged after the wearying winter months, in preparation for the wearying winter months that will surely follow.

Over the years the month of June has seen us enjoy the Cypress tree laden landscapes of the Tuscan hills, the understated charm and natural beauty of the Languedoc in Southern France and sun-drenched European coastlines from Porto to Sicily, Venice to Trieste, Barcelona to Cadiz, the Algarve to the Balearics.

I will happily recommend the ice cream in Dubrovnik or Zadar on Croatia's Dalmatian coast, a thirst-quenching pint with a spot of lunch in one of the welcoming cafes in the central square in Montenegro's Kotor, or a spectacular coach trip to Budva on the Montenegrin Riviera, all from experiences garnered during the month named in honour of the queen of the Roman gods.

Oh, and don't forget to try a gyros on the beautiful Greek island of Corfu if you ever get the chance. I had my first one for lunch sitting outside a pleasant little café on a baking hot day in June 2011, on the same cruise holiday we met our good friends Phil & Mollie Shrewsbury for the first time. Glorious. (Speaking of Phil, his fledgling football career with Notts County was cruelly cut short before it could get off the ground, courtesy of a broken metatarsal - in the days when it was still called a broken bone in the foot - decades before David Beckham made that the 'must-have' injury for any self-respecting celebrity footballer in the eyes of the British media. I suppose it also meant Mollie's own status as a WAG was similarly curtailed!).

And while I'm in the mood for making recommendations, may I suggest another book? 'Here We Go Gathering Cups in May' is one of many written and published following Liverpool's historic comeback in the Champions

League final in Istanbul in 2005, and features a chapter on each of our 5 European Cup wins (up to that point), and each from the experiences of a different fan.

Inspired by a famous Liverpool banner bearing the same triumphal message, and that a simple but clever play on the old English children's song 'Here we go gathering nuts in May', it harks back to a time – which doesn't feel *that* long ago when you're my age – when Liverpool FC regularly concluded the season awash with silverware.

Between 1964 and 1990 Liverpool won 27 major domestic and European trophies. At an average of one trophy (not including lesser trinkets like the Charity Shield and the European Super Cup) per season during that time, the haul included 6 doubles and a treble, with Bob Paisley alone presiding over the accrual of six League Championships, three League Cups, three European Cups and a UEFA Cup in just nine years as manager.

But that's May. From a football perspective, that's when most of the gongs are handed out. It's what May is for. Football wise, June is for pointless end of season international friendlies where exhausted players choose between pulling out of national squads and risking banishment to the international wilderness, or the potential for early burn-out and shortened domestic careers. It's for international tournaments which, despite – or maybe because of - the eager anticipation of national glory in the build ups, seldom do much for the national mood other than darken it.

A time to prepare for the important stuff which starts again in earnest in August, but really starts in July when the transfer window opens, and players return for pre-season training. June is a club football vacuum and I mostly welcome that. You have to go back to 1947 to find anything of significance happening on the pitch when, due to the extremely harsh winter which preceded it, the league title was decided in June.

Even then, Liverpool defeated title favourites Wolves 2-1 at Molineux in their final match on the last day of *May* to edge ahead of them and Manchester United by a single point. It wasn't until 14 June when Stoke City lost to Sheffield United in the final league game of the season that Liverpool were finally crowned the first post-war league champions. (On the same night we completed a treble of sorts by also beating Everton 2-1 at Anfield in the final of the Liverpool Senior Cup, having dispatched Bury by the same score line at Anfield in the final of the Lancashire Senior Cup the previous week. Let me recommend another excellent book – 'At The End of the Storm: The Remarkable Story of Liverpool FC's Greatest Ever League Title Triumph – 1946/47' – for the full story of that memorable season).

* * *

But then along came 2019...

Early in the year, San, as is her usual practice at that time, set about organising our summer holiday. We'd had our 'extra special' holiday the previous summer when, to celebrate our 60th birthdays which occurred 12 days apart in August and September, we'd sailed on the Queen Mary 2 from Southampton to New York.

Hiring a car, we then spent 10 days visiting Niagara Falls and Niagara On The Lake (a charming chocolate box of a town about half an hour from the Falls on the Canadian side of the border); Boston, where we stayed with a lovely, ever so slightly eccentric couple in their beautifully eclectic town house in Somerville (even managing to take in the Reds 2-1 win at Leicester City from the packed confines of The Phoenix Landing pub, home of the Boston branch of the LFC Supporters Club in Cambridge); and then Connecticut before we spent four hectic days revisiting the sights in Manhattan, where we'd lived for a few months back in 1982, to conclude our visit on American soil.

The weeklong return journey to Southampton on the same ship that brought us was a wonderful way to round off our dream trip and gave us the opportunity to recharge after our whirlwind tour of the North-Eastern States.

Our holiday *modus operandi* over a number of years has been to cruise one year and drive to Southern Europe the next, and though we'd driven (a lot) in America, the icing on the holiday cake, amongst many great experiences, was the two weeks cruising which started and finished it, so this year we planned to drive as far as Tuscany in Italy.

"I'm looking at the first 3 weeks in June" San informed me.

"June 1st is a Saturday, so we could leave then, spend a week on the drive down through France and northern Italy and arrive in Arezzo on Saturday the 8th. What do you think?".

"Sounds good to me" I replied.

"Season will be well over by then and I'll be more than ready for my jollies".

"Oh, actually, the Champions League Final is on the 1st, shall we hold off just in case?" San updated me optimistically.

"I think that's a bit of a long shot isn't it?" I continued the conversation. "Especially the way we're going in the League. Not sure we'll go all the way in both".

"Tell you what, we'll leave on the Monday instead. If we get to the final that'll give us the chance to watch it, and the following day to get over any celebrations!" concluded San.

And what a good job she did.

As we all now know, we enjoyed a record-breaking league runners-up season – small consolation – and made it all the way to the Champions League Final in Madrid. After coming through our group as runners-up to PSG, winning all our games at home and losing all of them on the road, superb away performances at Bayern Munich and Porto in the first two knock-out rounds deservedly put us through to a semi-final with Barcelona, the first leg of which took place at the Camp Nou.

I'd say we put in another superb away performance, dominating possession, creating and missing a plethora of excellent chances, and winning lots of admirers, not least from within the Barcelona dressing room. But we lost 3-0. A couple of goals from Messi and one from ex-red Luis Suarez seemingly making the second leg at Anfield a lost cause.

That sense of impending doom was only exacerbated on the day of the game by news of the loss through injury of two thirds of our first choice attacking trio – Mo Salah and Bobby Firmino – and who were then joined at half-time by our Scottish fullback revelation Andy Robertson, following some typical skulduggery from Suarez, though at least by then we did have a one goal advantage, courtesy of Firmino's replacement Divock Origi. It looked like at least some pride might be restored.

What followed is now writ large in Anfield folklore.

Gini Wijnaldum, affronted after being left on the subs bench at the start, replaced the injured Robertson, and proceeded to take his frustrations out on the hapless Catalonian defence, scoring twice within a couple of minutes to level the aggregate score before the second half was 15 minutes old. The already electric Anfield atmosphere, super-charged by the early Divock goal, was now at fever pitch, the crowd sensing the hitherto seemingly impossible outcome to be very much on.

With just over 10 minutes to go, following a largely sterile period – on the pitch if not in the stands - where Liverpool appeared to take a breather and Barcelona tried to clear their heads, local young prodigy Trent Alexander-Arnold, still only 20 years old and excelling at right fullback, with a second consecutive Champions League final firmly in his sights, cleverly won a corner at the Kop end.

Even more cleverly, following observations from the first leg in Barcelona where the home team appeared to lose concentration on occasion when the ball went dead, Trent feinted to leave the taking of the corner to Xherdan Shaqiri, before turning back quickly and drilling the ball to Origi, unmarked just outside the six yard box, to finish a still difficult chance into the roof of the net.

Anfield, eventually, erupted. Not only had Trent's feint taken the Barcelona players by surprise but seemingly a large part of the crowd as well, me included, with common refrains after the celebrations briefly subsided being 'Who scored?' and 'How did that happen?'.

The rest of the game was played out in a cacophony of celebration, a clearly shaken Barcelona doing little to threaten the away goal which would still have taken them through to the Final. The decibel level climbed again as the final whistle blew, confirming our 1st June date with destiny in Madrid, and San's prescience when finalising our holiday bookings.

The following Sunday we played our final home game of the season. Sandwiched between the two Barcelona games we'd won a thrilling game at Newcastle 3-2 with the latest of a number of late goals throughout the season, scored by Divock Origi. So tense had the conclusion to that game been that, not for the first time, I'd opted to avoid the last few minutes after Divock's goal by going for a long walk round the estate, only returning home when I received a text from San telling me that the game had finished in our favour.

That win had put us a couple of points ahead of Pep Guardiola's Manchester City at the top of the table, but they'd responded with a dramatic win themselves against Leicester City a few days later to take back top place with just the final league game of the season remaining for both teams. We now needed to beat Wolves at Anfield and hope City failed to beat struggling Brighton at the Amex Stadium on the south coast.

For a few brief disorienting minutes, it seemed the euphoria of the semi-final comeback might be repeated as a slightly lacklustre Liverpool took the lead, and rumours swept Anfield that Brighton had done likewise against City. By the time the rumours had been confirmed, City had recovered to take the lead themselves and we knew that dream was over, a fact underlined when City eventually ran out comfortable 4-1 winners.

Nevertheless, our own eventual 2-0 win against Wolves left us with an incredible 97 points, a tally only bettered twice in the history of topflight English football. City had done it with an unbelievable 100 points in the previous season and, unfortunately for us, with 98 points had bettered it this season too. We could only congratulate them as worthy champions before turning our thoughts to the looming Champions League final in Madrid (if looming is not too dramatic to describe a game still three weeks away).

Between us, the family have four season tickets. Two, which have been in the family since the mid-1970s and belonged to my parents until my dad became too infirm to attend regularly in the late noughties, are for seats a few rows behind the dugouts in the main stand and the other two, which we've had since 1987, give us access to the lower tier of the Sir Kenny Dalglish Stand close to the Kop.

Although we'd attended all the home games in the Champions League during the season, we hadn't attended any of the away games, which meant our only hope of getting tickets for the final was through the club ballot process. As we were due to leave on holiday shortly after the game, we were both happy to watch it on the box anyway, but unbelievably the Electoral Reform Services who ran the ballot came up trumps for us. As San doesn't fly, Tom's good friend Ryan, who we viewed as a lucky omen, was the grateful recipient of her ticket and I booked a day trip with a flight leaving from John Lennon Airport at 8.30 on the day of the game, returning in the early hours of the following morning.

There are a myriad of eloquent accounts available in the public domain of the pre-match build-up in Madrid, the game itself and the post-match celebrations, all of which do the occasion far more justice than I could possibly attempt to emulate here, so I won't. As I've mentioned elsewhere, it's always been all about the game and the result for me.

So, in that vein, Mo Salah scored a first minute penalty after Spurs Moussa Sissoko handled in the area, after which there followed 86 largely uneventful minutes - a brief 15 minute period aside where Alisson Becker demonstrated his mettle by keeping a couple of decent Spurs efforts out - until Divock Origi scored Liverpool's second goal to put the result beyond doubt with just a few minutes to go.

Uneventful though those intervening minutes may have been, each one felt like an age such was my nervousness throughout. As Divock's precise left-footed drive flew low past Hugo Lloris in the Spurs goal, the release of emotions from every Liverpool fan in the Wanda Metropolitano Stadium, home of Atletico Madrid, was palpable. I remember running at, jumping on, and bear hugging complete strangers, words and other sounds cascading from my mouth seemingly of their own volition, as if escaping the maelstrom of emotions fighting for dominance within.

When the final whistle sounded a few minutes later, signalling to the world that this Liverpool team were the new and worthy Champions of Europe, it was impossible to stop the tears from flowing. A guy next to me was with his young son and as he proudly proclaimed this to be his lad's first final, I recalled the last time we'd triumphed in this tournament, with a victory universally acclaimed as the Miracle of Istanbul.

That was Tom's first Champions League final (and mine for that matter – we made it to Athens a couple of years later as well), and we had celebrated together in the Ataturk Stadium, still disbelieving of what we'd just witnessed in a game which started and finished on two different days in a city which started and finished on two different continents. I like to believe that somehow somewhere Tom had managed to see this one. Hopefully with my dad and our Alan enjoying a celebratory drink beside him. Knowing Tom, nothing would surprise me!

A fantastic start to June then was supplemented by a three-week holiday basking in the afterglow of our 6th European Cup triumph, the highlights of which were a week spent on an organic Tuscan vineyard in Arezzo which we used as a base to visit Florence, Siena and Cortona, all of which we'd visited on previous holidays and all stunningly photogenic in their own way, and four nights in the tiny hamlet of Lezzeno on the shores of the peaceful and beyond beautiful Lake Como, from where we took a day out to visit Milan.

On the way down we also spent two nights and a day at Vernazza, one of the five towns which make up the ruggedly picturesque Cinque Terre in northern Italy. The thoroughly enjoyable day we spent there was book-ended by two contrasting experiences.

Cars are not allowed in the heart of Vernazza, so we parked at a small park & ride facility on the outskirts of town. As we'd risen a bit later than planned, we arrived after the early morning rush had passed and were the only passengers for the minibus which operated between the car park and the town. Just as we were about to leave, I realised I'd left my cap in the car and rushed back to retrieve it. It was the cap I'd purchased for the final in Madrid and was suitably monikered 'Madrid 2019'.

"Mustn't forget this" I said to our driver, and owner of the park & ride enterprise, who answered to the name Ivano. "Liverpool, Champions of Europe, mustn't forget it".

Ivano smiled for a moment and then, apparently realising what I'd just said, replied in heavily accented broken English "Liverpool, you are from Liverpool, yes?"

"Yes" I repeated, "Champions of Europe", basking again in the knowledge and the fact that Ivano appeared to be suitably impressed.

"Every day I meet people from England. From London, Birmingham, Cardiff" (I didn't have the heart to correct him). "Every time I ask – 'you are from Liverpool, yes?' – and always they say 'no'. Today I don't ask, and you are from Liverpool, yes" he beamed.

He was starting to get a little emotional at this point and explained that he hadn't seen his son for a couple of years. Named Alessio, his son worked in the 'Manhattan Bar' in Liverpool city centre (Fenwick Street to be precise). It turned out that Ivano had advised him to go to England to develop his English language skills and he'd ended up in Liverpool, which he loved. Ivano was so delighted that he'd eventually met someone from Liverpool in Vernazza that we promised to look Alessio up on our return, a pledge we kept a few months later when we stunned Alessio by turning up at the bar with a selfie of us with his dad, and he surprised his dad by sending him a selfie with us. More warm and fuzzies and we also got a free drink out of it. Everyone was happy.

Back on holiday in Vernazza, a touristic amble around the small town followed being dropped by Ivano in the centre, after which we decided to walk part of the 'Sentiero Azzuro' - the Cinque Terre trail - that being the High Trail which links Vernazza to Monterosso. The most striking views of the region are reportedly gained from the Ligurian Sea, an arm of the Mediterranean, but though it was a beautiful summer day, sunny, clear and seasonably hot, it was also quite windy and consequently the boat trip we had planned to take wasn't available. So, Shanks' pony it was.

As the crow flies it's a relatively short distance between the two towns, less than three miles, but as neither of us are crows it was far from a cakewalk. The rugged trail, starting with a set of rather steep man-made steps from the centre of Vernazza, climbs high and steeply above the Ligurian Sea, and provides many opportunities to pause and take in the spectacular views – of Vernazza as you edge away from the port, of Monterosso as you edge towards it, and all points in between.

At that time of year the trail was very busy, with visitors from all over the world, the terrain often less than completely firm underfoot, and the sun high and hot. Consequently, progress was a pretty slow and arduous ninety minutes or so and we were more than ready to refuel with a light Italian lunch and a long Italian beer (Diet Coke for San!) when we reached the busy Monterosso town centre. Following lunch, we again ambled around the town until a sudden, if brief, downpour turned our thoughts to getting back to Vernazza. Walking the trail again was never an option, so we purchased a couple of tickets for the short two- or three-minute journey to Vernazza and found a place on the platform to await the train.

A couple of minutes before the train was due, a message in Italian was relayed over the station speakers. The only bit of it I recognised was our platform number and as the train arrived at the appointed time, we climbed aboard. It wasn't long before we realised our mistake, as the train roared through Vernazza station a few minutes later. We were on the wrong one.

I'd had a similar personal previous experience, in the UK at least. Back in 2005 I was working in Birmingham when Liverpool drew Juventus in the Champions League quarter final, with the first leg to be played at Anfield. Unusually, Tom had asked for his ticket so he could travel to Liverpool early and sample the atmosphere around the city, so I just needed to concentrate on getting away from the office in plenty of time to catch my train, get home, changed and a bite to eat before jumping in the car for the 40 odd mile trip to Anfield.

Accordingly, I left the office early and arrived at Birmingham's New Street Station in reasonably good time for the next train to Crewe. Checking the departure boards, I noticed that the train earlier than the one I'd planned to get appeared to still be at the platform and as I approached it was clearly preparing to leave. A quick, short dash followed, and a helpful guard delayed the train's departure enough to allow me to jump on board before the doors closed almost immediately and the train set off. In the wrong direction.

In my haste, I'd obviously misread the departure board and jumped on the train leaving the platform before the train I needed could arrive. There was little I could do to remedy the situation. I explained my predicament to the ticket collector who sympathetically informed me that the next stop was Cheltenham Spa, getting on for 40 minutes away. Fortunately, the fact that I didn't have the correct ticket wasn't a problem, as he simply annotated it to indicate I had 'overrun' my stop and informed me I could simply cross the platform at Cheltenham and board the next train going in the right direction. No additional payment was required.

As it turned out, the train I needed from Cheltenham arrived almost immediately and took me all the way to Crewe where my car was parked. I was well behind schedule now and feared I wouldn't make kick-off but, perversely, the lateness of my eventual departure from home in Congleton coincided with more favourable traffic conditions than I would otherwise have expected, and I made it into Anfield, where Tom was already in situ, five minutes before kick-off.

It was a great omen for the game as Liverpool, in a cauldron of noise from the stands throughout, excelled against the tournament favourites to give themselves a narrow 2-1 lead to take into the return leg in a sure to be hostile Turin following the first game between the two clubs since the Heysel disaster almost 20 years earlier, with many of the Juve fans at Anfield in no mood to accept the belated communal apology from their Liverpool counterparts, however sincerely offered 'In Memoria E Amicizia' (in memory and friendship).

Back on the wrong train in the Cinque Terre 14 years later, the Italian ticket collector was also in no mood to cut us any slack for our simple error. Looking hot and harassed as he meandered through the carriage checking tickets, I anticipated his arrival with foreboding. One look at his face as he checked ours and it was clear he wouldn't be writing the Italian equivalent of 'overrun' on them, patting us on the head, and sending us on our way with a heartfelt 'arrivederci'.

"You do not have the right tickets for this train" he said. "You must pay 110 euros more".

"110 euros!" I exclaimed. "No chance, I'm not paying that. We just made a mistake".

"In Italy is not like in UK. You must pay more" he repeated.

I was fuming, but San was making it clear I needed to pay the fine and move on, so I begrudgingly proffered my credit card. Which only made the situation worse as the attempted payment was declined (Barclaycard connectivity issues as I was informed an hour or so later after a less than jovial call to their contact centre) and the ticket collector readied his mobile phone to call the Polizia Ferroviaria. Apparently my having an invalid ticket *and* an invalid credit card was ringing alarm bells for him.

Through my increasing disillusionment with the whole rapidly deteriorating situation I shrugged and half-heartedly mentioned I had another credit card and he could try that one "if you want". I was almost past caring. Fortunately however, he accepted the card, as did the card provider, and the fine was paid enabling us to leave the train at La Spezia, the end of the line, and get the next one back to Vernazza. For a few minutes the incident had left a sour taste, but I rationalised it as an extra 5 euros per day expense for the holiday as a whole and we'd managed to laugh it off by time we got back to the car.

Living in Congleton just north of the Staffordshire Potteries, themselves occasionally referred to as the 'five towns' (made up of Burslem, Hanley, Longton, Stoke and Tunstall but which are actually six towns which, with the inclusion of Fenton, amalgamated in 1910 to form the borough of Stoke-on-Trent), we found it interesting to compare the two regions. Okay, I jest. Suffice to say, in our opinion, the northern Italian version was by far the more attractive holiday destination. We do know where best to go for bloody good pottery too though. And it's not the Cinque Terre.

So, you know, swings and roundabouts.

* * *

...immediately followed by 2020...

Less than a month after we returned from our Italian adventure and under 6 weeks since Liverpool had celebrated winning the Champions League on that sultry, unforgettable night in Madrid, our first preparatory game for the forthcoming season took place, a gentle 6-0 victory stroll against Merseyside neighbours Tranmere Rovers on the same day that Dan's partner Lizzie gave birth to a beautiful daughter, our first grandchild, the wonderfully named

Hallie Hope.

The result, in what has become a regular pre-season opener at their Prenton Park home on the Wirral, was unimportant. Nevertheless, it was encouraging to see the team, such as it was at this early stage and with changes aplenty throughout the game, carry on seamlessly from where they'd left off a short time ago. It proved to be a good omen for the season to follow.

Liverpool opened the league campaign on a warm Friday evening in August, handing out a 4-1 thrashing to newly promoted Norwich City in front of a rapturous home crowd at Anfield. When we defeated Bournemouth 2-1 at Anfield the following March our league record read P29 W27 D1 L1 and we peered down from our soon to be regained perch at last season's champions Manchester City in second place 23 points adrift. Another 6 points in our favour – gained by us, lost by City or a combination of both – from the remaining 9 games would see us crowned as League Champions for the first time since 1990.

We'd also won the European Super Cup, defeating last season's Europa League Winners Chelsea on penalties in Istanbul back in August, and become the FIFA Club World Cup Champions in December for the first time in the club's history after beating Flamengo in the final in Qatar on Liv's birthday.

True, domestic cup disappointments remained but even then some light relief was provided when a very inexperienced side managed to knock Arsenal out of the League Cup on penalties after a thoroughly entertaining 5-5 draw at Anfield one side of Christmas, and our light relief cup joyously overflowed when a similarly inexperienced team defeated Everton 1-0 in the FA Cup at Anfield on the other side, 19 year old Curtis Jones' curling strike from the edge of the penalty area a memorable and worthy winner.

The only real downer as we prepared to put the finishing touches to our long-awaited Championship win was the relatively early exit from the Champions League at the hands of Atletico Madrid, our hosts for when we'd won it last season. Having narrowly, if deservedly, lost the first leg by the only goal at the Wanda Metropolitano, a superb 2nd leg performance at Anfield seemed sure to take us through.

A first half Gini Wijnaldum header levelled the aggregate score against an

Atletico side who were hanging on from pretty much the first whistle, and though they continued to hang on in the second half – and they really were hanging on – an early goal in extra-time from Bobby Firmino suggested their resistance was finally broken. Ten minutes later Liverpool had all but been knocked out, following two Atleti goals which most observers don't believe would have happened had our first-choice goalkeeper Alison Becker been available. As it was, his replacement Adrian's performance in extra time left much to be desired and Liverpool on their way out, an outcome confirmed when Atleti added a third on the break with a few minutes to go.

The Atleti fans in the Anfield Road End, some three thousand or so in number, were understandably ecstatic, as thoughts of the home fans turned back instantly to the holy grail of the Premier League. Surely now only a week or two away even though the calendar showed there were still 20 days remaining in March.

In the days and weeks leading up to the game against Atleti at Anfield, the simultaneously unlikely but increasingly most credible threat to Liverpool claiming their cherished league title started to emerge from beyond these shores. Millions, if not billions or trillions, of words have been and will be written on the subject of the coronavirus, it's impact across the world and how its effects were (mis-) handled by different governments, with those of the planet's supposed leading lights in that respect clearly, in my opinion, failing catastrophically.

I'll let you decide how I rate our government's efforts, but consider this: At the time Atleti arrived at Anfield for the second leg of that tie, Madrid was the Spanish epicentre of the pandemic raging throughout mainland Europe and more than three thousand Atleti fans were allowed to travel unchallenged, untested and untraceable to Liverpool, where many of them spent several days mixing with the local population, visiting sights, dining out and eventually celebrating in bars and pubs.

Back in Madrid, regional authorities had already imposed stringent lock-down measures which would severely restrict the day-to-day activities of their citizens and certainly prevent them from congregating in their own city, measures which would be underlined by a national lockdown the following weekend. In the UK it would be three months or more before even the lightest of restrictions on visitors from overseas would be put in place.

Before the weekend following the Atleti game, and only after the Arsenal manager Mikel Arteta had become the first Premier League 'participant' to test positive for the virus, the Premier League took matters into their own hands and indefinitely paused the season.

There followed a period, maybe of a couple of months, where the future of the season remained unclear. One or two clubs, with vested interests through their precarious league positions in simply cancelling the season, were rumoured to be pushing for it to be declared null and void. And predictably, social media was awash with fans of rival clubs wanting the same outcome simply to deny Liverpool the title win we craved and clearly deserved on the basis of this season's performances to date.

Mildly concerning though those noises were, simply voiding a season which was nearly three quarters complete was never a serious possibility. Worst case scenarios appeared to be the possibility of cancelling the remaining fixtures and having final league positions determined on a points per game basis, or simply leaving the league table as it currently stood. Either scenario would see Liverpool named as Champions and, to be honest, solving the 'Liverpool issue' as it was becoming known, was the least contentious one to be considered when determining the fairest way to conclude the season. Liverpool were already Champions elect in all non-partisan minds, and even in the minds of most of the partisans too I'd suggest.

Eventually, after a few weeks 'mid pre-season training' and a multitude of regular Covid-19 tests for all clubs which presented very few positive results, the season restarted in mid-June with all remaining games to be played in stadiums without fans present. Far from ideal, but in my opinion a reasonable solution under the circumstances. The social media warriors were reduced to limply suggesting our eventual proclamation as Champions should be accompanied by an asterisk (*).

Manchester City comfortably won their first two games following the restart while Liverpool started with a point from a drab 0-0 Merseyside derby affair at Goodison Park, meaning Liverpool could not now definitively win the league in our next game, to be played against Crystal Palace at Anfield.

Six years earlier, Palace had recovered from a 3-0 deficit with less than 15 minutes remaining at Selhurst Park to claim a point in a 3-3 draw which was to all intents and purposes the final nail in Liverpool's challenge for the title. Although Liverpool, surely, were too far ahead this time for any setback to have any kind of serious knock-on effect, a decent performance from the reds would suggest a welcome return to form after the disjointed derby performance. We needn't have worried.

'Decent' doesn't do the performance justice as Palace were swatted aside 4-0 at a deserted Anfield, in possibly our best performance since the turn of the year. Remarkably, Palace didn't manage to touch the ball on even a single occasion in Liverpool's penalty area during the game, such was our dominance. We now needed just two more points – and then only if City remained perfect for the rest of the campaign – with City due to play top four contenders Chelsea at Stamford Bridge the following evening.

Fast forward 24 hours to the evening of Thursday 25 June and Liv, who has joined us with fiancé Andrew for the day, is cracking open the bottle of champagne I'd placed in the fridge this morning 'just in case'. We've just come back in, me after running out of the house and loudly screaming 'Champions' accompanied by a number of expletives, at the top of my voice, Liv and Andrew after retrieving Hugo, their pet Westie, who escaped up the road after I'd obliviously left the front door open in my haste and determination to vent years of frustration into the sultry Cheshire evening. A few minutes earlier Chelsea had beaten City 2-1, a result not in doubt once City had been reduced to ten men when conceding the match winning penalty late in the game.

I'd seen us win the league 11 times previously, but the most recent win was thirty years ago, and though I was very happy, it also felt a bit surreal. I didn't feel quite as euphoric as I'd imagined I would. A combination of the decisive game not involving Liverpool, the outcome of the league being a pretty foregone conclusion for a number of months now, the lockdown enforced season interruption and the empty stadiums no doubt contributed to that. But the inability to share the moment with fellow reds – other than

San & Liv – I'm sure also played its part. In particular Dan, with his family in Liverpool and, of course, Tom watching from above.

So, for the second season running, silverware had arrived at Anfield in June (although technically the presentation of the trophy itself wouldn't take place until the final home league game against Chelsea in July). With seven games still to play, Liverpool had won the league earlier in this pandemic threatened season and later in the year than any club previously, and I was about to experience a couple of surrealism induced restless nights in the wake of it.

Put an asterisk next to that!

11

THE FUTURE'S BRIGHT

S o there you have it.

A glimpse into my past, the highlight reel I expect to flash before me when it's time to say my final farewell (hopefully with a few more highlights yet to be added). No sex, no religion, no politics. (Though, forgive me, if you still harbour any Tory or Trumpian sympathies after events of recent years, be sure to spare me that knowledge. There was a time when we may have been friends, when our differences may have been only matters of small degree to be discussed over a quiet drink, briefly, before moving quickly on to matters of greater import and common interest. No longer).

I have been blessed with a wonderful family and great friends, which I hope has been plain to see. Somebody (not Mark Twain apparently, though it is often attributed to him) once said that the two greatest days in your life are the day you were born, and the day you find out why. It resonated with me the first time I heard it, after which I was always on the lookout for my purpose, sensing it was tantalisingly within reach but refusing to make itself known. In the meantime, I quietly got on with the business of living my life, providing and caring for my family. It was the least I could do, the least they deserved.

And in the process of penning these few pages of recollection I must conclude that my purpose was there all along, hidden in plain sight. For what am I without San, Dan and Liv, and our shared memories of Tom?

They *are* my life. Past, present and future too.

Okay, so football, and Liverpool in particular, will always fill a need, the most important of the unimportant things in life. A decorative cherry atop a celebratory cake, completing the ensemble but totally unfulfilling on its own. Nevertheless, the club appears as healthy as it's been since the heady decades of the seventies and eighties, both on and off the pitch, with plenty of cause for optimism for continued success in the years to come.

Son Dan and his partner Lizzie have taken to parenthood like ducks to water, our beautiful little grand-daughter Hallie's happy countenance testament to that and more. Still in her second year, she is already growing into a beguiling sweetheart, and I into a besotted grandfather. Which is a relief to be honest. I had wondered, if not worried, when her arrival was pending and during her early days, if I would share those grandparental thoughts and feelings that grandfathers everywhere demonstrate so happily. How foolish I was to doubt it. With 'Lentil' well on the way to making an appearance I have no doubt that branch of the family tree will continue to grow and prosper.

As will our other one. The only fault I have found with Liv's fiancé Andrew (apart from the fact he's stealing my daughter away from me!) is his football allegiance. Newcastle indeed. He doesn't even sound like a Geordie! In all seriousness, I am looking forward to the covid-delayed day I will walk Liv down the aisle and formally welcome him into our family. We'll start work on his conversion after that.

And the last word, as always, for Sandra, my dear wife.

Thank You.

References

BOOKS:

Liverpool; A Complete Record 1892-1986
  – Brian Pead

Liverpool: The Complete Record
  – Arnie Baldursson, Gudmundur Magnusson

A Season on The Brink; Rafael Benitez, Liverpool and the Path to European Glory
  – Guillem Balague

An Epic Swindle; 44 Months With a Pair of Cowboys
  – Brian Reade

Hillsborough – The Truth
  – Phil Scraton

Here We Go Gathering Cups in May; Liverpool in Europe – the Fans' Story
  – Nicky Allt, Tony Barrett, Jegsy Dodd, Peter Hooton, Dave Kirby, John Maguire, Kevin Sampson

At The End of The Storm: The Remarkable Story of Liverpool FC's Greatest Ever League Title Triumph – 1946/47'

– Gary Shaw, Mark Platt

There She Goes
 – Simon Hughes

Far from Home; A True Story of Death, Loss and a Mother's Courage
 – Rosie Ayliffe

LINKS:

LFC History https://www.lfchistory.net/

Rev. H.O. Spink:
 ww1photos.com/Names/S/SpinkHORevArmy Chaplains.html

Printed in Great Britain
by Amazon